HERE'S THE CATCH

Additional Boulder Publications titles related to natural history include:

Atlantic Gardening

Birds of Newfoundland

Edible Plants of Atlantic Canada

Edible Plants of Newfoundland and Labrador

Explorations of the Interior of the Labrador Peninsula

Geology of Newfoundland

Newfoundland Gardening

Newfoundland and Its Untrodden Ways

Trees and Shrubs of the Maritimes

Trees and Shrubs Newfoundland and Labrador

Whales and Dolphins of Newfoundland and Labrador

Wildflowers of Newfoundland and Labrador

HERE'S *the* CATCH

The Fish We Harvest from the Northwest Atlantic

WADE KEARLEY

WATERCOLOUR ILLUSTRATIONS BY DEREK PEDDLE

Boulder Publications
Portugal Cove–St. Philip's, Newfoundland and Labrador

LIBRARY AND ARCHIVES CANADA CATALOGUING IN PUBLICATION

Kearley, Wade, 1956-
Here's the catch : the fish we harvest from the northwest Atlantic
/ Wade Kearley ; George Rose, introduction.

Includes bibliographical references and index.
ISBN 978-1-927099-08-7

1. Fishes--Atlantic Coast (Canada). 2. Fishes--Atlantic
Coast (Canada)--Identification. 3. Fisheries--Atlantic Coast
(Canada). I. Title. II. Title: The fish we harvest from the northwest Atlantic.

QL626.5.A84K42 2012   597.17609163'4   C2012-904898-4

Published by Boulder Publications
Portugal Cove–St. Philip's, Newfoundland and Labrador
www.boulderpublications.ca
© 2012 Wade Kearley

Editor: Sandy Newton
Copy editor: Iona Bulgin
Design and layout: Alison Carr, Sarah Hansen
Watercolour illustrations: Derek Peddle
Line drawings: Jess Kearley

Printed in China

We acknowledge the financial support of the Government of Newfoundland and Labrador
through the Department of Tourism, Culture and Recreation.

Newfoundland
Labrador

We acknowledge financial support for our publishing program by the Government of Canada
and the Department of Canadian Heritage through the Canada Book Fund.

To the past and to the future:
For my father, Albert Walter Kearley,
and father-in-law, John Gill,
and for my grandchildren, Luke and Annika.

Contents

Foreword

And for all this, nature is never spent.
— Gerard Manley Hopkins, "God's Grandeur"

S ince first encountered by native North Americans, then later by European adventurers and fishermen, the abundance of fish in the northwest Atlantic never failed to amaze. Some records are well known, almost clichés, having survived and been idealized by the passage of time. The pictographs of the Beothuk, the stories of Cabot's basket-hauling crew, and the writings of esteemed Captains John Davis, Jacques Cartier, and Richard Whitbourne have all survived to tell the tale. Countless more—perhaps most—no doubt have not. But it is easy, and at once brings a smile, to imagine Beothuk, Basque, French, and English fishermen around campfires or in far-off taverns in the dusky seaports of Europe telling tales of fish the likes of which they had never seen before.

In the centuries following the genesis of the European fisheries in the northwest Atlantic in the early 1500s, more than 250 million tonnes of cod alone have been taken from these waters—over half of that in the 20th century. For 450-odd years, come weather, gear changes, and the vagaries of nature, fish spawned, grew, fed, and survived—and the fishery remained sustainable. Oh, there were good and bad years, for sure, even decades when weather or war brought troubles, and the fishery was never good everywhere and all of the time, but for all that, stock collapses did not occur.

By the mid-20th century, it was near universally believed that the fish stocks of the northwest Atlantic could tolerate more fishing. In the jargon, they were "underutilized." Few saw what that belief would trigger, what was to come. No doubt it would have been nearly impossible to imagine the gross size of the European and Soviet fishing fleets that would set sail for the Grand Banks after the Second World War, to fish these "underutilized" stocks. It all happened so suddenly.

Within decades the major fish stocks were nearly gone. The measured response of North Atlantic countries was to demand control of fish stocks and fisheries within 200 nautical miles of their coasts, which was achieved under the U.N. Law of the Sea by 1977. This has worked well in some countries, such as Iceland and Norway, but less well in the northwest Atlantic. Off the Grand Banks, the continental shelf extends much further than 200 miles from the shores of Newfoundland. Continued overfishing, by both foreign and domestic fleets, laid waste to what remained there within a decade and a half of the U.N. extensions.

Forty years of excess has done its work. And a coinciding shift to poor productivity in many stocks has exacerbated the impact of the fisheries and undone the scientific models. To say that politicians, industry, and science were caught off guard would be an understatement.

But despite the 40 years of excess, the 450 years of sustainable production should not be forgotten, if for no other reason than a food-short world needs the hundreds of thousands of tonnes of the finest seafood protein that this region can sustainably produce. Of special importance is this: the basic ecosystem of the northwest Atlantic remains, with its extensive banks, ample production, and room for growth. And despite much opinion to the contrary, the fisheries that exploit this region are far from dead—badly wounded, for sure, but far from dead.

There are three basic problems facing the northwest Atlantic in the coming decades: continuing over-exploitation by Canadian and foreign fishing fleets, climate change, and the lingering ghost effects of poor past management. We can do something about current overfishing, and are mandated to do so under U.N. and national conventions. Climate change is harder to deal with, and with it will come winners and losers, shifts in distribution, and the arrival of new species (not all of which will be welcome). The ghosts of past management will continue to have their effect, and in some cases haunt us. The most anguished manifestations may be the persistence of foreign fisheries on the Grand Banks and seal herds that have grown to unparalleled levels at a time when fish stocks are at their lowest. These ghosts have become so big that easy solutions have become nearly impossible.

It is against this background that Wade Kearley has set this book. The northwest Atlantic, and the Grand Banks region in particular, form a remarkable ecological stage that has witnessed a plethora of human drama over the centuries. This drama has centred mostly on fish. In this well-researched book, Kearley puts all the players on stage, from the lowliest to the most exalted. Those interested in why some species declined to near exhaustion while others did not, or showed faster patterns of rebuilding, will here find clues and answers, based on the life histories and tolerances of those species.

The book is important not so much for the past but for the future, where the opportunity exists to have a positive influence on the rebuilding of the fish stocks and marine ecosystems on which they depend. And on which all life on Earth depends. Here is where the search for answers, and the future, begins.

There is no shortage of gallery pessimism with any fishery, and it is all too easy to believe that Kearley is writing an epitaph for what once was. Not so. All of the species covered exist, some in larger numbers than ever, many not. Unlike land animals, there have been almost no extinctions of marine fish. And habitat destruction is nowhere near as complete in the ocean as on land. It is far easier to envision rebuilt cod stocks than herds of bison on the North American plains.

Most important of all, in this book Kearley has given us a catalogue of knowledge with which to build a road map of what could be. The pieces are here. The map can be made. No doubt it will be a complex map, replete with winding turns and switchbacks with limited vision ahead. We should be prepared to be lost at times, with many roads leading to the same place, and many leading nowhere. But in this book we will find the legend, and a confirmation, that the biological parts of the ecosystem remain, their productivity latent. As Gerard Manley Hopkins wrote more than a century ago, "And for all this, nature is never spent." The question remains, are we?

Dr. George Rose
Aboard the *Celtic Explorer*, on the Grand Banks of Newfoundland, May 14, 2012

Preface

In 2010, in the office of illustrator Derek Peddle, my eye was caught by several vibrant watercolours he'd recently painted, now strewn about his desk. They were "portraits" of fish—commercially fished species of the northwest Atlantic, to be specific. I was immediately struck not only by their beauty but by how many of them I didn't recognize. I grew up on the shores of Conception Bay, Newfoundland, yet I was seeing some of these fish for the first time.

Neither Derek's nor my immediate family are fishers (as those who fish are now genderlessly labelled) but we felt a strong fascination for what swam beneath the seas around our home province. We had absorbed "fish culture," as anyone who has spent time near the water or listening to the talk or paying attention to the media here has. We both accepted as an obvious truth that it was because of the fish—and the money and livelihoods that could be made from them—that so many regions of coastal Atlantic Canada and the northeastern United States are as culturally rich and diverse as they are today.

So our talk turned to fish, instead of the business at hand. And as such conversations always seem to, these days, we also talked of our concern for the future of the fish, of the oceans, and of the regional industry that is founded on them. Landsmen both, we nevertheless felt that we'd like to give something back to our culture, to contribute in some way to the protection and value of our irreplaceable marine resource. Like many, we shared a belief that harvestable fish species can and should give our descendants reason to stay on our shores long after the oil crowd have packed it in and shifted to the Arctic or some other previously inconceivable frontier.

It didn't take long to realize that the "how" of this wish was staring us in the face. I write. Derek paints. We clearly *had* an opportunity—maybe even an obligation—to use our skills to pay homage to the northwest Atlantic fishery. We could collaborate in taking an honest and careful look at the fish that are being or have been harvested, all of which have a real and unique place in the ecosystem. And thus began more than two years of work to make this book.

Diving into the research, I soon discovered that there was no single source where people with a general interest in fish could find a layperson's overview of the four or five dozen species targeted by the commercial fisheries of the northwest Atlantic. This apparent gap further fuelled our resolve.

When I got to the writing, however, I sometimes felt as if I was penning a requiem for these same commercial species. It wasn't just the dire facts and figures that created that impression. Like everyone else in Atlantic Canada,

I had been watching in thrall as the fish disappeared. I am still haunted by the angry roar of the fishermen locked outside the doors of the news conference in which John Crosbie, federal Minister of Fisheries and Oceans at the time, announced the 1992 northern cod moratorium. On that day, a centuries-old rural fishing economy ended. In Newfoundland and Labrador, that was the official beginning of a mass exodus, the final results of which are still very much in question.

But gradually, the more I learned about the fish, the greater became my faith in the resilience of these species. Today, my hope is that if we can dedicate our efforts to understanding where and how the different species live and what they need to be healthy—and if fisheries' regulators can place protecting the fish ahead of protecting the fishery—then we will become better custodians and still be able to benefit from the harvesting of this amazing resource. And really, what other choice do we have?

Now that the book is done, I think what's impressed me the most is this: there is still so much to know. Despite all the research, past and present, and despite the wealth of experience gained from centuries of fishing these species for money, employment, and food, no one really knows what is going on out there under the vast blue lid. And that is the catch.

Wade Kearley
St. John's, 2012

Acknowledgements

In my email backup folder for the last 24 months there are 581 emails from my editor Sandy Newton. Each one of those emails is the result of significant, precise, and insightful work by her. Words are too imprecise to describe my appreciation but, nevertheless, I will say that I am deeply indebted to her for the support and for the professional guidance she provided. This book would not be what it is without her.

I would also like to acknowledge the generous and expert review of Dr. Richard (Dick) Haedrich. It was reassuring to know he was casting his experienced eye over the text and illustrations, helping us to ensure we had it right. My appreciation is not only for his broad, expert knowledge but also for his attention to detail, for the speed of his responses, and for his proactive approach to "reviewing." It was encouraging to know that not only was he supportive of the project but that he was also genuinely interested in it.

I happily acknowledge the work of illustrator Derek Peddle, who strove at every step of the process to render the best images possible and as a result has bequeathed to us this remarkable collection of images.

Humble thanks also to Dr. George Rose, who backed this project from the start, helping to identify the initial list of species and to identify accessible sources with the best and latest information.

And finally, to my wife, Katherine: Thank you, darling, for always being there to pick up the slack at home when I needed to hide away to do my fish research and writing.

Because of the Fish . . .

In an economy that seems to have turned its back on the once-dominant Atlantic industry, the fishery nevertheless persists. The voices of its fishers, of its plant workers and plant owners, can still be heard—in the news, at meetings for endless and ineffectual royal commissions, and on CBC's long-running regional radio program "The Fisheries Broadcast," which has been on the air since 1951. Independent and wary, these workers have a perspective on the fishery and the issues surrounding it that forms the bedrock of what actor Andy Jones has described as Newfoundland and Labrador's "galoot of a culture." And all along the coast of the northwest Atlantic—wherever the local economy was built on the necessity for people to wrest a living from a rich, cold, and often hostile sea—there persists a way of life that echoes the rhythms of the founding peoples and their challenging times that, without the fishery's endurance, might otherwise have been lost to history.

And it is through the coverage of their travails that I have glimpsed, as if through a foggy window, what it means to depend on the sea for a livelihood, to pursue an ancient and unpredictable way of life in a land that traditionally offered few other opportunities and was settled by Europeans mainly because of the fish. This fundamental underpinning is particularly true in Newfoundland and Labrador, where coastal settlements were isolated by rugged geography. Farther west and south, on the North American continent, expansion and centralization up the St. Lawrence River basin and down the Eastern Seaboard, fostered by a gentler climate and a vast hinterland, enabled a more diverse and resilient economy. Nevertheless, it was the abundance of the cod and other commercial species that fuelled European settlement in the first place along the North American coast of the northwest Atlantic.

Today, few would argue that the commercial fish of the northwest Atlantic are a shrinking resource or that they depend on a marine environment that is undergoing large-scale changes, the outcomes of which no one can predict. We need only look to the 1990s' cooling trend, which has been followed by general warming. In the trenches along the Labrador Shelf, where shrimp were abundant as recently as 2002, fisheries scientists report that temperatures have increased from 1° to 3° above the normal 2°C. As a result, the cold-loving shrimp are migrating to the top of the Shelf where the Labrador Current still keeps temperatures low. For those species of fish that depend on shrimp for food, this has enormous implications. And by default it also has enormous implications for those who depend on those fish (as well as on the shrimp) for their livelihoods.

Here's the Catch profiles the many remarkable commercial finfish in the northwest Atlantic marine ecosystem—their characteristics, biological patterns, harvesting, and current survival status. This information is presented along with a watercolour of each fish in the hope that it will contribute to a greater and wider knowledge of and respect for this resilient unseen resource that sustains us.

To help readers put each species and its fishery in perspective, the following pages present the larger context within which the fish and the fishery must be considered. "Drawing on Water" briefly sketches the ecosystem of the northwest Atlantic and its geography and how they have contributed to the abundance and distribution of fish in those waters, which was such a magnet for early European fisheries. "I Didn't Take the Fish Out of the Goddamn Water" examines the rise and fall of the fisheries up to the declaration of the northern cod moratorium and the subsequent fallout in rural economies. "Fish or Cut Bait" explores the possible causes for the collapse of the groundfish populations and asks whether or not good management can contribute to the long-awaited and still elusive recovery of the fish stocks. "Managing the Northwest Atlantic Fisheries" provides an overview of the development of international fisheries regulations and the origins of the Northwest Atlantic Fisheries Organization (NAFO); how the waters under its jurisdiction came to be divided into statistical divisions and economic exclusion zones; and how the data derived from these areas are used to set limits on the international fishing fleets. "Here's the Catch" considers whether or not the drive for profit, the ongoing adjustments in fisheries technology and techniques, and problems with regulation and monitoring are compatible with a sustainable fishery. Finally, in "Getting the Most out of This Book," the various conventions of the species profile pages are described to help ensure that all the information presented is accessible and useful.

DRAWING ON WATER

If Europeans came because of the fish, the fish were here because of geography. The waters of the warm Gulf Stream meet the frigid Labrador Current east of Newfoundland in very deep water off the Grand Banks. Part of the Canadian continental shelf, the Grand Banks are one of the widest continental shelves in the world. They extend up to 730 kilometres off the island's south and east coasts and sprawl over a total area of 285,000 square kilometres.

The floor of the Grand Banks consists of a series of relatively shallow marine plateaus between 35 and 185 metres deep, which are separated by deeper trenches. The contrasting temperatures and flow of the warm northbound and cold southbound currents over these shallow plateaus stir a nutrient-rich soup of phytoplankton, zooplankton, and shrimp-like krill. These serve as the foundation for one of the most distinctive and prolific marine ecosystems on the planet, traditionally supporting a range of fish species in numbers so vast that, until relatively recently, their populations were considered inexhaustible.

The Grand Banks are an important spawning, nursery, and feeding ground for many commercial fish species including Atlantic cod, Atlantic and Greenland halibut, capelin, haddock, redfish, flounder, and American plaice. The natural range of most groundfish species on the Grand Banks straddles the perimeter of the 370-kilometre (200-nautical-mile) economic exclusion zone, so these species are affected by both national and international fishing activity.

The Grand Banks are just one piece of a much larger network of ecosystems that includes all the western Atlantic

waters between the Davis Strait and Cape Hatteras, North Carolina. Within this immense and diverse stretch of ocean, commonly referred to as the northwest Atlantic, fishing nations and fishers for at least 250 years have recognized four overlapping ecosystems and three latitudinal boundary lines that divide them:

- Arctic and Nova Scotian regions, which overlap the boundary line of 47° N latitude. Beginning at Cape Race on the southeastern tip of Newfoundland, the dividing line runs east and bisects the Grand Banks into northern and southern halves;
- Nova Scotian and Virginian regions, which overlap on the boundary line of 42° N latitude. The dividing line runs east from Cape Cod, Massachusetts;
- Virginian and Carolinian regions, which overlap at 35° N latitude. The dividing line runs east from Cape Hatteras, North Carolina.

When I started my research for this book, I thought of the ocean as . . . well, "the ocean": a continuous blanket of water that wraps itself around the Earth and provides for fish a borderless habitat in which they can roam endlessly, stopping where the temperature or food supply seems most favourable. I quickly learned, however, that the ocean, like the continents that interrupt it, is subdivided by geography and climate, and that those factors, in turn, isolate populations. In fact, the same species of fish may thrive on two or more adjacent banks yet be separated by waters of such depth, current strength, temperature—or by hostile geology on the sea floor—that each sub-population represents a single reproductively independent stock.

"I DIDN'T TAKE THE FISH OUT OF THE GODDAMN WATER."

— John Crosbie, Minister of Fisheries and Oceans, July 1992

While the abundance of fish in the northwest Atlantic has rivalled the numbers in other more southerly ecosystems, the area's biodiversity is more limited: there are fewer species than in more southern environments. Of the species found in the northwest Atlantic, 52 have been or are now harvested commercially for their flesh, their oil, their eggs, and even for enzymes in their blood.

For centuries, these commercial species—especially Atlantic cod and haddock—have provided food for North Americans and Europeans, and eventually for people on every continent on Earth. Initially the fish were caught, split and gutted, soaked in brine, and either dried on shore or shipped "green" to distant markets. This industry of catching, salting, and shipping fish provided a foundation for many local economies, which grew in isolated pockets along the northeast coast of North America. Cod and haddock, the target species for much of that time, formed the basis not only of an ongoing sustainable industry, but of a time-tested way of life that endured the ebb and flow of fish populations and their fluctuating market prices.

Dependability, however, didn't last. The more easily captured species, such as sturgeon and alewife (which migrate into east coast river systems for part of the year), ran into trouble first. Offshore species were initially protected by the elements and by the limitations of fishing technology. As human ingenuity for capturing and refrigerating fish extended the industry's reach longer, farther, and deeper, the traditional offshore species became more vulnerable, and previously elusive species, such as the deepwater grenadier, became part of the harvesting mix.

Toward the middle of the 20th century, factory-freezer trawlers became a dominant force. Towing enormous nets and equipped with modern freezer technology, fishing vessels were transformed into an insatiable flotilla that harvested, processed, and froze fish far from land and far from the scrutiny of the regulators. When sophisticated fish-finding technology was added to those capabilities, there could be no doubt that humans had reached the apex of the marine food chain. Now neither the vastness of the northwest Atlantic nor the fecundity of the species that humans hunted could ensure a sustainable fishery.

The fishing fleets of Spain, Portugal, England, France, Russia, Newfoundland, Canada, the United States (and, later, Japan and others), all vigorously sought their share of the resources. Even when Canada finally declared its territorial waters in 1977, more than 30 per cent of the continental shelf still lay beyond its limit, including the Flemish Cap and the Nose and the Tail of the Grand Banks, all fertile areas essential to the life cycles of many commercial fish stocks.

Despite a growing international effort in the 1980s to manage the northwest Atlantic fishery (see page 21), it was headed for collapse on a massive scale. Some fishers and scientists in the 1980s, supported by a range of commissions (such as the 1980 report *Managing All Our Resources*, the 1982 Kirby report *Navigating Troubled Waters*, and the *Independent Review of the State of the Northern Cod Stocks: Final Report*, submitted by Dr. Leslie Harris for the Northern Cod Review Panel), made it clear that offshore stocks were in a dire situation and immediate action was necessary.

On July 2, 1992, John Crosbie, as the federal Minister of Fisheries and Oceans, declared Canada's moratorium on northern cod. By 1995, all significant groundfish and flatfish fisheries on the Grand Banks had been shut down and tens of thousands of fishers and plant workers were thrown out of work. So massive was this social dislocation that two decades later it still has not fully played out in the rural areas of Newfoundland and Labrador. Despite shifts to focus on other species (mainly crab and shrimp), industry workers continue to face limited fisheries and a continuing litany of plant closures.

Why did governments wait until trawlers on the Grand Banks were hauling empty nets—on what were supposed to be some of the best fishing grounds in the world—before they finally shut the fishery down?

FISH OR CUT BAIT

On Canada's east coast, the effort to modernize the commercial fishery was, after the 1970s, managed not for a sustainable fishery but to maximize the number of jobs for fishers and for fish plant workers. The revitalized fishing economy gained a momentum of its own as new boats, new plants, and thousands of new jobs were created. Even when they could no longer deny that the marine environment was in crisis, politicians were either reluctant or unwilling to step in and limit commercial activity to give the stocks a period of recovery—hoping that the crisis was temporary. It wasn't. And that is perhaps the biggest tragedy of the whole unfortunate affair: although environmental conditions may have played some role in the decline of fish populations, humans fiddled with the numbers and allowed species in crisis to be harvested long after it was clearly foolhardy to do so.

Researchers and fishers watched in disbelief as the number of Atlantic cod and other species plummeted. For example, in 1990, researchers identified 500,000 tonnes of cod migrating from offshore waters toward the bays and coves along Newfoundland's northeast coast. The very next year only 250,000 tonnes were tallied migrating in the same waters, and by 1992 that was reduced to just 125,000 tonnes. In 1993, it was virtually impossible to find a cod offshore. Not only that, the decline of cod appeared to affect many other fish species.

The rapid decline of the groundfish and other species is attributed to several factors and, as with any complex problem, there were contradicting theories about what really happened. Some people maintain to this day that the cooling ocean temperatures were most likely a major contributor. These proponents argue that the capacity of the cooling trend to profoundly affect biomass is demonstrated by the explosion in the populations of cold-loving northern shrimp and snow crab, which occurred even as the lower-than-normal temperatures were having the opposite effect on groundfish populations. Others, however, argue that this explanation is too simple. They point to studies that showed that the crab explosion occurred because the average size of cod had shrunk so far that the fish no longer ate crab. Compounding the downward pressure on fish populations, following a slowdown of the seal hunt, was the exponential increase in the number of harp and grey seals, voracious predators of these fish. But this does not absolve the fishing industry—either those who regulated it or those who prosecuted it. Far from it. Fishing pressure was the real culprit regardless of any rationales offered to somehow excuse the industry.

The total allowable catch for Atlantic cod, for example, was above the level of sustainability for years. The fishermen knew it. The researchers knew it. And the politicians, regardless of who they blame, most likely knew it, too. More than a decade after the moratorium was finally declared, the decline continued and the fish that could be found were stunted and reproducing two to three years earlier than normal.

In the years following the moratorium, the fishing industry shifted its focus and its gear to snow crab and shrimp. They were fished hard and now, 20 years later, the numbers of these species are also, predictably, declining. Meanwhile, research indicates that the cooling trend has reversed and the ocean is now warming quickly, even in the deep trenches off the Labrador Shelf. This may also be contributing to a decline in the shrimp biomass.

There is faint hope for a revival of cod stocks. On the Flemish Cap, in 2012, research by the Centre for Fisheries Ecosystems Research indicated slight increases in the population of Atlantic cod in different year-classes, though they are still in numbers far below those that would justify reopening a fishery. Capelin returned to the beaches around Newfoundland in mid-June (in 2012), as they have done historically, instead of in late July or even August, as they have been doing over the past dozen or more years. But it is far too early to speculate on whether or not any of these observations represents a reliable trend. On a larger scale, however, one could speculate that it is not individual species that are adapting but the entire ecosystem that is changing in some profound but as yet poorly understood process.

Can a change in management strategy lead to full recovery? The jury is out. There are precedents for nursing a fish stock back to health. In the 1970s, Europeans extirpated the spring herring in many areas of the northeast Atlantic. The collapse, caused by an unsustainable level of fishing, necessitated a four-year moratorium on the herring fishery in the North Sea. Stocks began to recover rapidly—and fisheries were allowed to gear up too quickly. The stocks declined once more in the 1990s, and it was then that new international rules were introduced. In 1996, herring fishery quotas were cut. Then common-stock management guidelines were introduced and adopted by all nations fishing in these waters. As a result, North Sea herring stocks have returned to levels where a sustainable fishery is once again possible.

But that kind of recovery takes a strong commitment by governments to fund continuing scientific research and politicians with the courage to make tough decisions and support effective management techniques.

Will we see such a recovery in the northwest Atlantic for the threatened species? Much hangs in the balance. And to complicate the matter further, many of these stocks—such as cod, tuna, swordfish, Greenland halibut, and dogfish—straddle international boundaries, so international cooperation is essential for recovery in the long-term.

MANAGING THE NORTHWEST ATLANTIC FISHERIES

Fisheries management today is based on the approach that good statistical data on population trends are critical to successfully regulating a sustainable fishery. For its fisheries in the northwest Atlantic, the United States began to generate statistics as early as the 1890s. The Americans collected data on fish numbers, which they correlated with the general areas in which those species were harvested. By 1920, Canada also had a limited program in place. It was not until the 1930s, however, that an international body first subdivided the northwest Atlantic in a way that allowed fish-harvesting numbers to be consistently matched with specific offshore locations. The purpose was to generate meaningful statistics about individual fisheries.

This advance was still limited by the geographic divisions separating biologically independent fish stocks from one another. Reproductive isolation makes the apparently simple challenge of estimating the population health of a single fish species much more complex. Researchers must first know where the dividing lines are between separate stocks, then collect and analyze samples from all stock locations. The data for independent stocks must be considered independently to calculate a true picture of the health of a species. The importance of this is shown, for example, by the fact that high numbers of cod in inshore waters do not indicate that offshore stocks are recovering.

In 1932, delegates to the North American Council on Fishery Investigations (NACFI)—an international body—developed a macro-grid of the northwest Atlantic, basing it on then-current research on the distribution of two species: Atlantic cod and haddock. These two groundfish dominated the region's northern and southern fisheries, respectively. NACFI's research data were biased toward stocks on the relatively shallow banks and also reflected the separation of groundfish stocks by deep trenches such as the Laurentian and Fundian channels. Where biological data were absent, other criteria such as oceanography—and even politics—guided the pen of the cartographers.

The grid imposed on the northwest Atlantic (called the Convention Area) continued to evolve through ensuing international meetings, even when NACFI ceased to function during the Second World War. The source of scientific knowledge that member countries used to determine the precise locations of statistic boundaries does not appear in any documentation, but the guiding principles for the boundaries appear to be the distribution of commercial fish stocks and the location of barriers to their migration. The natural division into the four regions mentioned above may have influenced the creation of divisions and subdivisions within the NACFI Convention Area, but the determining factor in how well this was done was a limited and (we now know) sometimes incorrect understanding of species distribution, behaviour, and migration patterns.

In January 1949, European and North American government representatives convened in Washington, D.C., and replaced NACFI with a new international fisheries management organization. They also drafted the *International Convention for the Northwest Atlantic Fisheries*. As part of that agreement, they created the International Commission for the Northwest Atlantic Fisheries (ICNAF). Its purpose was "the investigation, protection, and conservation of the fisheries." (One wonders how different the northwest Atlantic ecosystem might be today if their purpose had been "the protection and conservation of the fish populations.") By collecting and standardizing commercial fishery statistics, governments declared their intention to chart population trends for various stocks and, if required, to maintain these stocks by regulating the respective fisheries.

ICNAF first met in April 1951. Canada came to the table with a renewed mandate: included in its territory for the first time were the extensive fishing grounds of the former nation of Newfoundland, which had only recently become a part of the Canadian confederation.

At the convention, delegates agreed on new perimeters for the Convention Area. The easternmost limit was set at 42° W (west), which corresponded to the western boundary of the Permanent Commission responsible for the Northeast Atlantic fishery (based in Europe). Thus the entire North Atlantic fishery was now under the statistical eye of one commission or the other.

The agreed western boundary (71°40' W) was the westernmost limit of the haddock fishery. Canada proposed a southern limit of 40° N latitude, based on traditional ground fisheries, but delegates approved a southern boundary of 39° N latitude, which added the continental slope south of Georges Bank and the Nantucket Shoals to the Convention Area. To the north, the boundary, which included northwestern Greenland, was set at 78°10' N latitude and 73°30' W longitude.

Under this agreement, which was made at a time before the declaration of national 370-kilometre economic exclusion zones, Canada and the United States retained jurisdiction and regulation of the relatively narrow band of water then claimed for their domestic fisheries. The internationally agreed-upon boundaries, and the regulations governing the fisheries within them, applied everywhere else.

With the outline of this vast area of ocean decided, delegates then imposed an irregular grid of fisheries "Divisions" on the waters. Once again, these gridlines were determined in reference to the distribution of a limited number of fish stocks. And although the Divisions each covered enormous areas of ocean, they were the smallest areas ICNAF used to collect data. But because the data were collected as if they came from a single stock (when they may actually have represented two or more independent stocks), the resulting data were flawed and may even have been wrong altogether.

The need for a geographical scale that respected individual fish stocks helped inform crucial decisions in 1953 about ICNAF Divisions. However, in this pre-digital age, practical considerations, particularly the difficulty of obtaining accurate, comprehensive statistics by small areas, also influenced the larger size of the grid. Scientists and others at the time used Divisions to provide an adequate basis for fishery science and management. They relied on historical data from the same regions to help create a clear picture of species and population trends and catch rates. This status quo alters rapidly, however, when new technology is introduced or fishing methods change. The introduction of factory-freezer stern trawlers in the 1950s revolutionized the fisheries and may have even been a catalyst for the creation of economic exclusion zones two decades later. This extension of territory, in turn, radically altered traditional patterns in the fisheries.

In 1970, in the midst of foment over national and international boundaries and the implications for sustainability of new fishing capabilities, ICNAF introduced the concept of Total Allowable Catch (TAC). Under this system, calculating a TAC for each species and assigning portions of that TAC to various countries became the method of attempting to control the biomass of each commercial species within the Convention Area. Later refinements, such as the Individual Transferrable Quota, increased the complexity of regulating and managing the process of developing each species' TAC.

Refinements of the grid into which the Convention Area was divided continued over time, as the international fisheries body reorganized itself. At the 26th annual meeting of the ICNAF in June 1976, the United States and Canada declared their intention to extend their economic exclusion zones (EEZ) to 370 kilometres as of March 1, 1977, and January 1, 1977, respectively. Denmark followed suit, extending its jurisdiction around Greenland to 370 kilometres, and France similarly extended its sovereignty around the islands of St. Pierre and Miquelon.

At conferences held in Ottawa in 1977 and 1978, international delegates hammered out the Convention on Future Multilateral Cooperation in the Northwest Atlantic Fisheries. It came into effect January 1, 1979, and provided for the establishment of the Northwest Atlantic Fisheries Organization (NAFO). During March 1979, NAFO held its inaugural meetings in Montreal; its first annual meeting was in Halifax that June. After a twelve-month transitional overlap between the two organizations, ICNAF ceased to exist on December 31, 1979.

In 1980, NAFO consisted of 13 contracting parties. Their objective, through this organization, was to "contribute through consultation and cooperation to the optimum utilization, rational management, and conservation of the fishery resources of the Convention Area." Headquartered in Dartmouth, Nova Scotia, NAFO's members today include Canada, Cuba, Denmark (Faroe Islands and Greenland), European Union, France (St. Pierre and Miquelon), Iceland, Japan, Republic of Korea, Norway, the Russian Federation, Ukraine, and the United States of America.

The fishery resources covered under the Convention, within the agreed boundaries of the northwest Atlantic, include:
- Atlantic cod in Divisions 3NO
- redfish in 3LN and 3O
- American plaice in 3LNO
- yellowtail flounder in 3LNO
- witch flounder in 3L and 3NO
- white hake in 3NO
- capelin in 3NO
- skate in 3NO
- Greenland halibut in 3LMNO
- independent stocks of Atlantic cod, redfish, and American plaice in 3M (Flemish Cap)

A few commercial species—including salmon, tuna, and marlin—are outside the jurisdiction of NAFO and managed by other bodies. Also outside NAFO's jurisdiction are whales, which are managed by the International Whaling Commission, and sedentary invertebrate species such as shellfish.

One of NAFO's reforms was to extend the Convention Area to include statistical areas south and north of the area inherited from the ICNAF. The first addition, outlined in 1967, extended the Convention Area south from the Nantucket Shoals to a new Subarea 6 Division (between 39° N and 35° N latitude). In 1974, NAFO added a second extension to the north: the Baffin Island Area—labelled Statistical Area 0. It encompassed newly delineated habitat for Greenland halibut

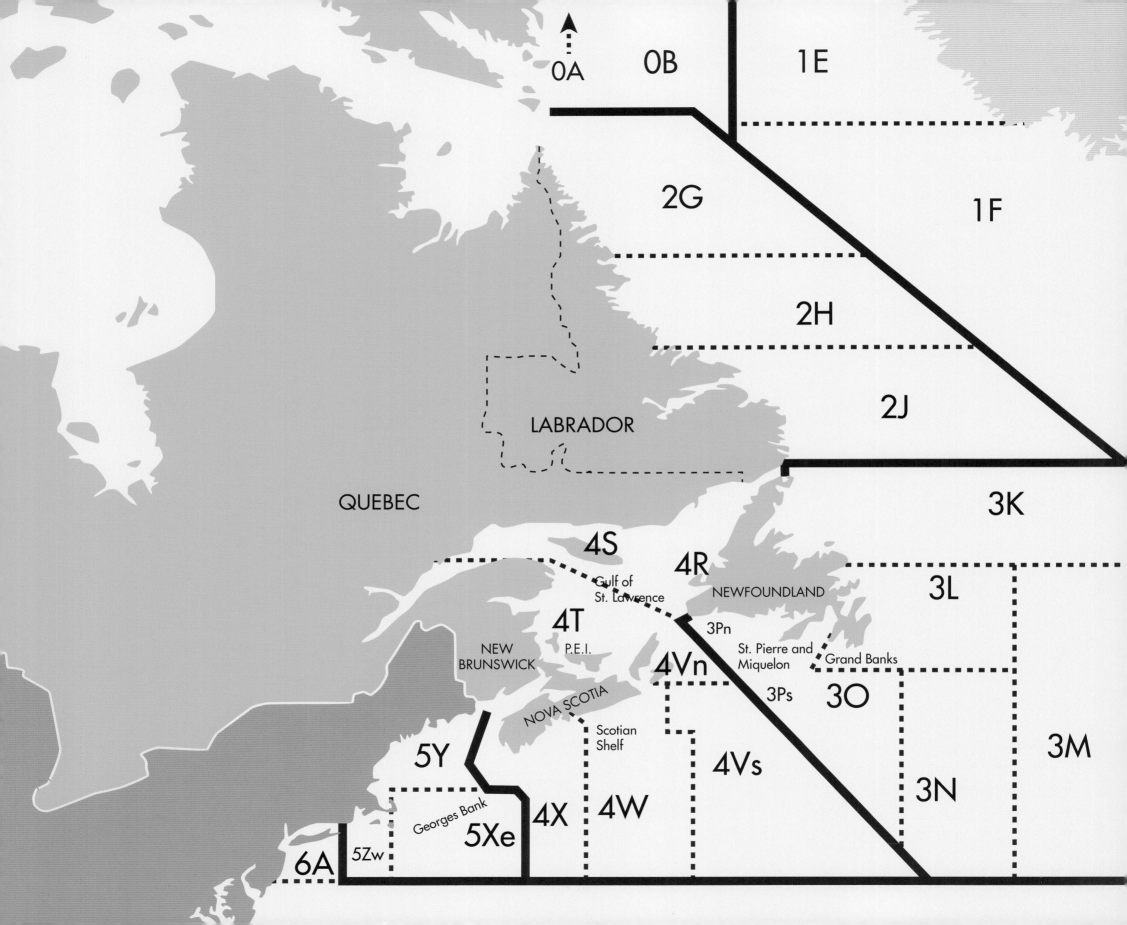

and roundnose grenadier stocks, which extended into deep waters off eastern Baffin Island. The border of this new area was extended north again in 1978 (to 78°10' N latitude) and the area further divided into Divisions 0A and 0B.

Management areas have continued to evolve. In each case, changes to NAFO fishing area boundaries have reflected the desire of coastal states to rationalize statistical collection activities with newly defined jurisdictional areas. This desire recognizes that effective monitoring of the results of regulatory action is an integral and necessary ingredient for successful fisheries management at both the national and international levels. With the advent of electronic data processing and global positioning systems, it is increasingly possible to collect data on any scale. Coastal states now capture data for their own use on a scale substantially smaller than the area of a NAFO Division.

TAC is still the foundation for the management of marine resources in the modern fishery. Its flaws, however, may actually be contributing to the lack of sustainability in most fisheries. Catch quotas are still set based on a limited understanding of stock abundance and population dynamics. Onboard and onshore monitoring and enforcement are also ongoing challenges: fishery observers continue to be intimidated and obstructed in their attempts to carry out their duties at sea, for example.

In addition to lack of knowledge and inconsistent enforcement, at least two much more serious factors help explain why the TAC management approach has failed to guarantee sustainability in the fisheries. First: setting TAC is an interdependent process in which different interests and institutions—which often have conflicting interests, ethics, and strategies for influence—lobby policy-makers to skew the quotas to suit their own ends. Second: policy-makers, being elected members of government (or directly dependent on elected members), often favour decisions that help assure re-election and they avoid unpopular moves that may be needed to ensure sustainability of the stocks.

HERE'S THE CATCH

What is the state of the ecosystems in the northwest Atlantic today? For the strongest clue, consider what comes up in the nets. Right now, the quality and quantity of the catch is not encouraging. Make no mistake, the modern fishery is a business and the technology has one purpose: to take fish from the surface or the mid-waters or drag them from the bottom, and to do it for a profit. As late as the 1970s and early 1980s, when valued species (Atlantic cod, flounder, haddock) were still plentiful, trawl tow times were short and each haul delivered a high proportion of the targeted species. In the first decade after 2000, however, most—if not all—stocks were either fully exploited or, more often, over-exploited.

The perilous decline of the traditional groundfish species in the 1990s has resulted in changes in the trawl fisheries that have serious implications for both the industry and the northwest Atlantic ecosystem. Few fisheries today target a single species. Instead, with long tow times (averaging three hours), trawlers rake their way through a diversity of habitats, take many different species, and increase the mortality rate of "non-target" species.

Deploying fishing gear that does not target specific species guarantees bycatch. It also puts traditionally different fisheries in competition with each other because the species taken and retained overlap. In the dredge fishery for scallops, for example, money from the sale of monkfish and yellowtail flounder bycatch (once sold by fishers for cash on the wharf) now makes up a portion of the vessel's revenue—and is necessary as scallop populations decline.

Generic fishing and the related lengthened tow times have created other problems, as well. Small or prohibited commercial species—and those with no commercial value—are inevitably entangled in fishing gear. By law, they must be thrown overboard—a senseless waste of marine life for no commercial gain. The gear and the approach also kill untold numbers of seabirds, marine mammals, and sea turtles.

So it seems, at this writing, that the sustainability and diversity of the northwest Atlantic fish stocks are now badly compromised—by overexploitation, by high rates of dumping, and by temperature fluctuations. The result may be an overall disruption of the northwest Atlantic ecosystem. If that is the case, then it is too difficult for anyone to predict how it will all play out. As terrifying as it may be, that thought has to be confronted and we need to do more.

The only fisheries worth preserving are those that depend on a sustainable harvest rate while striving for greater productivity. But this cannot come at the expense of the ecosystem. Harvesting techniques must be adapted to take fewer non-target and juvenile fish. The only way to ensure that all stakeholders comply with a revised approach, however, is to continue to rigorously monitor these fisheries at sea. Doing so will allow us to document and assess which management measures are most effective at reducing bycatch and rates of discard. And with that information, policy-makers can be better prepared to implement policies that ensure that those measures are enforced, provided, of course, that politicians can be persuaded to keep their hooks out of the process.

There will be no quick fixes, and honesty must play a role. Scientists have proven that increasing mesh size decreases bycatch and its unwanted consequences. Accurate management of all species, however, also relies on truthful bycatch and discard data. Currently, the reporting of this information is self-regulated and the fleet is international. In some fisheries, such as for the internationally regulated bluefin tuna, at least one country has been accused of misrepresenting undersized-fish bycatch data in order to skew calculations and make it appear as if the species is recovering. So even the impartiality of ships' logs is in doubt, as evidence mounts of the unreliability of some countries' catch records. And international news stories continue to report on the intimidation of fisheries observers at sea.

Thousands of vessels return each year to the waters where many generations have fished before, to the Labrador Shelf, the Grand Banks, the Gulf of St. Lawrence, the Scotian Shelf, the Bay of Fundy, the Gulf of Maine, and Georges Bank. The names of these fishing grounds, like an often-repeated mantra, are woven into the history of European and North American nations. They were the breeding grounds for fish—and also the training ground for fishers and sailors, whose lives have contributed so much to the prosperity of what we today call Atlantic Canada and the Eastern Seaboard. If we can find the will to use these resources responsibly, then, for those who fish and for those who remain ashore, the northwest Atlantic represents an opportunity—to continue an honourable tradition and to pass on a sustainable future for the generations yet to come.

Getting the Most out of This Book

The profiles of the 52 species of commercially harvested fish included in this book are presented alphabetically by scientific (Latin) family. Within each, they are in alphabetical order by the most widely accepted English name. An index lists the species alphabetically by all common English names—a reference aid for readers who are more familiar with those names.

Derek Peddle's watercolour illustration of each profiled species is complemented by several visual elements, including a range map, key-feature diagram, fact icons, statistical fishery charts (for major commercial species, where available), and occasional additional illustrations. The accompanying text provides a general introduction to the profiled species and describes its physical appearance, habitat, prey and predators, and life cycle. There is also a summary of the fishery and current at-risk status of each species. In most cases, there is also a short list of interesting facts. Pages 141–148 present detailed tables listing vital statistics of each species, enabling easy comparison of similarities and differences.

This approach was chosen to be as self-explanatory and easy to use as possible. The following sections explain the conventions and codes we adopted to convey the most information in the space available for each species.

THE PARTS OF A FISH

Each species profile describes and illustrates a fish's appearance and key physical characteristics. Specific biological terms have been used, many of which are defined in the glossary (pages 155–157), along with other technical terms that have been used throughout. The most commonly cited elements of fish anatomy, however, are illustrated on page 28.

THE PARTS OF A FISH

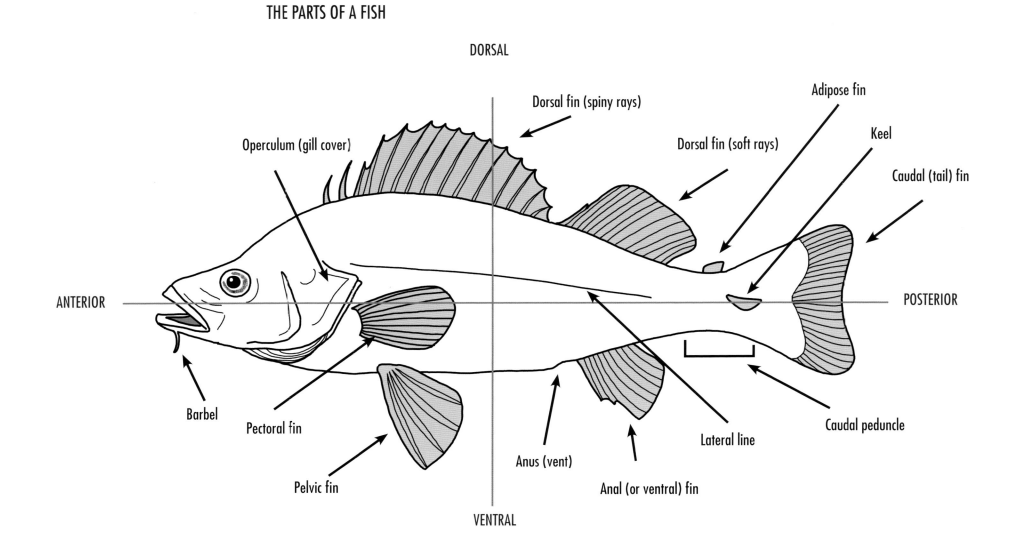

DORSAL

Dorsal fin (spiny rays)

Adipose fin

Keel

Operculum (gill cover)

Dorsal fin (soft rays)

Caudal (tail) fin

ANTERIOR

POSTERIOR

Barbel

Pectoral fin

Caudal peduncle

Pelvic fin

Anus (vent)

Lateral line

Anal (or ventral) fin

VENTRAL

TAIL TYPES

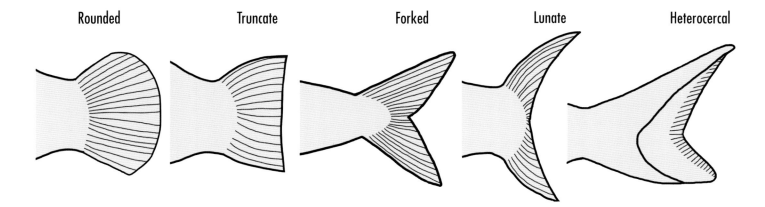

Rounded   Truncate   Forked   Lunate   Heterocercal

AT-RISK DESIGNATIONS

Designations indicating the conservation status of each species are drawn wherever possible from the database of Canada's Committee on the Status of Endangered Wildlife in Canada (COSEWIC). Legally established in 2003 by the *Species at Risk Act* (SARA) as the authority for assessing the conservation status of wildlife species that may be at risk in Canada, COSEWIC has nevertheless been operating since 1977 and first assessed the status of species at risk in 1978.

COSEWIC investigates wildlife species suspected of being at risk of extinction or extirpation. It does so by adding them to its prioritized Candidate List of species, drawing on candidate lists put forward by species subcommittees. Also on COSEWIC's prioritized Candidate List are species previously designated as being at risk but later found to be at lower risk, species for which new information suggests an increased risk in Canada, and species for which there is not enough data to confirm or deny their status.

Before a priority species on the Candidate List can be assessed and a conservation designation applied, a status report must be commissioned to provide information about distribution, extent of occurrence, area of occupancy, population and habitat trends, and factors or threats that have an impact on its conservation status. There are three Prioritized Candidate Lists: Group 1 is highest priority; Group 2 is intermediate priority; Group 3 is lowest priority.

To date COSEWIC has listed 500 species of plants, animals, and fish as being at some level of survival risk in Canada. Each year new status reports are commissioned and others are updated. Based on the information gathered in these, COSEWIC assigns a risk category to newly assessed species and determines whether or not an existing conservation status should change.

The higher-risk COSEWIC designations and their meanings are:
- **Extinct (X):** A wildlife species that no longer exists.
- **Extirpated (XT):** A wildlife species that no longer exists in the wild in Canada (or a specific region), but does exist elsewhere.
- **Endangered (E):** A wildlife species facing imminent extirpation or extinction.
- **Threatened (T):** A wildlife species that is likely to become Endangered if nothing is done to reverse the factors that are leading to its extirpation or extinction.

Information gathered during the preparation of a status report may show that a wildlife species is at less risk than suspected or at a lesser risk than when previously assessed. Newly assessed and re-assessed wildlife species, where such findings are the case, may be designated to the following lower risk-status categories:
- **Special Concern (SC):** A wildlife species that is particularly sensitive to human activities or natural events but is not currently Endangered or Threatened.
- **Not at Risk (NAR):** A wildlife species that is not at risk of extinction or extirpation in current circumstances.

When assessing some species for the first time, COSEWIC may determine that the status report does not provide enough information to allow a determination to be made. In such cases, the status is listed as **Data Deficient (DD)**.

WHAT THE ICONS MEAN

On each page, a set of icons provides at-a-glance information about species movement, behaviour, habitat, reproduction, and egg buoyancy. The following paragraphs describe how to interpret each one, when it appears.

Migration

Fish species exhibit a range of migratory behaviours that include crossing oceans and moving between salt and fresh water. These icons indicate the type of migration a species undertakes:

 a species that migrates from salt to fresh water to spawn (anadromous)

 a species that migrates to and away from specific areas of its ocean range for spawning (oceanodromous)

 a species that migrates from fresh to salt water to spawn (catadromous)

 a species that moves between fresh and salt water for spawning and other reasons (amphidromous)

Species that spawn within their home range are considered non-migratory and no migration icon is shown on their profiles.

Schooling

Fish of a single type often form groups that act and travel in a similar direction and exhibit similar behaviour. This behaviour is called "schooling." A group (or "school") of such fish may include several individuals, as in the case of tuna, or billions of fish, as in the case of herring. Other species lead solitary lives. They may accumulate in significant numbers in a given environment, as cunner do, or, like wolffish, remain solitary throughout their lives, They are considered to be non-schooling. The two types of behaviour are indicated like this:

 a fish species that forms schools

 a fish species that does not form schools

Water Depth

Fish have specific preferences for depths of water and proximity to the surface or bottom.

 a pelagic fish species, which lives in the water column away from the bottom

 a demersal fish species, which lives on or near the bottom

Numerals beside these icons indicate the depths in metres that the species in question normally prefers. In certain circumstances, individuals may occur in a much greater range of depths than this "preferred depth."

Egg-Laying or Live-Bearing

The ways that fish give birth are complex but they can be divided into two general types. The first, called "spawning," involves the release of eggs by a female into the environment to be fertilized by males and hatch outside the body. The second, most notably by sharks and redfish, involves mating and the internal fertilization and hatching of eggs inside a female prior to the release of live larvae or juvenile fish into the environment. Such species are said to be live-bearing fish. These two types of behaviour are indicated like this:

 a species that produces eggs that hatch outside the body

 a species that gives birth to live young

Egg Buoyancy

Most fish reproduce by spawning. The females' eggs are fertilized either internally by male sperm or released into the water column or on the bottom to be fertilized by male sperm (milt). In some cases, the eggs stick to a substrate—rock, seaweed, sand, or gravel. No matter where they are laid, once fertilized, eggs may sink, remain where they are, or become semi-buoyant and rise in the water column to the near surface, where temperature and currents favour their development and distribution. The various properties are indicated like this:

 eggs are spawned in the water column and sink

 eggs are spawned on or near the bottom and rise into the water column

 eggs are spawned and remain floating in the water column

eggs are spawned on or near the bottom and remain there

 eggs are spawned in the water column and rise to the surface

ABOUT THE MAPS AND GRAPHS

Each species profile has a map of the northwest Atlantic Ocean that shows the area throughout which that fish can be found with a high degree of probability. If the species' natural range extends beyond the area shown, this is indicated in the text.

Several of the species also have graphs indicating catch statistics in recent decades. The data in these graphs are derived from information supplied by the Fisheries Department of the United Nations' Food and Agriculture Organization.[1] The information and periods in the graphs vary from species to species.

COMPARING THE SPECIES

Following the species profiles are comprehensive tables in which the vital statistics for each species are captured. This tool allows you to more easily compare the biological statistics that distinguish one species from another. In its way, it depicts the intricate web of life that stretches throughout the northwest Atlantic Ocean.

---

[1] Capture production 1950-2008. FISHSTAT Plus—Universal software for fishery statistical time series. Version 2.3. 2000. Available online at www.fao.org/fishery/statistics/software/fishstat/en.

THE FISH WE HARVEST FROM THE NORTHWEST ATLANTIC

} 10 to 50 m

Atlantic sturgeon

Acipenser oxyrinchus
Black sturgeon, common sea sturgeon, common sturgeon, *esturgeon, esturgeon noir*

Threatened
(COSEWIC, 2011)

When Europeans first arrived on the east coast of North America, the Atlantic sturgeon was common in estuaries and large rivers from Hamilton Inlet in Labrador south along the coasts of Atlantic Canada, New England, and America as far as the east coast of Florida. In some regions, Aboriginal cultures made an annual rite of harvesting these fish during their spawning runs. Colonial records show exports of sturgeon to Europe as early as 1628.

The Atlantic sturgeon has been hunted for both its flesh and its eggs, which are served as highly prized caviar. It is, however, extremely vulnerable to human disturbance because of the late timing of sexual maturity, late maximum egg production, and infrequent spawning. All of these life-cycle characteristics contribute to a low to moderate lifetime fecundity, as does the Atlantic sturgeon's dependency on clean, cool, moderately flowing fresh water for spawning.

HABITAT AND APPEARANCE

The sturgeon family of fish dates from more than 65 million years ago. The Atlantic sturgeon is of more recent origin but is still primitive, with a skeleton of cartilage, not bone. Instead of true scales, it has five rows of bony plates (scutes). Its heterocercal tail fin resembles that of some sharks, with an upper lobe that is much longer than the lower one.

Atlantic sturgeon are blue-black and olive green on the back, fading to white on the belly. Individual fish can grow to more than 4 metres in length and 368 kilograms in weight.

For most of their lives, this species prefers estuaries and shallow nearshore waters (10 to 50 metres deep) with gravel and sand bottoms; there are, however, records of sturgeon being taken by trawlers fishing Newfoundland's offshore waters. When spawning, they move farther upstream in their natal rivers. In Canada, the Atlantic sturgeon is known to spawn only in the

St. Lawrence and Saint John river systems.

Atlantic sturgeon overlap in some geographic areas with the shortnose sturgeon (*Acipenser brevirostrum*). Adults of the two species are easily distinguished based on size: shortnose sturgeon reach a maximum of 1 metre in length. In addition, the snout of the Atlantic sturgeon is narrower and longer than that of the shortnose sturgeon, and the mouth is proportionally much narrower. The Atlantic sturgeon has a set of enlarged, bony plates between the base of the anal fin and the side rows of scutes, which are absent in the shortnose sturgeon. Internally, the intestine of Atlantic sturgeon is a lighter colour than that of shortnose sturgeon.

Because of their size, adult Atlantic sturgeon have few predators other than sharks and humans. They have evolved to be effective bottom-feeders. Using four barbels on the underside of the long snout to detect prey, these fish forage by rooting in the sand and mud with their snout, thrusting out their toothless mouth to take in sea-bottom mud and organisms such as molluscs, polychaete worms, gastropods, shrimp, isopods, and amphipods. Atlantic sturgeon will also eat small bottom-dwelling fish such as sand lance.

LIFE HISTORY

Atlantic sturgeon can live for 60 years or more. Slow to reproduce, the population native to Atlantic Canada takes from 19 to 35 years to mature.

Like salmon, Atlantic sturgeon return to the rivers in which they hatched to breed. However, unlike salmon, sturgeon are not known to leap low barriers. So dams, no matter how small, pose a serious threat to the species during migration. In unobstructed rivers, the migration begins when the fresh water reaches 6° to 8°C—usually in May in Atlantic Canada—with the males preceding the females by a week or more. The sturgeon migrate upstream, seeking the area between the salt front and the fall line. Females return to spawn every three to five years, males return every one to five years.

Ovoid eggs, released in batches, are amber in colour. They adhere to bottom gravel and vegetation. Smaller females may lay as many as 400,000 eggs, while larger females can lay 8 million or more. After spawning, females usually return to the ocean within six weeks. Males may remain in the river or estuary until fall.

Within 10 days, the new larvae hatch and begin feeding as they migrate downstream, hiding in gravel beds to escape predators. Sturgeon larvae have teeth but lose them very early in the life cycle. Juveniles 4 centimetres or longer and all adult sturgeon are toothless.

Juvenile Atlantic sturgeon migrate to the brackish estuaries. The farther south they are located, the more rapidly they grow in the rivers until, over a period of several years, they reach 76 to 92 centimetres. At this length, they move to coastal waters, where they range over great distances. Genetic evidence indicates, for example, that sturgeon from the Atlantic Canadian stock reached the Baltic Sea sometime before the Middle Ages, displacing the local stock (which is now considered extinct). Some researchers in Russia believe, however, that there is a single large North Atlantic sturgeon species and the Atlantic sturgeon is a subspecies of the European sturgeon.

FISHERY STATUS

Sporadic episodes of intense commercial fishing followed by population crashes characterize the history of Atlantic sturgeon in Canadian and American waters. This large fish has also experienced significant habitat degradation as a result of pollution and hydroelectric dam construction.

The heavy exploitation of the species reached its peak in the last decades of the 19th century. In the United States the harvest was reduced by 99 per cent by the 1920s; all American Atlantic sturgeon fisheries have been closed since 1997.

Since 2010, the species has been listed as Threatened in the United States; there is even pressure to have it listed under the *Endangered Species Act*. Among the dangers the species faces is significant bycatch by the east coast ground fishery.

In Canada, Atlantic sturgeon was listed as Threatened by COSEWIC in May 2011. Here, despite its relatively small breeding population, the species is exploited in regulated commercial and recreational fisheries that undergo limited monitoring for their effects on the species. As a result, the viability of Atlantic sturgeon in Canada is uncertain.

Did You Know . . .

- Atlantic sturgeon can leap completely out of the water—a breathtaking show of strength and beauty.
- On average, Atlantic sturgeon achieve half their maximum lifetime egg production at age 29— three to ten times later than bony fish species.
- The Baltic Atlantic sturgeon population was extirpated in the early 1900s. In 2009 a German–Polish project began releasing Atlantic sturgeon from New Brunswick's Saint John River into the Oder River, which flows in part between the two European countries.

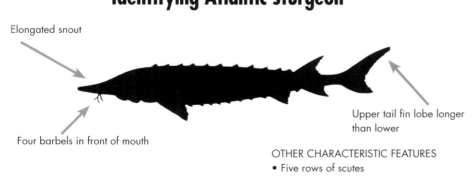

Identifying Atlantic sturgeon

Elongated snout

Four barbels in front of mouth

Upper tail fin lobe longer than lower

OTHER CHARACTERISTIC FEATURES
• Five rows of scutes

Landings — Total landings

Tonnes

150
120
90
60
30
0

1920 1930 1940 1950 1960 1970 1980 1990 2000

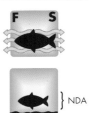

} NDA

Special Concern
(COSEWIC, 2005)

Shortnose sturgeon

Acipenser brevirostrum
Bottlenose, buzgus, little sturgeon, mammose, pinkster, roundnoser, soft shell sturgeon, *esturgeon à museau court*

The shortnose sturgeon is found in 18 Atlantic-coast rivers in the United States, as far south as the St. Johns River in Florida. In Canada, the species inhabits only New Brunswick's Saint John River system.

One of five sturgeon species in Canada, shortnose sturgeon was important for the Atlantic region's Aboriginal people. After the arrival of Europeans, the stock also supported a commercial fishery for several generations.

These slow-growing fish are late to mature. The species' survival depends on the success of informed conservation efforts, even as the quality of their habitat steadily declines.

HABITAT AND APPEARANCE

The shortnose is one of the smallest sturgeon species. Its elongated body is heavily armoured with five rows of bony scutes instead of scales. The abdomen is cylindrical. The head is short and least prominent in older fish. The eyes are small and the mouth is ventral and inferior. It can be extended like a tube to suck food off the bottom. Four barbels dangle about halfway between the tip of the snout and the mouth.

Shortnose sturgeon have large fixed pectoral fins; the foremost ray is thick and ossified. The dorsal fin is toward the tail end of the fish, behind paired pelvic fins. The caudal peduncle is narrow and the caudal fin, like that of the Atlantic sturgeon, is heterocercal.

The back and head of the shortnose sturgeon show a dark mottled chain pattern over an olive brown or green background. The sides are lighter, the belly white. The scutes on the back are a lighter brown; those on the sides and belly are tinged with yellow. The colour along each fin's leading edge is light, occasionally white.

In the rivers of the southern United States, the shortnose sturgeon is anadromous. In the Saint John River system, however, it is amphidromous: fish range from the brackish tidal zone to the upper freshwater reaches of their natal river and tend to spend most of their lives in fresh water.

Only very rarely are shortnose sturgeon caught in coastal waters. Anecdotal evidence suggests that a landlocked population exists above the Mactaquac Dam, but research has not yet confirmed the claim.

LIFE HISTORY

Much of the life history of the shortnose sturgeon remains a mystery, particularly the larval and juvenile stages (when fish are less than 45 centimetres long). The mean size of juveniles decreases in upriver locations, which suggests that younger fish use the more upstream habitats. Larger juveniles and adults overwinter in lower river areas, in deep holes influenced by tidal activity. Northern populations grow more slowly than fish in southern rivers.

Because they migrate within their natal river system, shortnose sturgeon needs unhindered access to upstream freshwater spawning grounds. The species' preferred rivers feature fast-flowing water over a bottom of boulders and gravel.

On the spawning grounds, females release black to brown eggs, which, when fertilized by the male, adhere to the bottom. In five to thirteen days, embryos (averaging 9 millimetres in length) emerge with a large yolk sac. They have a strong instinct to seek cover, an essential survival strategy given their poor sight and limited ability to swim. In about two weeks they double in size and enter the swimming larval stage. By the time they reach 20 millimetres long, they resemble adults and begin feeding. In this juvenile stage, they drift downstream in the deeper channels, remaining in fresh water for the first year.

Before they reach 40 centimetres in length, juveniles generally move to the areas where fresh and salt water mix; they move up and down the river with the brackish water as the tide rises and falls.

FISHERY STATUS

The shortnose sturgeon has been harvested for its meat, skin, swim bladders, and eggs, which are eminently suitable as caviar. Because it is a freshwater fish, populations were depleted early and have never rebounded, so commercial interest is low. Modern developments that threaten shortnose sturgeon include hydroelectric dam construction, poaching, and bycatch in freshwater alewife and shad fisheries.

Considered a species of Special Concern by COSEWIC, shortnose sturgeon is listed as Endangered under the American *Endangered Species Act* (March 1967) and has had International Union for Conservation of Nature (IUCN) Red Book status since 1996 (assessed as Vulnerable at that time). It is also currently listed in Appendix 1 of the Convention on International Trade in Endangered Species of Wild Fauna and Flora (CITES).

Identifying shortnose sturgeon

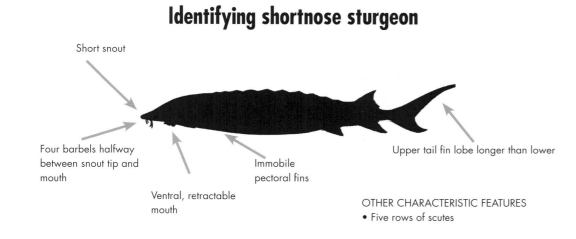

Short snout

Four barbels halfway between snout tip and mouth

Ventral, retractable mouth

Immobile pectoral fins

Upper tail fin lobe longer than lower

OTHER CHARACTERISTIC FEATURES
• Five rows of scutes

} 0 to 73 m

American sand lance

Ammodytes americanus

Inshore sand lance, lawnce, launce, sand eel, sand lance, *lance, lant, lants*

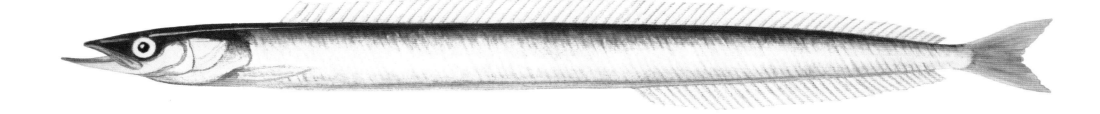

Schools of American sand lance gather along the eastern coast of North America from northern Labrador to Cape Hatteras, North Carolina, and are found most often in shallow water of 2 metres depth or less. The American sand lance swims with an undulating motion that resembles that of an eel. One of the northwest Atlantic's most abundant species—with schools ranging in size from a hundred to tens of thousands of individuals—American sand lance are a vital link in the food chain for many predatory species.

HABITAT AND APPEARANCE

The elongated American sand lance has a toothless and relatively large mouth; the bottom jaw projects beyond the upper. The dorsal fin is low, extending from above the pectoral fins almost to the base of the forked caudal fin. The anal fin resembles the dorsal but is less than half its length. In the water, the back appears blue-green to olive brown; sides are silver and the belly is white. These colours dull and lose their luminescence when sand lance are removed from water.

One way to distinguish the American sand lance from the northern sand lance is by the number of fin rays. The American sand lance has 51 to 62 dorsal fin rays compared to the northern sand lance, which has 56 to 68. It has 23 to 33 anal fin rays (compared to the northern sand lance's 27 to 35). There are also internal clues: the American sand lance has 61 to 73 vertebrae (northern sand lance has 65 to 78). Though similar to small eels in appearance, the two species are unlikely to be confused with them because they have separate dorsal, anal, and caudal fins; eels have continuous dorsal and anal fins that merge seamlessly with the rounded caudal fin.

An inshore species, the American sand lance is found mainly in shallow coastal waters and protected bays and estuaries, as well as in shallower areas of the Grand Banks, where the bottom has sand or light gravel. It emerges from sea-bottom burrows in the daytime to form schools and feed. It is frequently uncovered on sandy beaches when people dig for clams.

The American sand lance feeds on phytoplankton, invertebrate eggs and larvae, and tiny crustaceans, which makes it an important link in the food chain between plankton and the fish-eating organisms of the northwest Atlantic. Among its predators are salmon, herring, mackerel, yellowtail flounder, Atlantic cod, silver hake, and pollock. American sand lance is also important in the diet of such marine mammals as fin and humpback whales.

LIFE HISTORY

The American sand lance grows quickly in its first five years. It matures during its second year: males at around 84 millimetres, most females at 90 millimetres. Growth slows in later years; fish reach a maximum of 170 millimetres at 8 to 12 years of age.

Unlike most other fish species, the American sand lance does not seek deeper, warmer water when temperatures fall in winter. While they are not known to migrate over large distances, American sand lance make daily trips from their protective burrowing areas to feeding grounds in search of the small crustaceans that form the greatest portion of their diet. Returning after feeding, they wiggle 15 centimetres into the sandy bottom, snout first, to shelter from strong tidal currents and from predators.

American sand lance spawn in late fall and winter. Deposited on the ocean bottom, the eggs adhere to grains of sand and gravel. Incubation can take from 62 to 69 days. On hatching, the larvae rise to the surface where they remain for a few weeks. At just over 2 centimetres in length, they become juveniles, adopting not only adult coloration but also the daily feeding and hiding behaviours.

FISHERY STATUS

Aside from a small bait fishery, the American sand lance is not fished commercially in North America. The burrowing capability of sand lance renders them difficult to catch with trawls—they simply dive right through the mesh to escape.

This species' status is not assessed. The American sand lance does appear to undergo substantial changes in total numbers, which is likely driven by population surges and crashes among predators such as mackerel and herring.

Identifying American sand lance

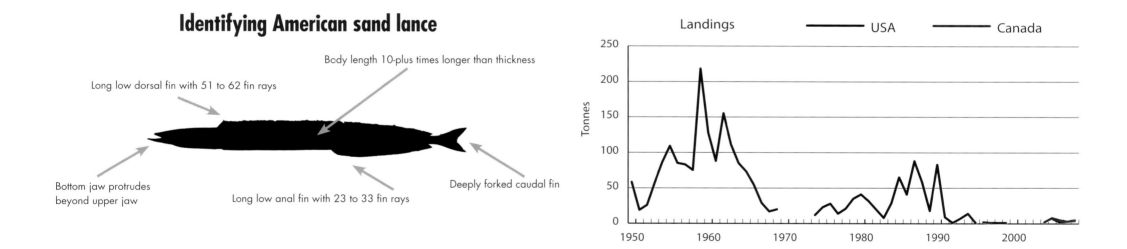

Body length 10-plus times longer than thickness

Long low dorsal fin with 51 to 62 fin rays

Bottom jaw protrudes beyond upper jaw

Long low anal fin with 23 to 33 fin rays

Deeply forked caudal fin

Landings — USA — Canada

} 0 to
108 m

Northern sand lance

Ammodytes dubius

Arctic sand lance, Greenland sand lance, offshore sand lance, *lançon du nord*

Although the northern sand lance inhabits deeper offshore and more northerly waters than the inshore American sand lance, there is some overlap in the distribution of these closely related species. Both occur in temperate to colder regions on both sides of the North Atlantic. The northern sand lance is common in the northwest Atlantic, ranging from west Greenland to Cape Hatteras, North Carolina, in both offshore and inshore areas, particularly around Hudson Bay, the Labrador Shelf, Georges Bank, the Grand Banks, and the Gulf of Maine. High-density populations of northern sand lance are found on the eastern and southeast shoals of the Grand Banks.

HABITAT AND APPEARANCE

Resembling a small eel, the northern sand lance is an elongated fish: its body is about one-tenth as thick as it is long. It has a relatively long head, sharply pointed snout, and wide gill openings.

The lower jaw of its large toothless mouth protrudes beyond the upper jaw.

Pelvic fins are absent and the pointed pectoral fins are low on the body. The low dorsal fin is more than twice the length of the anal fin and extends from above the pectoral fins to the base of the forked caudal fin.

The northern sand lance has 56 to 68 dorsal fin rays (more than the American sand lance's 51 to 62), 27 to 35 anal fin rays (the American sand lance has 23 to 33), and 65 to 78 vertebrae (the American sand lance has 61 to 73). It may also be distinguished from the inshore species by its skin folds: northern sand lance has only 124, American sand lance has 147.

The northern sand lance inhabits only the moderately deep offshore waters where it can burrow into the sand or light gravel on the bottom. It emerges from the sand in enormous numbers during the day to pursue plankton, invertebrate eggs and larvae, and tiny crustaceans. Like the American sand lance, it is an important link in the food chain between zooplankton and predatory fish, mammals, and birds.

When the sand lance is used for bait, many species are hooked in both commercial and recreational fisheries, including salmon, herring, mackerel, yellowtail flounder, Atlantic cod, silver hake, and pollock. The northern sand lance is also important in the diet of marine mammals such as seals and fin and humpback whales.

LIFE HISTORY

Northern sand lance grow quickly in their first few years, with no discernible difference in the growth rate between the sexes. Growth slows in later years; fish reach their maximum length (37 centimetres) at 8 to 12 years, their maximum life expectancy.

Maturation comes during the first or second year of life. Males usually mature at around 84 millimetres, most females mature at 90 millimetres.

Like the American sand lance (but unlike many other species), northern sand lance do not seek warmer water in winter. Their migrations are basically limited to daily trips between burrowing areas and feeding grounds.

The northern sand lance spawns in late fall and winter. Eggs are deposited on the ocean bottom, where they adhere to grains of sand and gravel. As with American sand lance, the volume of eggs laid makes up 45 per cent of the total female body weight.

On hatching, after 62 to 69 days incubation, the larvae drift up toward surface waters, where they remain for a few weeks. Those that survive the ensuing heavy predation to reach 20 milliimetres in length descend as juveniles to the ocean floor (with adult coloration) as they adopt the daily routine of burrowing and feeding.

FISHERY STATUS

Except for a small bait fishery, northern sand lance is not fished commercially in North America—despite strong interest in the Atlantic region. The problem is that the species is notoriously difficult to catch. In fact, no efficient means of harvest has yet been devised. Because of their prowess for burrowing, northern sand lance can quickly dive through all but the smallest net mesh. The status of this species is not assessed.

Did You Know . . .

- Sand lance are so effective at digging with their snout that, if swallowed whole by cod or other large fish, they can burrow through the predator's stomach wall. They have even been found encysted in predators' body cavities.
- In the early months of the year, sand lance larvae are the most plentiful and widely dispersed fish larvae in the northwest Atlantic.

Identifying northern sand lance

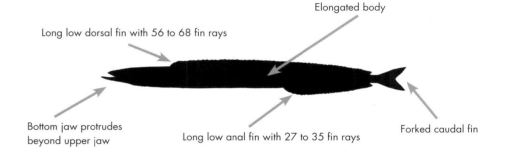

Long low dorsal fin with 56 to 68 fin rays

Elongated body

Bottom jaw protrudes beyond upper jaw

Long low anal fin with 27 to 35 fin rays

Forked caudal fin

} 150 to 350 m

Atlantic wolffish

Anarhichas lupus

Atlantic catfish, catfish, ocean catfish, ocean whitefish, ocean wolffish, rock salmon, sea cat, sea catfish, striped wolffish, *loup atlantique*

Special Concern
(COSEWIC, 2004)

With prominent canine-like teeth at the front of its jaws, a blunt rounded snout, and small eyes, the Atlantic wolffish looks formidable. But this fearsome appearance has done little to protect it from overfishing and the destruction of its habitat. Found across the North Atlantic, its range in the west extends from western Greenland and, in Canada, southern Labrador to Cape Cod in Massachusetts, and rarely, as far south as New Jersey.

HABITAT AND APPEARANCE

The Atlantic wolffish has a long stout body, firm muscular flesh, and heavy rounded pectoral fins but no pelvic fins. Its head is relatively small for its body size. The dorsal fin is long, extending to the base of the small rounded caudal fin. Its colouring varies from slate blue to dull olive green or purple-brown, but the underside of the head and belly are a muted white tinged with the upper-body colour.

The wolffish has developed an impressive set of teeth, which help it devour its hard-shelled prey and make it a key species in controlling the population of invertebrates such as sea urchin. The upper jaw has a line of large tusk-like teeth with smaller canine teeth behind. In the lower jaw, large tusk-like teeth in front are backed by rows of molars. A solid plate of crushing teeth lines the roof of the mouth. Even the throat has small teeth.

The Atlantic wolffish prefers shallower and more southern waters than the other two wolffish species also found in the North Atlantic. Juvenile Atlantic wolffish are prey for Atlantic cod, haddock, spotted wolffish, Greenland shark, and grey seal. Larval cannibalism is also a significant form of predation. The Atlantic wolffish feeds on whelks, sea urchin, brittle star, crab, scallop, and occasionally redfish.

LIFE HISTORY

The slow-growing Atlantic wolffish is a late-maturing species. Living as solitary individuals, mature Atlantic wolffish form bonded pairs during the spring and summer. Depending on location, most Atlantic wolffish mature at around 6 years of age and 40 centimetres in length—but for more than half the population, maturation takes 8 to 11 years. Although fecundity is low, internal fertilization, nesting habits, and egg-guarding behaviour increase the potential for egg survival.

Females spawn in September after four to nine months of incubation. Larger females lay more than 37,000 eggs in clusters on the sea bottom, often in rocky crevasses. Males guard the egg masses and have been observed aerating them with their fins. Male fish shed their teeth and stop eating during this stage. The fierce-looking tooth plates are sometimes found washed up on beaches.

When they hatch, larvae are about 20 to 25 millimetres long and have small intact teeth. Initially they remain close to the bottom, in the area of the nest. Within days, however, as they exhaust the contents of the yolk sac, they begin to rise and occasionally to feed pelagically, until they are about 40 millimetres long. They then begin the bottom-dwelling stage, which lasts for the rest of their life cycle.

FISHERY STATUS

Currently, there is no directed fishery for any of the three wolffish species in Atlantic Canada. All are common bycatch in other fisheries, but the species most frequently taken is the Atlantic wolffish.

Though generally a solitary species, wolffish may congregate in large enough numbers to support a commercial fishery. Biomass for this species has been in decline for some time, however, and the 1990s saw a precipitous decline in populations. At the close of that decade, the biomass had shrunk to just 8 per cent of the 1968–88 average in most areas of the Atlantic wolffish range. It is likely that declining ocean temperatures contributed to this alarming decline, but the main threat to this species is overfishing and bycatch in trawl fisheries.

There is a significant amount of ongoing research to adapt aquaculture techniques to support this species and also the spotted wolffish.

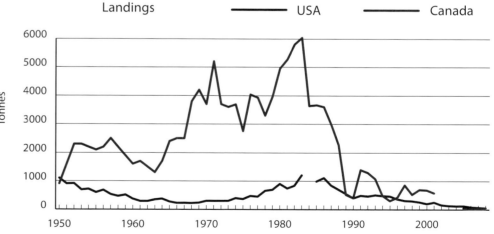

Did You Know . . .

- Divers often see the Atlantic wolffish close to shore, but never the other two North Atlantic wolffish species.
- An antifreeze compound in its blood allows the Atlantic wolffish to live in water colder than 0°C. This compound may have applications in preserving or shipping human organs for transplant.

Identifying Atlantic wolffish

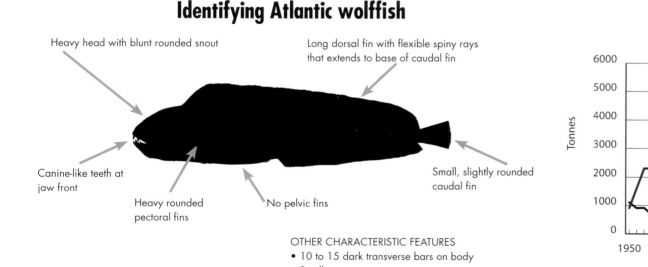

Heavy head with blunt rounded snout

Long dorsal fin with flexible spiny rays that extends to base of caudal fin

Canine-like teeth at jaw front

Heavy rounded pectoral fins

No pelvic fins

Small, slightly rounded caudal fin

OTHER CHARACTERISTIC FEATURES
- 10 to 15 dark transverse bars on body
- Small eyes

Landings — USA — Canada

500 to 1,000 m

Northern wolffish

Anarhichas denticulatus
Broadhead wolffish, bullheaded wolffish, catfish, jelly cat, rock turbot, *loup à tête large*

Threatened
(COSEWIC, 2001)

The northern wolffish occurs as far north as the Davis Strait (northern limit: the Nunavut area) and off southwest Greenland, as well as on the northeast Newfoundland and Labrador shelves (its centre of concentration), on the Flemish Cap, in the Gulf of St. Lawrence (uncommon), and on the Grand Banks. It may very occasionally be observed on the Scotian Shelf.

Between 1980 and 1984, northern wolffish could be found in significant numbers north of the Grand Banks—covering much of its shelf, the eastern Grand Banks shelf edge, and the Flemish Cap. From 1985 to 1993, there was a steep decline in both the number of fish and the areas in which the species could be found. As recently as 1995 to 2003, populations were low and locations few on the Newfoundland and Labrador shelves. Currently, the remaining northern wolffish are confined to the edge of the Labrador Shelf, the southern edge of the Grand Banks, and the Flemish Cap.

HABITAT AND APPEARANCE

The northern wolffish is a large, sturdy, thick fish with a big head and impressive canine-like teeth in front and rounded or pointed teeth behind. The front teeth are smaller but sharper than those of the other two wolffish species found in the northwest Atlantic. Northern wolffish can grow to 146 centimetres long and weigh 20 kilograms or more.

The body colour is dark grey to dark brown to purple-black for all year-classes. Occasionally the skin has a violet tint and indistinct dark spots. The upper jaw's palatine teeth extend farther toward the throat than the vomerine (central) teeth. The dorsal fin is a uniform width along its entire length. The anal fin begins approximately halfway along the body. Pectoral fins are medium-sized and there are no pelvic fins.

This deepwater fish is native to near-freezing northern waters. Scientists believe northern wolffish prefer a rocky or muddy sea floor, but the species is found over all types of ocean bottoms and is thought to frequent the water column.

Northern wolffish larvae feed pelagically on larvae, eggs, and small crustaceans. From the juvenile stage onward, they feed on pelagic fish and invertebrates. Unlike the other two wolffish species in the northwest Atlantic, juvenile and adult northern wolffish leave the bottom to hunt for lower and mid-level pelagic fish. Like the other wolffish,

however, they also consume bottom-dwelling creatures such as crab, sea urchin, and starfish. The sharp, dangerous teeth of the northern wolffish discourage predators.

LIFE HISTORY

The sedentary northern wolffish occupies a limited territory during its life—tagging suggests a maximum radius of 8 kilometres. In the northeast Atlantic, northern wolffish have been observed defending an area around bait; acoustic tracking also shows a restricted territorial behaviour.

At around 5 or 6 years of age and 70 to 80 centimetres in length, female northern wolffish release a single cohesive egg mass. It settles to the ocean floor where, according to some sources, adult males guard the eggs (this has not been observed for this species

in a scientific and verifiable way). Incubation time is unknown. Larvae usually emerge in the late fall; they measure 26 millimetres and have a small yolk sac, large eyes, dark pigmented skin, and well-developed fins.

FISHERY STATUS

From the Grand Banks to the Labrador Shelf, the northern wolffish is at risk. Populations declined by more than 90 per cent during the late 1970s to early 1990s, most drastically in the northern part of the species' range. Although there is no targeted commercial fishery, northern wolffish are frequently taken as bycatch in other fisheries. Because of its characteristic jelly-like flesh, the species' commercial value is virtually nil and it is dumped at sea. Bottom trawling continues to disrupt this species' environment.

Identifying northern wolffish

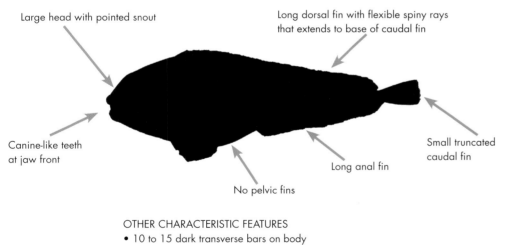

Large head with pointed snout

Long dorsal fin with flexible spiny rays that extends to base of caudal fin

Canine-like teeth at jaw front

Small truncated caudal fin

No pelvic fins

Long anal fin

OTHER CHARACTERISTIC FEATURES
- 10 to 15 dark transverse bars on body
- Small eyes

} 100 to 400 m

Spotted wolffish

Anarhichas minor

Catfish, leopard fish, spotted catfish, spotted sea cat, wolffish, *loup tacheté*

Threatened

(COSEWIC, 2001)

The spotted wolffish is native to the Arctic Ocean and the North Atlantic from the Barents Sea to Labrador; Baffin Bay is its northern Canadian limit. It is most commonly found off Greenland, on the Labrador Shelf, on the Grand Banks, and, less frequently, on the Scotian Shelf.

Before 1986, the spotted wolffish covered much of the Grand Banks shelf and was also found, less often, on the Flemish Cap. Between 1985 and 1993, local populations disappeared, leaving only low concentrations along the shelf edge and in deep channels. More recent studies (1994 to 2001) show no significant concentrations throughout its former range.

HABITAT AND APPEARANCE

A large marine fish that can reach lengths of 2 metres, the spotted wolffish has a prominent head with a blunt rounded snout and pronounced canine-like teeth. Vomerine teeth on the upper jaw extend back toward the throat as far as the palatine teeth do (see diagram). The long, firmly muscled body and fins have irregular-sized dark spots.

Like the other wolffish of the northwest Atlantic, this species has a single dorsal fin with flexible spiny rays extending the length of its body to the base of the slightly rounded caudal fin. Its pectoral fins are also rounded and there are no pelvic fins.

Juvenile wolffish are grey-brown but may have a purple tinge. Adults are usually light grey with dark brown blotches, but their colour can range from yellow-brown and grey-brown to dark brown.

The spotted wolffish inhabits intermediate depth and temperature niches compared to the other two species of North Atlantic wolffish. It is found over ocean bottoms of solid rock, small rocks, pebbles, sand, and even mud.

The wolffish's diet consists mainly of the creatures it forages from the bottom, including echinoderms, crustaceans, molluscs, and tube worms. Finfish make up a small part of its diet. The main predators of the spotted wolffish include Atlantic cod, pollock, and Greenland shark.

LIFE HISTORY

The spotted wolffish is slow to mature. It does not begin to breed until males and females reach 7 years of age. It is not considered as solitary a fish as the Atlantic wolffish, although it congregates only in small schools for local and very limited migrations. With its slow maturation and low rate of fecundity, the species is highly vulnerable and can take about 14 years to double its population.

Although larval spotted wolffish can be found in the pelagic zone, this species lives exclusively on the bottom from the time it becomes a juvenile (50 millimetres or longer) and throughout the adult life stages. Juvenile spotted wolffish prefer habitats such as rough bottoms, in areas with scattered rocks that can provide shelter.

FISHERY STATUS

Although it is only of minor commercial value, the spotted wolffish is a Threatened species. The fishery in northern Europe has been primarily for the skin, which is used as high-end leather; in Greenland, it is regarded as a food fish.

In the 1990s, the spotted wolffish population was 10 per cent of what it had been in the 1970s. Threats to the species include overfishing, commercial fisheries that disturb its marine habitat, and mortality as bycatch in other fisheries. It is also caught as a game fish.

Did You Know . . .

• The skin of the spotted wolffish can be tanned to make durable, high-quality leather.

Identifying spotted wolffish

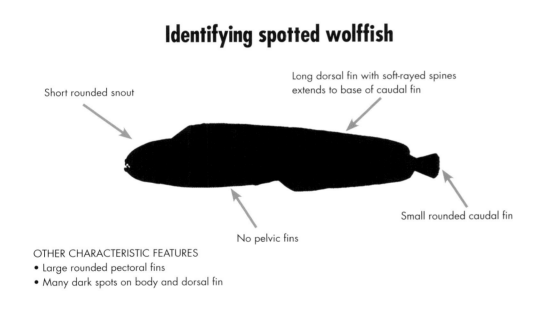

Short rounded snout

Long dorsal fin with soft-rayed spines extends to base of caudal fin

Small rounded caudal fin

No pelvic fins

OTHER CHARACTERISTIC FEATURES
• Large rounded pectoral fins
• Many dark spots on body and dorsal fin

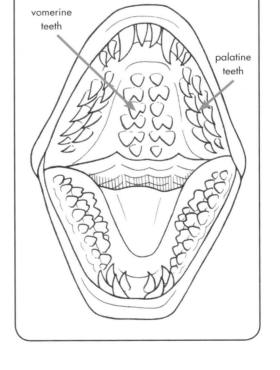

vomerine teeth

palatine teeth

} 0 to 35 m

American eel

Anguilla rostrata

Atlantic eel, black eel, Boston eel, bronze eel, common eel, green eel, silver eel, snakefish, yellow eel, yellow-bellied eel, *anguille, anguille argentée, anguille d'Amérique, kat*

Threatened
(COSEWIC, 2012)

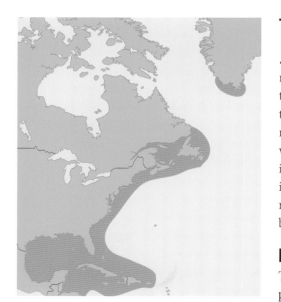

No matter how far American eels may travel during their lives, they all return to the Sargasso Sea to spawn. From there, young eels drift with ocean currents west and north along the east coast of North America, and farther north to the southwestern tip of Greenland. Others are carried south from the Sargasso to the north coast of South America. By the time they reach these far-flung locations, the eels have matured to the point where they actively migrate into fresh water, swimming upstream into rivers, streams, ponds, and lakes, and in some cases as far inland as the Great Lakes. Depending on temperature and food resources, it may take from 10 to 25 years before they mature and begin the return migration to the Sargasso Sea.

HABITAT AND APPEARANCE

The American eel has a distinctive long, snake-like body and pointed head. Its large mouth with many teeth opens as far back as the midpoint of the eye or farther. The gill opening is just in front of the pectoral fins.

Eels have no pelvic fins. The dorsal fin extends as a continuous structure from one-third of the way along the dorsal side of the body to the vent on the underside, merging seamlessly with the caudal and anal fins. Rudimentary scales are embedded deep in the eels' tough skin. The skin secretes mucus (hence the phrase "slippery as an eel").

Mainly nocturnal, American eels spend much of their lives in freshwater rivers and estuaries. Their preferred habitat has heavy vegetation in which they hide, and sandy bottoms in which they burrow tail first, re-emerging only under cover of darkness.

Eels eat insect larvae, fish eggs, small fish, crabs, worms, clams, and frogs. They will also feed on animal carcasses by biting the flesh with their small blunt teeth and using forceful forward and backward movements to pull off small pieces.

Fish that prey on eels include large oceanic predators such as Atlantic cod, haddock, sharks, and swordfish. In fresh water, they are prey to striped bass. Cormorants, many species of gulls, and even eagles include the American eel in their diets.

LIFE HISTORY

Every American eel belongs to the single breeding population that spawns in the Sargasso Sea, east of the Bahamas. Once released, the eggs float to the surface and hatch willow-leaf-shaped larvae (leptocephali). These drift west with the Antilles Current, the Florida Current, and the Gulf Stream for 6 to 18 months along North America's continental shelf, where they morph into colourless "glass eels" (55 to 65 millimetres long). As they migrate into brackish estuaries, they develop skin pigmentation and become "elvers."

Glass eels and elvers reach the Atlantic Canadian coast in May and early June, feeding at night and resting near the bottom by day. They move in and out of the estuaries with the tides, slowly transforming from pelagic oceanic fish to demersal freshwater fish.

Within a year of entering fresh water, elvers reach 13 to 14 centimetres in length. Over the next several years, they travel up to 1,000 kilometres inland. Dams may interfere with migration but are not necessarily barriers. Eels can wriggle along the damp side of smaller obstructions to reach and continue on in the river above. On the return trip, however, they often follow the flow through the dam turbines, with tragic results. In the St. Lawrence River system, 40 per cent of mature eels that pass through the turbines are killed.

Not all elvers migrate upstream. Those that remain in the estuaries grow more quickly, but all develop into "yellow eels," which have a dark back and a yellow-tinged belly.

Eels that remain in the estuaries or live in warmer southern waters reach sexual maturity as early as 3 (male) or 4 years (females). Eels from inland waters in more northerly regions may be as old as 22 years before maturing.

Before undertaking the return migration, adult eels change physically: their eyes and pectoral fins grow larger and their bodies change colour as they become "silver eels." They stop eating and their gut begins to degenerate.

Beginning in February and continuing into April the entire migrating adult population of American eels converges in the Sargasso Sea in water as deep as 4,000 metres. There they spawn in what is presumed to be the final act in a complex life cycle that remains shrouded in mystery. No spent eels have ever been taken.

FISHERY STATUS

Historically, the American eel was found in all coastal and accessible inland waters of eastern Canada as far north as the Lake Melville estuary in Labrador. Today, its survival is under threat from many quarters. Some experts believe that a northerly shift in the Gulf Stream system is diverting eggs and larvae away from the coast; others doubt this claim. Dams and other river barriers are fragmenting habitat. Turbines kill and injure mature eels on their downstream migration. Highly sensitive to water quality, eels also face chemical contaminants and, as ever, arriving elvers and the departing adults must run the gauntlet of

commercial river fisheries.

Aboriginal people caught the American eel for at least 3,000 years. Records of a commercial fishery date to 1900 in the St. Lawrence River. With annual landings peaking at more than 1,000 tonnes in the 1930s, and declining since then to less than 86 tonnes in 2007 (the lowest level ever recorded), the protection of eels seems to be beyond the capabilities of management agencies. This is, in part, because managing this single stock, which straddles international boundaries, requires international cooperation. The American eel's status was changed from Special Concern to Threatened in 2012.

Identifying American eel

Pointed head

Long dorsal fin merged with caudal and anal fins

Large mouth

No pelvic fins

Landings — USA — Canada

Tonnes

1200
1000
800
600
400
200
0

1950   1960   1970   1980   1990   2000

} 0 to 750 m

Basking shark

Cetorhinus maximus

Bone shark, elephant shark, sun fish, sun shark, *pélerin*

Special Concern
(COSEWIC, 2009)

The earliest basking shark fossils date to between 29 and 35 million years ago. Today this species—the only member of its family—is the second-largest fish in the world and among the most docile of sharks.

These huge fish are often sighted during the summer but seem to virtually disappear in the other seasons. Found around the globe, they generally gather in temperate coastal shelf waters where plankton—their primary food—tends to concentrate. Recent tagging studies have extended the distribution to tropical waters of the Caribbean and south to the northeast coast of South America.

Basking sharks in Atlantic Canada are most abundant south and west of the Newfoundland Shelf, but their range may extend north to 51° latitude (which crosses the south coast of Labrador).

The Bay of Fundy is a rich environment for this species and sightings are reported every year.

The number of basking sharks in the northwest Atlantic is difficult to estimate. This is reflected in the suggested population range: from a low of 1,771 individuals to a high of not more than 10,125 individuals.

HABITAT AND APPEARANCE

The distinctive physical features of the basking shark make it easy to identify: enormous size, extremely large gill openings nearly encircling the head, and a huge, sub-terminal mouth with minute hooked teeth. The inside of the gill arches are covered with large gill rakers that filter microscopic food from the water. The caudal peduncle has prominent side keels and the caudal fin is heterocercal.

Basking shark body and fin colour ranges from black to grey-brown, grey, or blue-grey. The belly may be lighter with irregular white blotches. Basking sharks often swim with their huge mouths gaping wide. Underwater, the basking sharks' large gill slits are clearly visible.

This enormous fish seeks out waters where tides and currents encourage the growth of zooplankton, on which it feeds. Shrimp and small herring, however, have also been found in the gut of basking sharks.

Basking sharks live on continental and coastal shelves—often close to land but just off the surf zone—and will enter bays. To feed, they swim slowly at the surface, usually in groups of three or four, along headlands, around islands, and in regions where two or more currents meet. Although their shallow-water behaviour has been known for some time, recent evidence suggests that these giant fish also descend as deep as a kilometre below the surface.

The adult basking shark can grow to be as long as a city bus (10 metres) and, not surprisingly, has no known predators. Juveniles may, however, be prey for other large shark species.

LIFE HISTORY

Named for its conspicuous behaviour—feeding at the surface—the basking shark nevertheless has a poorly understood life history. Most details are derived from a few sightings or even a single observation—as well as the assumption that this species probably behaves as do other large plankton-feeding animals.

Basking sharks are highly migratory between seasons; individuals tracked over four months travelled from the Gulf of St. Lawrence more than 2,500 kilometres south to waters off Jacksonville, Florida, and between Jamaica and Haiti. This evidence supports the theory of a single basking shark population along the Eastern Seaboard of North America.

In addition, a recent study provides evidence of transatlantic migration: a female tagged off the Isle of Man in the far northeast Atlantic swam 9,600 kilometres before the tag surfaced off eastern Newfoundland. This suggests that basking sharks in Atlantic Canadian waters may be part of an Atlantic basking shark population that is shared with the United States, the Caribbean, northern South America, and Europe.

From the observed courtship behaviour of males and females—

Identifying basking shark

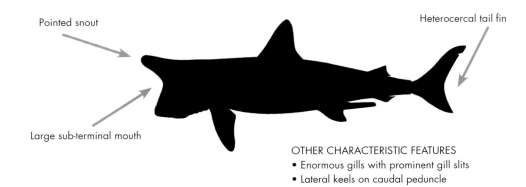

Pointed snout

Heterocercal tail fin

Large sub-terminal mouth

OTHER CHARACTERISTIC FEATURES
• Enormous gills with prominent gill slits
• Lateral keels on caudal peduncle

swimming in circles, nose to tail—basking sharks mate in early summer. The gestation period is long—between 30 and 42 months. Embryonic basking sharks may survive by eating unfertilized eggs produced in the mother's ovaries. The time between successive litters is two to three years. Nothing is known about the immature stages in this shark's life history because only one juvenile basking shark sighting has ever been recorded.

Basking sharks periodically shed their gill rakers. During the four to five months it takes to re-grow them, it is likely that these sharks stop feeding. At this time they probably rely for nourishment on nutrients stored in the massive liver, which serves as a biological "larder" until the gill rakers regenerate and feeding can resume.

FISHERY STATUS

The basking shark is harvested for its liver (a highly valued source of rich oils), its fins (for soup), its hide (for leather), and its large carcass (for fish meal). Of these, the oil is by far the most valuable and sought after. The commercial value of basking shark fins in Asia supports a lucrative trade to those countries. Harpooning is the main means of capture. Even with that modest effort, basking sharks are susceptible to over-fishing, which has happened repeatedly in local populations around the world.

In the northwest Atlantic, fisheries bycatch is the most significant threat to this species, although ship collisions are also a factor. From 1986 to 2006, the foreign and domestic offshore fisheries in Atlantic Canada had an annual average bycatch ranging from 164 to 172 tonnes. The total catch during those two decades was 3,444 tonnes. This suggests that 3,444 basking sharks may have been harvested,

since the average weight of a basking shark is 1 tonne.

According to COSEWIC, the decline in fishing activity in both offshore and inshore Canadian waters has brought a decline in basking shark bycatch. The annual average bycatch between 1997 and 2006 was 78 tonnes, down significantly from 1990's maximum recorded level, 741 tonnes.

A recent stock assessment used a population model based on the most recent population size, known bycatch over two decades, and life-history parameters. It suggests a relatively low likelihood of basking shark population decline over the past 20 years and low probability of decline to extinction levels in the next 100 years. This model, however, is highly speculative because of the high degree of uncertainty about actual population numbers. As of 2009, basking shark was listed as a species of Special Concern by COSEWIC.

Despite this stock assessment, other agencies believe the basking shark population may be more vulnerable to human impacts than any other marine fish. The IUCN has given the species Red List assessment—this flags worldwide basking shark population as Vulnerable, and the northeast Atlantic and north Pacific populations as Endangered.

}50 to
150 m

Alewife

Alosa pseudoharengus

Bigeye herring, branch herring, river herring, greyback,
white herring, saw belly, *kiack, ki'ak, gaspareau*

Special Concern

(NATIONAL MARINE
FISHERIES SERVICE, U.S.)

The alewife is native to the northwest Atlantic—as well as to some of the lakes and rivers that feed into it—from Newfoundland and Labrador south to North Carolina. Its range includes the Gulf of St. Lawrence, the outer east coast of Nova Scotia, the Bay of Fundy, and the Gulf of Maine.

The alewife is also found as an invasive landlocked species in the Great Lakes, where it was first recorded in 1931, having apparently gained access through the Erie Canal. The species can adapt easily to a wide range of salinity and prefers cooler water than some anadromous fish (although some species in the trout family, such as Arctic char, are found in colder water).

HABITAT AND APPEARANCE

With a thin body that is more than three times as long as it is high, the alewife is built for migrating in large densely packed schools—which it does in the tens of thousands up and down the coastal waters of the northwest Atlantic and into fresh water, where it migrates to spawn.

Alewives have a triangular head and large eyes with adipose eyelids. The lower jaw projects slightly beyond the upper when the mouth is closed. Young fish have a few small teeth at the front of both jaws. They disappear as the lower gill rakers grow, increasing the fish's ability to filter-feed.

The single dorsal fin is directly above the small pelvic fins. The caudal fin is deeply forked. The anal fin is relatively long with up to 19 rays. The pectoral fins, low on the sides, can have up to 16 rays. The lateral line is barely visible. Scales on the belly's midline form scutes that line up in a serrated keel (this no doubt gave rise to the nickname "saw belly"). Males are smaller and generally do not live as long as females.

Alewives, which shed their scales, are silver overall with a grey-green back. Immediately behind the head at eye level is a black spot. In the ocean, adults develop a golden cast on their head and upper body.

Alewives avoid light, descending to deeper water during the day and rising to the surface at night, following the daily vertical migration of zooplankton. In fresh water, they feed on plankton, tiny crustaceans, shrimp, and small fish. In the marine environment, the shrimp-like northern krill and related species make up more than 82 per cent (by volume) of their total stomach contents.

The alewife is prey for fish such as striped bass, salmonids, smallmouth bass, eel, perch, bluefish, and walleye. The birds that feed on them include terns, eagles, osprey, herons, and gulls.

Adult alewives can withstand water temperatures up to 25°C and young-of-the-year can live in waters up to 30°C. In fresh water, alewives are usually found in deeper water but they venture into shallows and tributary streams in the spring to spawn

before returning to the deepest parts of a lake to overwinter.

LIFE HISTORY

Alewives spend most of their lives in the coastal waters of the northwest Atlantic. Each spring, from April to July, adults use their sense of smell to find and migrate up the rivers in which they were born. They then spawn mainly in freshwater lakes, ponds, and streams, and sometimes in brackish water.

The species moves into coastal areas in February. Once river temperatures begin to warm, males (and later, females) enter fresh water by day and spawning under cover of darkness in warmer, slow-moving, shallow sections of rivers, streams, or lakes.

Females release their eggs over sand, gravel, or even aquatic vegetation. Males quickly fertilize them. Demersal in quiet water, the eggs float in areas with a current. Many alewives die after spawning. Survivors return to the sea within a few days.

Three to five days after hatching, the larvae have absorbed the yolk sac and are

beginning to feed on tiny zooplankton. They have schooled by the first week but remain in freshwater nursery areas until summer's end. By early fall they are 3.8 to 12.5 centimetres long. As water temperatures dip in mid-fall, the young-of-the-year swim downstream to brackish water, where they feed on small invertebrates. The mortality rate to this stage is daunting—only three fish from every batch of 100,000-plus eggs make it to the ocean.

Little is known about alewife life history from the time juveniles enter the ocean until they re-enter the rivers to spawn. Recent research, however, is filling in some gaps. For example, ocean-going alewives grow heavier and longer (from 25 to 35 centimetres) than landlocked individuals (which average 15 centimetres). Though smaller, however, landlocked alewives mature faster than their saltwater counterparts. In addition, alewives feed on visible zooplankton at sea, when they are in sufficient numbers, and filter-feed on microscopic zooplankton only when larger prey cannot be detected.

Research off the coast of Nova Scotia shows that feeding activity—and the proportion of feeding fish—is greatest in water 200 or more metres deep. In summer, the Bay of Fundy is the region where alewives most often had full stomachs; in winter,

feeding activity shifts to the Scotian Shelf, confirming the theory that these two regions are seasonally important foraging areas.

FISHERY STATUS

Important to northeastern Aboriginal people as a crop fertilizer before the colonial period, the alewife has also played a role in the lives of North American settlers. It has been the basis of a directed commercial fishery in lakes, rivers, and estuaries since the early 1800s and is a bycatch species in ocean fisheries. The commercial fishery has declined significantly, however, because of overfishing, loss of spawning habitat, and restriction of migration routes following dam construction. In addition, recreational catches of alewife have decreased dramatically since the mid-1970s. Although not assessed by COSEWIC, the National Marine Fisheries Service in the United States lists the alewife as a Species of Concern.

Identifying alewife

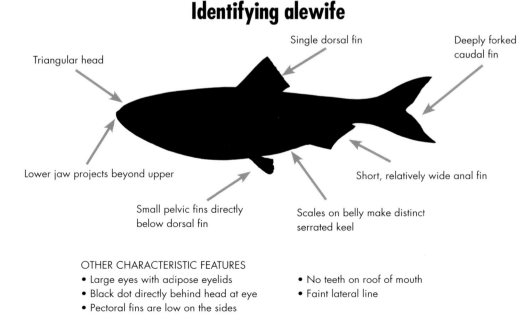

Triangular head

Single dorsal fin

Deeply forked caudal fin

Lower jaw projects beyond upper

Small pelvic fins directly below dorsal fin

Scales on belly make distinct serrated keel

Short, relatively wide anal fin

OTHER CHARACTERISTIC FEATURES
• Large eyes with adipose eyelids
• Black dot directly behind head at eye
• Pectoral fins are low on the sides

• No teeth on roof of mouth
• Faint lateral line

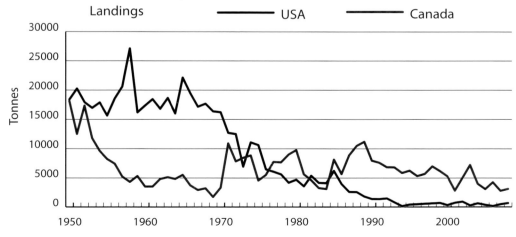

Landings   —— USA   —— Canada

} 0 to 120 m

Prioritized Candidate List

(COSEWIC, GROUP 2)

American shad

Alosa sapidissima
Atlantic shad, common shad, gate, shad, white shad, *alose savoureuse*

A swift and agile swimmer, the American shad has a natural coastal range from Nain in Labrador to southern Florida. Shad have been reported from every coastal region of the Maritimes—from the Bay of Fundy to Labrador—and they also occur in waters off the island of Newfoundland. In the Gulf of St. Lawrence, shad are most abundant in the Miramichi River in May to mid-July, consistent with a spawning run. Declines related to pollution and dams have been noted, and restoration projects have been established. It is likely that stocks can be identified in relation to specific river systems.

HABITAT AND APPEARANCE

The American shad has a thin body, fin rays, and a deeply forked caudal fin. Its large mouth and many gill rakers enable filter-feeding on plankton. Females are usually larger than males.

At sea, silvery adult shad may be iridescent brown-black through blue-green on the back. Up to three rows of dark, progressively smaller spots run along each side from the gill cover to the area below the dorsal fin. Shortly after entering their natal rivers for spawning, shad take on a bronze or copper tone. The head and belly become red, especially in males. If an American shad is not handled cautiously, the row of sharp scutes that runs along the lower edge of the abdomen can inflict a serious cut.

American shad migrate over vast distances: northward in summer and back to the southern part of their ocean range in winter. Most shad migrate between offshore North Carolina and the Gulf of Maine, following preferred ocean temperatures in the 13° to 18°C range. They congregate on the surface at various times during the year but are hard to find in winter. They prefer deeper water before spawning season.

Like other herring species, American shad feed mainly on plankton in the water column but will also consume small shrimp and fish eggs. They will also (rarely) prey on small fish. Predators include Atlantic cod, dogfish, sharks, bluefin tuna, kingfish, porpoises, and seals. Young shad in fresh water are prey for bass, American eel, and birds.

LIFE HISTORY

American shad spend most of their lives at sea, schooling by the thousands. Every summer, these migrating members of the herring family congregate in the upper Bay of Fundy or along Canada's east coast, including the mouth of the St. Lawrence River. Spawning populations migrate as far north as Nain but may be found as far south as Florida.

As a true anadromous fish, the American shad spawns in the river of its birth. In eastern Canada, spawning runs enter rivers when the water temperature is between 8° and 12°C, usually from April to late June. Males arrive first, following deep channels with moderate to strong currents. Females arrive soon after and begin to spawn when the water temperature is above 12°C. Spawning peaks when waters reach 16° to 20°C.

Every night during the spawning season, female shad, each accompanied by several males, spawn at the surface, releasing transparent amber eggs in batches of about 30,000. Large females will release as many as 400,000 eggs, which are 2.5 to 3.5 millimetres in diameter and slightly heavier than water. They settle individually and drift with the current. When the eggs hatch, transparent, slender larvae 10 millimetres long emerge. American shad reach mature lengths of 40 to 60 centimetres between 4 and 5 years of age.

FISHERY STATUS

American shad are landed in commercial, recreational, and First Nations fisheries, all of which tend to be local with small landings. These factors make total landings difficult to track. In Atlantic Canada, the species is a Group 2 candidate for assessment by COSEWIC. It is suspected of being at risk of extirpation in some regions because the fish mainly return to the river where they hatched—and population declines are closely related to conditions in spawning rivers. The presence of dams or dangerous levels of pollution top the list of threats to the species' survival. Active restoration efforts in the United States seem to be producing positive results.

Did You Know . . .

- The American shad's large scales are easily shed in salt water but become firmly embedded after the fish enters fresh water.

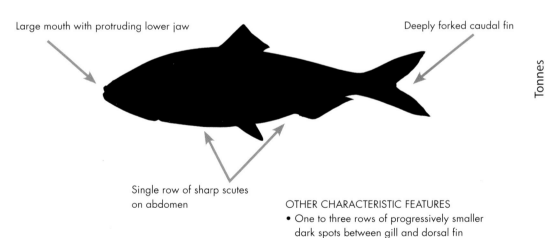

Identifying American shad

Large mouth with protruding lower jaw

Deeply forked caudal fin

Single row of sharp scutes on abdomen

OTHER CHARACTERISTIC FEATURES
- One to three rows of progressively smaller dark spots between gill and dorsal fin

Landings — USA — Canada

Tonnes

5000
4000
3000
2000
1000
0

1950   1960   1970   1980   1990   2000

Atlantic herring

Clupea harengus

Bloater, Digby chick, kipper, Labrador herring, mattie, sea herring, sea stick, skadlin, sperling, spring herring, summer herring, yawling, *hareng atlantique*

S   S

} 1 to 200 m

The Atlantic herring is among the most abundant fish species in the ocean. Although not considered an Arctic species, herring can be found across the entire North Atlantic and into the Arctic Ocean, wherever plankton concentrate in rich layers just below the surface. Enormous schools can be found in the Beaufort Sea, Davis Strait, Labrador Sea, Gulf of St. Lawrence, Bay of Fundy, and the Gulf of Maine. When the ocean is calm, herring schools can be detected by rippling on the surface that can be seen from as far away as 2 kilometres.

HABITAT AND APPEARANCE

Atlantic herring is a small fish with a dark blue back and uniformly silver sides. Its slender elongated body has a rounded belly and a keel of scutes. The caudal fin is deeply forked. The base of the pelvic fin is below or just behind where the dorsal fin begins; the single anal fin has a low profile. The lower jaw projects slightly beyond the upper jaw, and gills are large with an evenly rounded border.

Herring schools, which can include millions or even tens of millions of individuals, react rapidly to avoid and confuse predators—of which there is no shortage. Atlantic herring usually school in deeper waters by day and rise to the surface at night.

This species, high in fats and protein, plays a vital role throughout its life cycle in the region's marine ecosystem. It serves as forage for a wide array of the ocean's key predators. Many species of demersal fish, including Atlantic cod, haddock, red hake, and winter flounder, feed on clusters of herring eggs on the bottom. As juveniles, herring are eaten by pelagic fish, marine mammals, and seabirds. Adult Atlantic herring are a key species in the diet of a number of larger fish, sharks, skates, marine mammals, and seabirds.

During the first year of life, Atlantic herring is the main predator of small planktonic copepods. Later it broadens its diet to include krill, tiny fish, and arrow worms. When food density and particle size are suitable, this species can switch from small prey to microscopic organisms, which it captures using gill rakers.

LIFE HISTORY

Juvenile Atlantic herring congregate in shallow water near the banks where they were spawned. At 2 years of age they form vast schools and seek out deeper water. Adopting a precise three-dimensional formation, these schools cruise at a constant speed of just under 4 kilometres an hour along a triangular route from spawning grounds to nursery grounds to feeding grounds and back to spawning grounds. Such wide triangular journeys help to minimize cannibalism of herring larvae by reducing encounters between herring at different life stages.

Spawning strategies differ among Atlantic herring populations. Generally, however, both males and females constantly rub against one another and against the sea bottom during spawning. Mucus-coated eggs remain on the bottom, sticking in layers or clumps to rock, stones, gravel, sand, or even algae beds. Eggs that lodge in crevices or beneath solid structures appear to have the highest survival rate. Wave action and turbulence from coastal currents help keep the eggs oxygenated—but if the egg layers settle too thickly on the sea floor, the eggs at the bottom of the pile may be suffocated.

Even with a 75 per cent mortality rate, a single aggregation of larval herring in early spring—when they measure just 40.5 millimetres—may be 2 to 3 kilometres long and 10 to 20 metres deep. These concentrations thin out in late spring as larvae reach the juvenile stage and begin schooling.

FISHERY STATUS

Excessive harvests of Atlantic herring in the northwest by international fishing fleets during the 1960s—with landings topping out at 470,000 tonnes in 1968—led to a collapse of the stock in the 1970s. International fishing was then phased out, and the herring stock began to recover. Total landings increased from the mid-1980s through the 1990s.

In the mid-1990s, a fleet of mid-water trawlers was introduced into the fishery: 50-metre-long, industrial-scale vessels that can hold 500,000 kilograms of fish. To catch herring, these trawlers drag a 5-centimetre-mesh net the size of a football field (but six stories deep) through the herring spawning

grounds; sometimes two vessels are used to maximize the take.

The fisheries' combined totals peaked in the 1970s. From 2002 to 2005, total landings averaged 109,000 tonnes, followed by 116,000 tonnes in 2006 and more than 90,000 tonnes in 2008. Underlying the declining catches is a 24 per cent decrease in Atlantic herring biomass between 2000 and 2008.

In the first decade of the 21st century (see the FAO landings graph), Canadian landings exceeded those of the United States by more than 100 per cent.

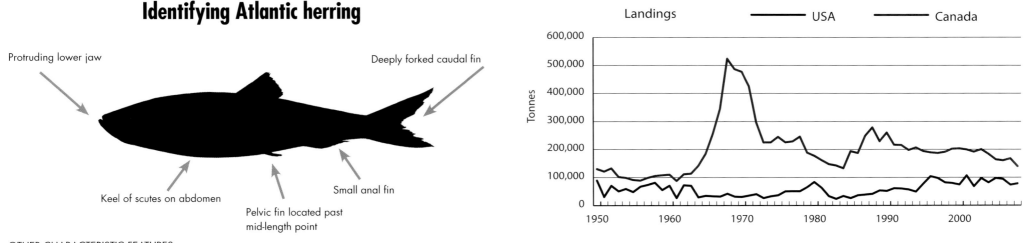

Identifying Atlantic herring

Protruding lower jaw

Deeply forked caudal fin

Keel of scutes on abdomen

Pelvic fin located past mid-length point

Small anal fin

OTHER CHARACTERISTIC FEATURES
• Large gills with evenly rounded edge

Landings — USA — Canada

Tonnes

Lumpfish

Cyclopterus lumpus

Blue lump, henfish, lumpsucker, paddle-cock, red lump, sea cock, sea hen, sea owl, *lompe, poule de l'eau, lepisuk, nipisa*

} 50 to
150 m

Lumpfish are found near the ocean bottom throughout the North Atlantic. In the northwest Atlantic, the species ranges from Hudson Bay and James Bay south along the coast of Labrador, through the coastal waters of Atlantic Canada, to the waters off New Jersey and (rarely) to Chesapeake Bay.

HABITAT AND APPEARANCE

The lumpfish, half as deep as it is long, has a short head and an arched dorsal profile. The teeth are small and the gills large. The body has seven rows of large, pointed, usually dark-tipped tubercles. The one on the dorsal ridge is a cartilaginous flap that encloses the first dorsal fin and then divides in two until it reaches the second dorsal fin. Three more rows run along each side: over the eye, just above the pectoral fin, and along the line that delineates the side from the belly. Between the rows of large tubercles, the skin is thickly studded with tiny tubercles.

The large, rounded pectoral fins (bigger on males than females) meet at the throat. The caudal fin is broad and square-tipped. The pelvic fins, each with six pairs of fleshy knobs surrounded by a circular flap of skin just behind the throat, are uniquely adapted to function as suction disks.

Adult lumpfish can be blue-grey, yellow-green, chocolate

brown, or slate blue. The belly, usually pale, is sometimes whitish, sometimes a yellowed tint of the body colour. Males are more vividly coloured than females. Their bellies and suckers turn red during the breeding season. Though they can grow to 61 centimetres and weigh more than 9 kilograms, lumpfish usually only reach one-third that size.

Lumpfish prefer stony bottoms between 50 and 150 metres deep but may also be found in floating seaweed. Some evidence suggests that once they move to the open ocean, lumpfish often feed pelagically at 50 to 60 metres. In winter, they are found at depths of 400 metres or more, as feeding intensifies and they seek water of about 8°C.

Their diet includes crustaceans, segmented worms, small fish, and jellyfish. A sluggish swimmer, lumpfish are prey to seals, Greenland shark, whales, and seabirds.

LIFE HISTORY

Lumpfish are solitary benthopelagic fish that migrate inshore in the spring and early summer to spawn. In the northwest Atlantic, they choose shallow coastal waters of 27 metres or more, with seaweed or stone bottoms. Males migrate first and establish territories. Females arrive later and lay eggs in batches every 8 to 14 days. After spawning, the females migrate to deeper water, leaving the fasting brood males to guard the egg masses.

At first, the male fans the eggs with its fins almost continuously, then gradually less frequently. This behaviour is believed to promote oxygenation and remove silt, but recent research suggests that the initial intensity may also help disperse the potentially toxic ammonia that is released when the eggs clump together.

The developing eggs slowly change from pink to pale green, then become dark. Only when the tadpole-shaped larvae finally hatch does the emaciated male's vigil end. The larvae are active swimmers and quickly learn to cling to seaweed. At 34 millimetres, the fry exhibit most adult features.

Adult lumpfish hide in seaweed, using their ventral suckers to secure themselves to rocks and other bottom objects. They have occasionally been found clinging to foreign objects, such as lobster traps—there is one historical record of a lumpfish affixing itself to an unfortunate mackerel.

It was once assumed that the lumpfish was primarily a demersal feeder in rocky nearshore areas. Studies now indicate that these fish spend much of their adult lives in the pelagic zone far from land, but little is known about their offshore distribution.

FISHERY STATUS

The lumpfish fishery is directed at females, for the caviar market. Demand is weak for the flesh because it is high in water content and low in protein and fat. The fishery runs from April to July in shallow inshore waters. Lumpfish management is based not on total allowable catch but on regulations of mesh size, number of nets, and length and timing of the fishing season. Fishers with boats of less than 10.7 metres use gill nets with a minimum mesh size of 26.7 centimetres. The level of effort depends entirely on market demand, which can vary significantly from year to year.

Whole lumpfish are landed in Division 4T, but only roe is landed in Northwest Atlantic Fisheries Organization (NAFO) subdivision 3Pn and divisions 4R and 4S. Scientific knowledge about lumpfish is limited, but research projects help to give some perspective. Landings dropped from 264 tonnes in 2005 to just 11 tonnes in 2009, then increased slightly to 36 tonnes in 2010. The 2009 value was the lowest since 1993 and represents a 95 per cent

decrease in just over four years.

The alarming decline in landings, effort, and yields indicates a significant decline in the lumpfish population. The long-term effects of harvesting spawning fish may have caught up with the fishery, but there is no direct evidence to support this because the exploitation rate is unknown. Despite uncertainties, however, DFO reports that this assessment indicates the status of this resource is "very weak and likely over-exploited."

This observation follows a pattern with other groundfish, in particular the Atlantic cod. In addition to overfishing and poor management, it seems clear that the cold water of the 1990s also negatively impacted the lumpfish population. With no research on this stock after 2005, current baseline data are not available.

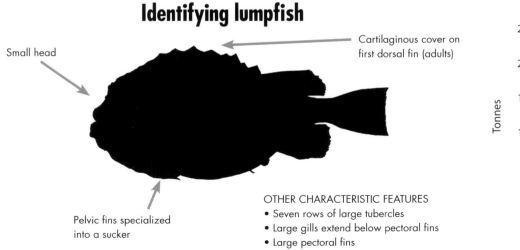

Identifying lumpfish

Small head

Cartilaginous cover on first dorsal fin (adults)

Pelvic fins specialized into a sucker

OTHER CHARACTERISTIC FEATURES
• Seven rows of large tubercles
• Large gills extend below pectoral fins
• Large pectoral fins

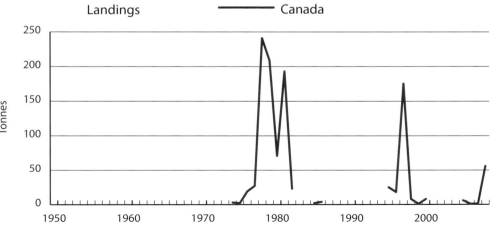

Landings — Canada

Tonnes

250

200

150

100

50

0

1950   1960   1970   1980   1990   2000

Arctic cod

} 0 to 400 m

Boreogadus saida

Arctic tomcod, polar cod, *morue polaire, saïda franc, ogaq, equaluaq, itok, ôgark, ovac*

Circumpolar in distribution, the Arctic cod inhabits the Arctic seas off Canada, Alaska, northern Russia, and Greenland. Within Canada's boundaries, it is found in the Beaufort Sea, throughout the Arctic Archipelago, in Hudson Bay and Baffin Bay, along the Labrador coast, off Newfoundland's eastern coast, on the northern and eastern Grand Banks, and, very rarely, in the Gulf of St. Lawrence.

HABITAT AND APPEARANCE

With a maximum length of 40 centimetres, the Arctic cod can be distinguished from Atlantic cod, rock cod, haddock, and tomcod by the slenderness of its body, its deeply forked caudal fin, the small size or even absence of the barbel, and a projecting lower jaw (in the other species the upper jaw projects past the lower). Palatine teeth are always absent.

Like the other cod, however, this species has three dorsal and two anal fins. The pectoral fin extends beyond the end of the first dorsal fin. The pelvic fin has a slightly elongated ray. A light lateral line runs along each side from the head to the caudal fin. The small embedded scales do not overlap. The Arctic cod has a brown back with many fine dots. The sides and belly are silver.

Arctic cod can be found inshore among ice floes and offshore to depths of 1 kilometre. Where the ocean is ice-covered, Arctic cod seek out ice with irregular undersides, where it is more difficult for predators to find them.

Larvae prefer temperatures between 2° and 5°C, which accounts in part for the higher mortality rate of larvae from eggs hatched before mid-July (in cooler water) than those hatched later. Fry thrive in temperatures ranging from 5° to 7°C.

Juvenile Arctic cod, 4 to 6 centimetres long, feed on small crustacean eggs and larvae. At 8 to 12 centimetres, they eat shrimp-like crustaceans and arrow worms. The mature Arctic cod's diet includes tiny lipid-rich plankton, small fish, and smaller Arctic cod.

This species has a key role in the food chain as a forage fish for predators that include narwhal, beluga, ringed seal, and seabirds, some of which depend on it as a primary food source. Other predators include Atlantic cod, Arctic char, Greenland halibut, and Atlantic salmon.

LIFE HISTORY

Arctic cod congregate at the surface in autumn, then migrate into coastal waters; however, they have also been found deep offshore and in ice-free waters, where they form enormous schools.

Arctic cod grow more slowly in the Arctic Ocean than off Labrador, but growth can be equated with age. Both males and females reach maturity after 3 years of age, at 20 centimetres, after which the growth rate slows considerably. Maximum length is 40 centimetres, and the maximum recorded lifespan is 7 years.

Arctic cod spawn only once. In the late fall and early winter, they school in large numbers, migrating beneath the shore ice, where females spawn and males release milt from gonads that make up 10 per cent of their body weight. The first larvae appear from May to early July but continue to hatch into late summer.

FISHERY STATUS

There is no directed Canadian fishery for Arctic cod for human consumption, but the species is harvested in Russia and north European countries as a bycatch in the capelin fishery (and is considered excellent fare). Arctic cod is also used for fish meal and oil.

Identifying Arctic cod

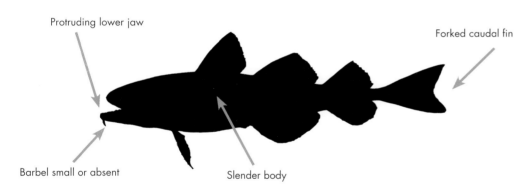

Protruding lower jaw

Forked caudal fin

Barbel small or absent

Slender body

150 to
200 m

Endangered
(VARIES BY STOCK)

Atlantic cod

Gadus morhua
Codfish, cod, fish, northern cod, rock cod,
morue commune, morue de l'Atlantique

It is difficult to overestimate the international economic and social impact of cod. For centuries, Europeans came to harvest the seemingly inexhaustible species, settling close to the fishing grounds. In the northwest Atlantic, the greatest concentrations of Atlantic cod were off Newfoundland, in the Gulf of St. Lawrence, and on the Scotian Shelf, although it ranges from shallow inshore waters to the edge of the continental shelf and from the coast of Greenland, across the Davis Strait to Frobisher Bay and Ungava Bay and south to Cape Hatteras, North Carolina.

The Atlantic cod population in the northwest Atlantic today is estimated to be 3 per cent of its 1960 numbers—in some offshore areas where it once flourished, nets are being hauled empty.

HABITAT AND APPEARANCE

The Atlantic cod's streamlined body tapers at both ends, typical of fish that can swim at moderate speed for long distances. It has three dorsal and two anal fins. The caudal fin is almost square. This species has a large mouth with a protruding upper jaw, wide gill openings, and a single, well-developed barbel. Its scales are so small they feel smooth.

Atlantic cod vary in colour from brown to green to grey. Small, dark spots dot their backs. A pale lateral line curves above the pectoral fins.

They vary in size/age ratios by stock location. On average, they measure 60 to 70 centimetres and weigh 2 to 3 kilograms, only rarely exceeding 30 kilograms.

This epibenthic-pelagic species occupies a range of habitats in unique populations, from the nearshore to the continental shelf. The omnivorous Atlantic cod schools at dawn and dusk to feed on invertebrates such as crab and shrimp and fish such as capelin, herring, and even juvenile cod. It consumes just about anything it can swallow—including sea anemones.

As juveniles, cod are eaten by spiny dogfish, winter skate,

silver hake, sea raven, squid, Atlantic halibut, flounder, and adult cod. Because of the adults' large size, their predators are mainly large sharks and seals.

LIFE HISTORY

The Atlantic cod is among the largest of the 100-plus varieties of codfish. Its several independent North Atlantic stocks share some common migration and spawning features and larval and juvenile behaviours.

Observers have identified a regular pattern of spawning and seasonal migrations in the Newfoundland stock: huge schools leave deep oceanic wintering areas following seams of deep, relatively warm water to nearshore summer feeding grounds. In late summer, these fish migrate north along the Newfoundland coast before returning to offshore areas to overwinter. The largest individuals lead the migrating fish; smaller fish are at the rear. Migrating cod occasionally disperse to pursue prey before massing again.

Ninety per cent of spawning occurs between mid-November and mid-May, peaking around mid-March depending on location. Spawning begins along the southern flank of Georges Bank and progresses north and west. Egg viability depends on the condition and age of females. Unhealthy or underfed fish and first-time spawners produce less viable eggs than older, larger, and healthier cod.

After hatching, larvae drift with currents. Once the yolk sac is empty(within two weeks), they begin to feed on plankton. Many of the year-class are eaten or starve. Those that survive learn to swim and seek conditions that improve their chances of survival.

The growth rate is likely influenced by water temperature and by zooplankton presence at depths from near-surface to 75 metres. Juvenile cod—2 centimetres or longer, with all fin rays present—move into deeper water as they grow. Once they reach 2.5 to 6 centimetres long, most Atlantic cod adapt to the demersal feeding patterns of mature cod.

Juveniles tolerate a wider temperature range than adults; their survival is more closely associated with ocean-floor type. Favourable are cobble substrates, solid bottoms with attached fauna such as sponges and amphipod tubes, and nearshore nurseries with eelgrass beds, in which young fish can avoid predation.

At 1 year, juveniles are 15 centimetres long; over the next two years they double or triple that length. The "tomcods" that escape nets and predators mature by the fourth or fifth year (or earlier) and are ready to spawn.

FISHERY STATUS

The Atlantic cod population is a small fraction of its former size, and no wonder—in the early 1980s, 810,000 tonnes were harvested from the northwest Atlantic. Despite this huge level of harvesting, how¬ever, it still came as a shock to many when, in July 1992, much of the Canadian Atlantic cod fishery was closed. The precipitous decline in the number of fish may be due in part to the cold ocean temperatures, but poor management and over-fishing decimated the stocks.

Offshore stocks remain at record low levels and scientists are uncertain about a recovery schedule for some stocks. COSEWIC lists all Atlantic cod populations in the northwest Atlantic as Endangered except the Arctic Lakes (Special Concern) and Arctic Marine (Data Deficient) populations.

Biologists maintain that, in the complex offshore environment, regulations alone are not enough to rebuild the cod population. They say serious international conservation efforts are needed for the

species to rebound. Suggested measures include no-catch zones for spawning areas and migration routes—both of which include Canadian and international waters.

Also puzzling is a decline in size, age, and general health at maturity in some stocks of Atlantic cod in recent decades. Theories include a general decline in stock biomass caused by colder water and intense overfishing, less available prey, increased competition for food resources, and a genetic shift to smaller individuals in response to selective pressure from the sustained harvest of larger fish.

Age and size at maturity declined by half and by two-thirds, respectively, in the 20 years after 1959. This trend continued into the 21st century in all zones between Georges Bank and Labrador—35 centimetres is the new length and 2.8 years the new age marking juveniles from adults.

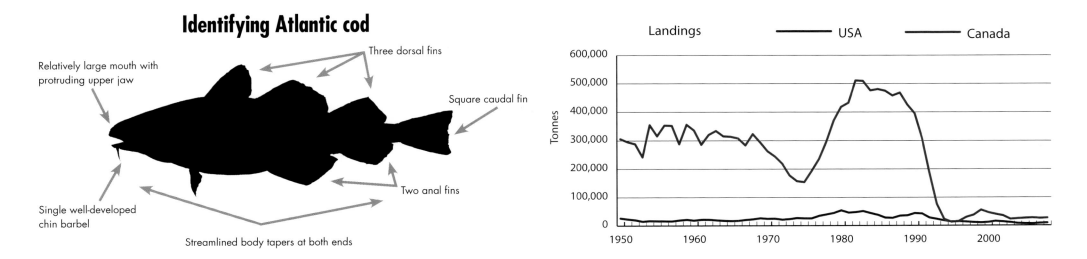

Identifying Atlantic cod

Relatively large mouth with protruding upper jaw

Three dorsal fins

Square caudal fin

Two anal fins

Single well-developed chin barbel

Streamlined body tapers at both ends

Landings — USA — Canada

Tonnes

600,000
500,000
400,000
300,000
200,000
100,000
0

1950   1960   1970   1980   1990   2000

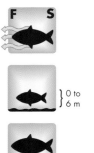

}0 to
6 m

Atlantic tomcod

Microgadus tomcod
Frostfish, London trout, tomcod, *poulamon*

This northwest Atlantic species is indigenous to waters from southern Labrador to Virginia. An inshore fish, Atlantic tomcod is abundant in estuarine habitats such as river mouths and salt marshes—it seldom descends more than 5 metres below the surface, and spends its life within 2 kilometres of shore. It inhabits brackish water much of the time but will swim farther into fresh water during the winter months. Landlocked tomcod have also been found in northeastern lakes.

HABITAT AND APPEARANCE

The Atlantic tomcod bears a strong resemblance to the Atlantic cod: it has the same elongated body and pale lateral line but is much smaller. As with cod, its upper jaw projects past the lower and there is a barbel on the chin. However, Atlantic tomcod can be easily distinguished from *Gadus morhua* by several physical features. The shape of the pelvic and caudal fins, particularly, provides definitive clues.

The pelvic fins of the Atlantic cod are moderately broad and rounded; the filament at the tip is less than a fourth of the total length of the fin. The pelvic fins of the Atlantic tomcod, however, are narrower, more tapered, and have a filament equal in length to the rest of the fin. It is actually more suggestive of a feeler than a fin. The shape of the tomcod's caudal fin is rounded compared with the squared or slightly concave fin of the cod. In addition, because it lives in shallower water than the cod, the Atlantic tomcod's eyes are relatively much smaller than the cod's, and its body is more slender. The tomcod's first dorsal fin originates above the middle of the pectoral fin (or farther back) and the pectoral fins stretch back to the middle of the first dorsal fin.

Overall olive green, olive brown, or dark green, the tomcod has some yellow on its back. The lower sides have a yellow cast, particularly in larger individuals. The belly is grey or yellow-white. The dorsal fins are mottled with dark blotches and the edge of the anal fin is olive green or olive brown.

The Atlantic tomcod is found at the high-tide mark of salt marshes and mud flats (to a depth of 6 metres), in eelgrass beds, and in bays, estuaries, and inshore coastal waters within 2 kilometres of shore. Tomcod have also been caught in the freshwater portion of rivers far above the saltwater mark.

The Atlantic tomcod feeds on shrimp, amphipods and other small crustaceans, worms, molluscs, squid, and fish fry such as alewife, cunner, herring, sand lance, smelt, sculpin, stickleback, and striped bass. Little is known about predation on tomcod by other fish species, but Atlantic tomcod may serve as an alternative prey species for any larger fish in the estuaries.

LIFE HISTORY

The Atlantic tomcod spawns in shallow estuaries, river mouths, and other locations where water may be brackish or salt. The reproductive season lasts from November to February, peaking in early to mid-winter.

Fertilized tomcod eggs sink to the bottom (unlike the pelagic eggs of the Atlantic cod), where they clump together in masses. The eggs may also adhere to seaweed, stones, or debris. Incubation takes about a month, depending on water temperature. When they emerge, tomcod larvae are larger and more developed than emerging Atlantic cod larvae.

The fry likely spend the summer in the waters where they hatch, reaching 5.2 to 7.7 centimetres by fall. The rate of growth after this period has not yet been recorded. They return to bays and harbours in the fall and migrate into the estuaries to spawn in the late fall or early winter. In the spring, tomcod move away from shore to cooler water.

FISHERY STATUS

The Atlantic tomcod was the target of a regionally important commercial fishery in northern estuaries in the 19th century, but that fishery declined during the first half

of the 20th century. Today, it is taken as bycatch in the smelt fishery in Atlantic Canada and is sometimes targeted by handline and hoop net. It is also taken in a winter ice fishery in the St. Lawrence River. The species has not been assessed by COSEWIC, but estimates rate it as having low vulnerability. The FAO has no American statistics for this species.

Identifying Atlantic tomcod

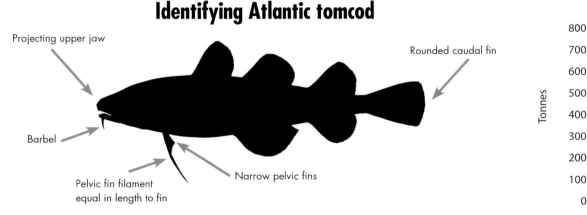

Projecting upper jaw

Rounded caudal fin

Barbel

Pelvic fin filament equal in length to fin

Narrow pelvic fins

OTHER CHARACTERISTIC FEATURES
• Small eyes (one-fifth to one-sixth as long as head)
• First dorsal fin starts above midpoint of pectoral fins
• Pale lateral line
• Pectoral fins extend to midpoint of first dorsal fin

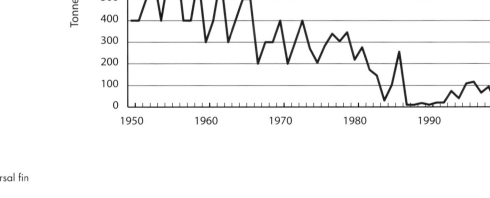

Landings — Canada

} <200 m

Greenland cod

Gadus ogac
Rock cod, *ogac, uvak*

The Greenland cod is known in northern Canada by its Inuktitut name, *ogac*. Found from Alaska to West Greenland, the Greenland cod also appears farther south along the Canadian coast and in the Miramichi estuary, the Gulf of St. Lawrence, and off Cape Breton Island. The tough texture of its flesh makes the Greenland cod undesirable as a commercial species for international markets, but it is caught and eaten locally.

HABITAT AND APPEARANCE

With its relatively broad head, two anal fins, and three dorsal fins (the first of which is rounded), the Greenland cod profile closely resembles that of the Atlantic cod. But, unlike the more widely known species, the Greenland cod has no dark body spots and is much smaller, seldom reaching more than 60 centimetres (except in Greenland's waters, where individuals 70 centimetres long have been recorded).

The upper jaw of the Greenland cod protrudes slightly and there is a thin, well-developed barbel under the lower jaw. The eyes are large. Body colour is brown to black, with pale yellowish blotches, and a grey to white belly. A light lateral line extends the full length of the body.

The Greenland cod inhabits waters close to the coast that are no more than 200 metres deep and is rarely found offshore. Though it can tolerate low salinity, it is unlikely to enter fresh water. Its main prey are fish such as capelin, Arctic cod, and Greenland halibut. Greenland cod also eat crustaceans, molluscs, starfish, and worms. Their own cannibalistic tendencies aside, Greenland cod have few predators.

LIFE HISTORY

Greenland cod live on the ocean bottom in relatively shallow water and, unlike Atlantic cod, do not migrate and do not congregate in schools.

The Greenland cod is small for a cod. Individuals may reach 50 centimetres in length by age 6. They usually die by age 9, but in the waters off Greenland they sometimes live to age 11.

Female Greenland cod spawn annually after maturation (3 to 4 years of age) in frigid Arctic waters. Spawning occurs between February and May. Eggs are laid in batches that sink to the bottom.

FISHERY STATUS

Once abundant in the coastal waters of Greenland, the Greenland cod stock has been greatly reduced in recent years despite its limited commercial value. Low rates of recruitment are a significant part of the problem. Intensifying the poor health of the stock is the decreasing mean weight and length of mature Greenland cod, which has dropped by more than 48 per cent since the 1970s.

Did You Know . . .

• Like the Vikings before them, Greenland cod may have migrated to southern Greenland from Iceland — but much later than their seafaring human counterparts: around the late 1800s.

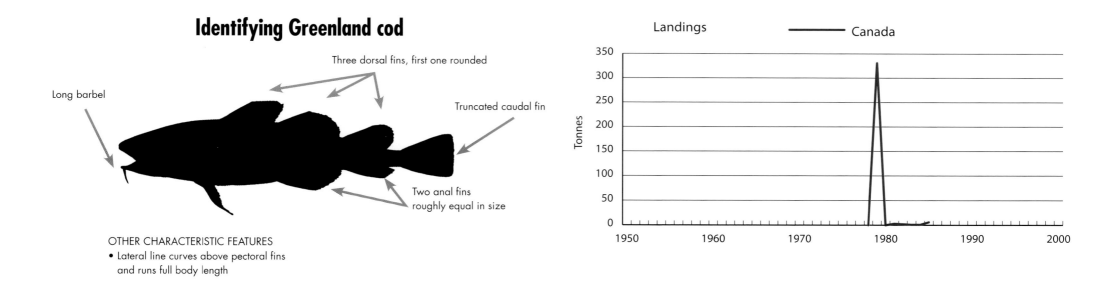

Identifying Greenland cod

Three dorsal fins, first one rounded

Long barbel

Truncated caudal fin

Two anal fins roughly equal in size

OTHER CHARACTERISTIC FEATURES
• Lateral line curves above pectoral fins and runs full body length

Landings — Canada

Tonnes

350
300
250
200
150
100
50
0

1950   1960   1970   1980   1990   2000

} 20 to 549 m

Threatened
(COSEWIC, 2003)

Cusk

Brosme brosme
Brismark, brosme, moonfish, torsk, tusk

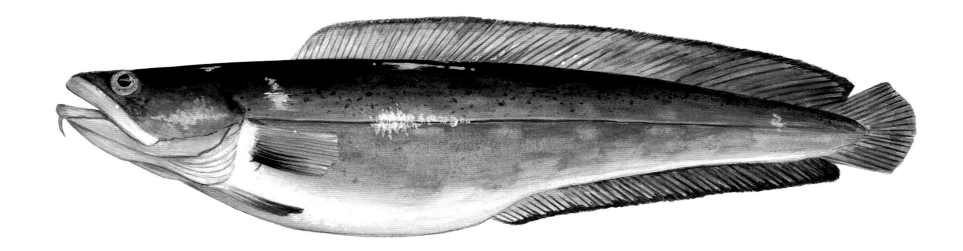

The cusk is a large, slow-moving bottom-feeder. In the northwest Atlantic, it is commonly found in the Strait of Belle Isle, on the Grand Banks of Newfoundland, and south to New Jersey. The northernmost limit of this Threatened species is probably southern Greenland, where it is caught infrequently. Since 1970, the main cusk population—in the Gulf of Maine and on the southeast Scotian Shelf—has declined by more than 90 per cent.

HABITAT AND APPEARANCE

Solitary and bottom-dwelling, cusk can grow to approximately 100 centimetres and weigh 14 kilograms. In Canadian waters, these offshore fish primarily congregate in small schools over rocky, pebble, or gravel bottoms. They avoid smooth sand.

The single elongated dorsal and anal fins are separated from the rounded caudal fin by deep notches; these fins distinguish the cusk from other fish in the Gadidae family. The fleshy pelvic fin has no elongated rays. The ventral fins have a characteristic dark margin rimmed with white.

Though skin colour varies on the dorsal side, cusk tend toward red-brown or green-brown, fading to yellow toward the pale belly. A continuous lateral line runs from the pores on the head along the sides to the start of the caudal peduncle. Younger fish are easily identified by six transverse yellow bands on their sides.

Sporting a barbel on the lower jaw, which is slightly shorter than the upper jaw, cusk feed primarily on crustaceans, shellfish, flatfish, gurnard, and starfish. They are relatively easy prey for offshore seals. Large cusk are becoming increasingly rare, as is the species generally. In the northwest Atlantic today, the cusk found are usually no more than 50 to 80 centimetres long.

LIFE HISTORY

This slow-growing fish takes up to eight years to reach maturity. There is no clear evidence of seasonal onshore or offshore migration, and it is unlikely that cusk move from bank to bank. Within their territory, however, they do migrate vertically from greater to lesser depths. Cusk are generally solitary but will form small schools.

A mature female cusk can produce 2 million eggs or more. Eggs float at or near the surface. The fry remain near the surface, feeding pelagically, until they reach 5 centimetres in length. They then descend to begin their demersal life.

FISHERY STATUS

Based on the findings of a 2003 assessment and status report, COSEWIC listed cusk as a Threatened species. Following a drastic decline in population—which, by 1998, stood at just 10 per cent of the 1970 population—protective measures were finally put in place.

In 1999, a bycatch cap of 1,000 tonnes was placed on cusk landings in the 4VWX Division fixed-gear fishery. In 2003, the cap was further reduced to 750 tonnes. Despite these restrictions and escalating concerns over the future of the stock, cusk is still harvested, mainly as bycatch in trap fisheries and longline fisheries for other groundfish. And despite its Threatened status, it is still sold in Atlantic Canada.

Did You Know . . .

• It is difficult to determine what cusk eat because their stomachs often turn inside out as they are being hauled to the surface.

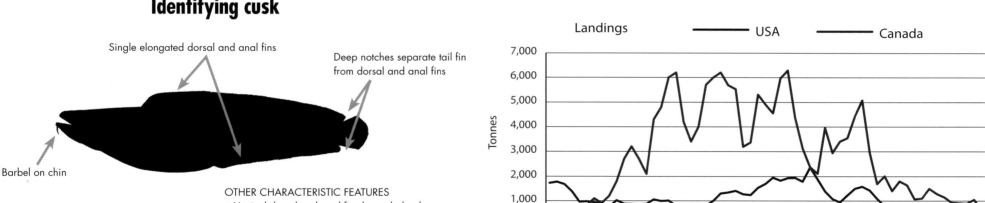

Identifying cusk

Single elongated dorsal and anal fins

Deep notches separate tail fin from dorsal and anal fins

Barbel on chin

OTHER CHARACTERISTIC FEATURES
• Vertical dorsal and anal fins have dark edge rimmed with white
• Continuous lateral line curves above pectoral fins
• Fleshy pelvic fin with no elongated rays

Landings — USA — Canada

75 to
200 m

**Prioritized
Candidate List**

(COSEWIC, GROUP 1)

Haddock

Melanogrammus aeglefinus
Chat, gibber, jumbo, pinger, ping pong, scrod,
snapper haddock, *églefin, poisson de St. Pierre*

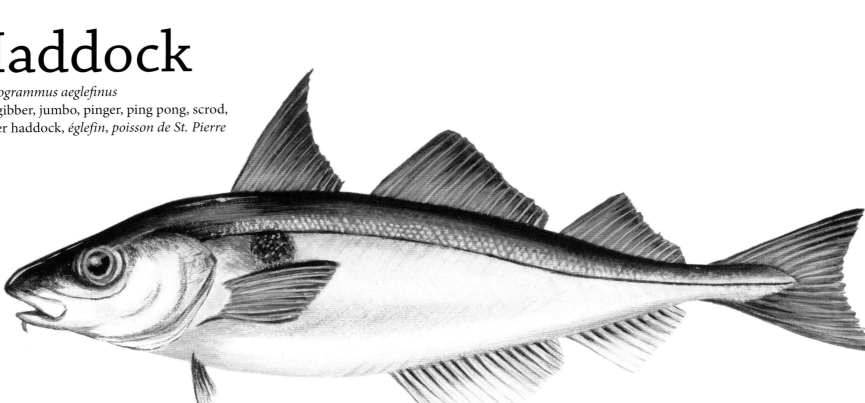

The haddock is a groundfish of the North Atlantic. It is also occasionally found along the southern tip of Greenland. In the northwest Atlantic, it ranges from the Strait of Belle Isle south to Cape May, New Jersey. Within this region, six distinct haddock stocks have been identified.

In Atlantic Canadian waters, haddock frequent the continental shelf from the Bay of Fundy along the east coast of Cape Breton Island and east to the Grand Banks.

Historically, haddock had the highest biomass of any groundfish on the Grand Banks. Intensive year-round fishing from the 1940s to the 1960s and high rates of discard for juvenile haddock, however, took a heavy toll on the stocks as the remaining fishery focussed along the Scotian Shelf and in the Bay of Fundy and Gulf of Maine.

HABITAT AND APPEARANCE

Haddock have three dorsal fins; the first is the highest, rising steeply to a point and sloping down gradually toward the back. The first of two anal fins has the longest base. There is a black blotch just above each pectoral fin. From the pores on the head, a distinct black lateral line slopes downward in a slight curve to the caudal peduncle. The caudal fin is forked. The top of the head slopes steeply to a protruding upper jaw. Beneath the lower jaw is a small chin barbel.

Its overlapping scales give the haddock a dark purple-grey sheen on the head and back. Below the lateral line, the colour lightens to silver grey with a pink tint.

The larvae and early juvenile haddock feed on plankton, copepods, and invertebrate eggs nearer the ocean's surface.

When juvenile haddock make the transition to demersal feeding, they seek out a pebble-gravel sea bottom. This environment reduces predation and provides an abundance of demersal prey, including small crustaceans (primarily copepods and krill), marine worms, and small fish.

Haddock eggs and larvae are a significant part of the diet of herring and mackerel. Juvenile haddock are also prey to spiny dogfish and skate, as well as many other groundfish species including other members of the Gadidae family, such as cod, pollock, cusk, and several species of hake. Other predators include goosefish, halibut, sea raven, and grey seals.

LIFE HISTORY

The haddock of the northwest Atlantic is most commonly found at depths between 75 and 200 metres, over rock, sand, and gravel bottoms in the offshore. Juveniles prefer shallower water than adults do.

Although adult haddock migrate over long distances, juvenile haddock do not. Seasonal movements to and from spawning grounds, however, occur across all age groups.

Males and females have similar growth rates up to their fourth year, after which females become the larger of the two sexes. Males reach maturity earlier, however. The growth rate also varies among the various haddock stocks. Historically, haddock matured in year 4, but now female haddock on average mature by their second year. Haddock more than 80 centimetres long are rare.

Spawning in the northwest Atlantic occurs at depths of 50 to 150 metres from January to late June and peaks from the end of March to early April. Haddock are highly fecund spawners, broadcasting eggs over rock, gravel, sand, or mud. A female 55 centimetres long releases as many as

900,000 eggs (in batches) near the bottom, where they are fertilized by males. The fertilized eggs rise to the surface and are carried over great distances by the currents.

After hatching, juvenile haddock are pelagic for three to five months, migrating to the bottom after they reach 6 to 10 centimetres in length. The eggs and larvae from first- and second-time spawners are smaller and less viable than those from multiple-year spawners.

FISHERY STATUS

Because of poor stock conditions, there are no directed fisheries for haddock in Divisions 3LNOP. The species is taken as bycatch, however—in cod (3PS) and yellowtail flounder (3NO) fisheries, and also in longline fisheries for skate, white hake, and Atlantic halibut. Bycatch landings of haddock averaged approximately 180 tonnes annually between 2000 and 2003.

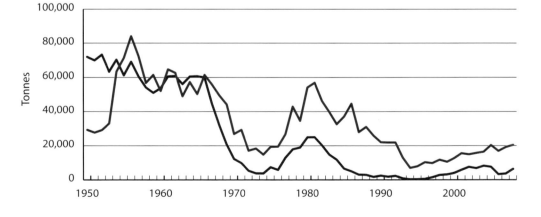

Did You Know . . .

- Historically, some fishers called the black spot above the haddock's pectoral fins "the devil's thumbprint." Others termed it "the mark of St. Peter."
- In warmer water, haddock may be the main mid-sized predatory fish. Cod takes that role in cooler water.

Identifying haddock

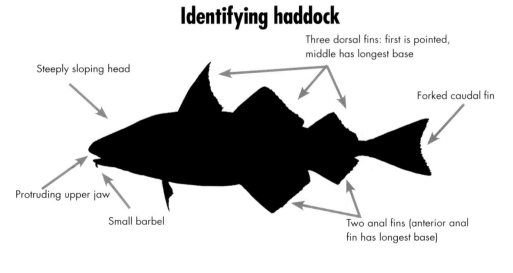

Steeply sloping head

Three dorsal fins: first is pointed, middle has longest base

Forked caudal fin

Protruding upper jaw

Small barbel

Two anal fins (anterior anal fin has longest base)

OTHER CHARACTERISTIC FEATURES
- Dark blotch above both pectoral fins
- Distinct curved black lateral line along body length

} 100 to 125 m

Prioritized Candidate List

(COSEWIC, GROUP 2)

Pollock

Pollachius virens

Black cod, blister back, Boston bluefish, coalfish, coley, colin, green cod, harbour pollock, poodler, rock salmon, saithe, *gorberge, lieu noire, merlan, merlan-noir*

The pollock is found on both sides of the North Atlantic. In the northwest Atlantic they range from southern Labrador to Cape Hatteras, although they are rarely encountered at either the northern or southern extremes of that range. They concentrate on the Scotian Shelf, on Georges Bank, and in the Gulf of Maine. This group includes a slower-growing eastern stock and a faster-growing western stock.

HABITAT AND APPEARANCE

Atlantic pollock have a deep body that tapers to a slender caudal peduncle. The medium-sized mouth has a slightly projecting lower jaw (in juvenile fish, jaws are similar in size) and a small barbel (often missing in larger fish). Pollock have three dorsal fins: the first is triangular and higher than the other two; the second (also triangular) is the longest. The third dorsal fin and second anal fin are the same shape and size, and the first anal fin is considerably longer at the base than the second. The caudal fin is deeply forked. Pectoral fins are high on the sides. The pelvic fins begin a little in front of them and are only half as long.

Atlantic pollock are easily distinguished from cod by their greenish hue—hence the British name "green cod." They are deep olive green or brown-green on their backs, paling to yellow-grey or smoky grey on their sides, below a white or pale grey lateral line. The belly is silver grey. Fins are olive green except for the pelvic fins, which are white, tinged with red. Young fish are darker, and their sides are tinged with yellow.

Pollock eggs and larvae are found in the water column at depths of 50 to 250 metres. Juveniles are common inshore. They begin migrating offshore as they reach 2 or 3 years of age. The Atlantic pollock is reported over a wide variety of bottoms including sand, mud, rock, or vegetation. Adults show little preference for specific types of bottom habitat.

Pollock migrate extensively between the Scotian Shelf and Georges Bank and, to a lesser extent, between the Scotian Shelf and the Gulf of Maine. In these waters they are an important but not a dominant predator. Their diet includes small herring, young cod, young haddock, young white hake, silver hake, and other small fish, as well as pelagic crustaceans such as krill.

In the regions where pollock school, fishers often see them chasing schools of herring. Once they reach 0.5 kilograms, juveniles commonly swim up estuaries in pursuit of smelt in the autumn. A range of fish species eats juvenile pollock, but the size and agility of adult pollock limits its predators to spiny dogfish, monkfish, and larger pollock.

LIFE HISTORY

The Atlantic pollock spawns in batches over hard, rocky, or stony bottoms. The fertilized eggs rise in the offshore water column, drifting with the currents as they hatch. Larvae remain in the column for three to four months. Then, as small juveniles ("harbour pollock"), they swim to rocky inter- and sub-tidal zones, where they remain until the end of the second year. At this point, they migrate offshore.

Active feeders, pollock school in both inshore and offshore waters, migrating to spawn in deeper waters in late fall to mid-winter and returning to coastal waters in spring. Evidence suggests that different year-classes do not mix but form large, size-segregated schools.

Pollock grow rapidly and, by the end of the first year, juveniles are 20 centimetres long. They nearly double in length after two years, reach 50 centimetres by age 3, and 60 to 65 centimetres by age 5. Growth slows at maturity, but by year 10 pollock may reach lengths of 95 centimetres. This general size pattern can vary, however, because growth is affected by habitat, genetics, and many other variables: pollock 70 to 100 centimetres long can be anywhere from 6 to 20 years old.

FISHERY STATUS

A variety of fishing gear is used to fish pollock, primarily otter trawl and gill nets but also handlines and longlines. Pollock are also landed as bycatch in the small-mesh silver hake and redfish fisheries.

Total stock size of Atlantic pollock increased in the late 1970s and early 1980s, then markedly declined in the 1990s, while catch rates peaked in the mid- to late-1980s then steadily declined.

In recent years, the poor status of the pollock resource—as described in the Department of Fisheries and Oceans' 2005 assessment, for example—was inconsistent with reports from fishers, who were seeing abundant signs of pollock (in 2006) throughout the stock area. Catch rates since 2003 have been less than 10,000 tonnes.

Did You Know ...

- A pollock just 25 centimetres long can eat 77 herring (up to 5 centimetres long) in a single feeding.
- Pollock can be caught from shore with rod and fly or other bait and provide nearly as good sport as an equal-sized salmon.
- As with other North Atlantic fish, the age and size of pollock at maturity are declining (see table below), which may be an effect of size-selective overfishing and/or other complex factors such as declines in stock abundance or near-starvation conditions.

Year	MALES Length / Age of maturity		FEMALES Length / Age of maturity	
1961	58 cm	48–84 months	62.5 cm	60–84 months
1970–1984	50.5 cm	42 months	47.9 cm	38 months
1986–1988	41.8 cm	27 months	39.1 cm	24 months

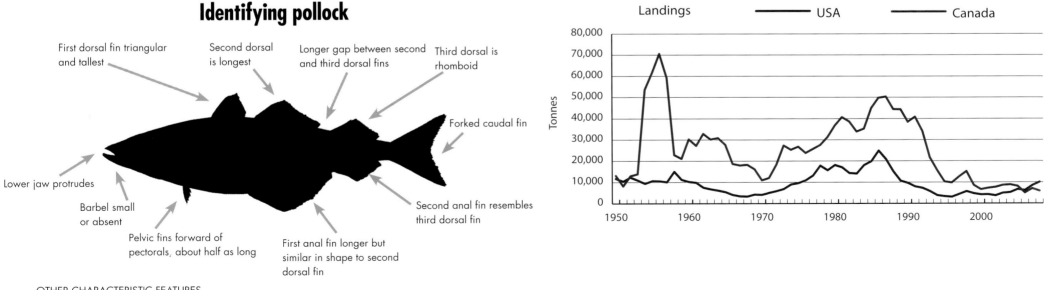

Identifying pollock

- First dorsal fin triangular and tallest
- Second dorsal is longest
- Longer gap between second and third dorsal fins
- Third dorsal is rhomboid
- Forked caudal fin
- Lower jaw protrudes
- Barbel small or absent
- Pelvic fins forward of pectorals, about half as long
- First anal fin longer but similar in shape to second dorsal fin
- Second anal fin resembles third dorsal fin

OTHER CHARACTERISTIC FEATURES
- High pectoral fins with rounded lower corners and pointed tips

Landings — USA — Canada

Tonnes: 80,000 / 70,000 / 60,000 / 50,000 / 40,000 / 30,000 / 20,000 / 10,000 / 0

1950 1960 1970 1980 1990 2000

} 55 to 375 m

Prioritized Candidate List
(COSEWIC, GROUP 1)

Silver hake

Merluccius bilinearis
Atlantic hake, hake, New England hake, whiting

Slender, fast-swimming members of the Gadidae family, silver hake are most abundant in the waters from Nova Scotia to New Jersey but are also caught on the southern edge of the Grand Banks to the Gulf of St. Lawrence, on the continental shelf and south to the southern Georges Bank (Middle Atlantic Bight), and off North Carolina. Although silver hake do not swim in definitive schools, they do, nevertheless, mass in large numbers.

HABITAT AND APPEARANCE

Based on differences of head and fin lengths, scientists have separated silver hake into southern and northern stocks. On average, adults normally measure 35 centimetres in length. The slender body is six times longer than it is deep.

Silver hake have two well-developed dorsal fins, the first much shorter than the second. The caudal fin is slightly forked. The anal fin is extended; pelvic fins lack the long feelers of other hake species. The long pectoral fins reach the origin of the anal fin.

Silver hake have two or more rows of sharp curved teeth in a relatively large mouth. The projecting lower jaw has no barbel. The lateral line stretches from the head to the caudal peduncle. The glistening greyish brown on the back fades to silver white on the belly.

Voracious nocturnal predators, silver hake rest on the bottom during the day, preferring sand, mud, or pebble bottoms for camouflage. Between sunset and midnight they swim up the water column to feed, then return to the bottom. Their diet includes smaller fish, crustaceans, and squid—depending on the season, their age, and possibly their gender. Juvenile silver hake (less than

20 centimetres long) eat crustaceans such as shrimp. As silver hake grow, the percentage of finfish in their diet increases until, at around 34 to 36 centimetres, they eat finfish almost exclusively, including any juvenile silver hake they can cannibalize. The main predators of silver hake include cod, haddock, dogfish, and winter skate.

The oldest recorded age of a silver hake is 15 years. In recent decades, few silver hake older than 6 years are caught.

LIFE HISTORY

Both juveniles and adult silver hake migrate to the deeper waters of the continental shelf as water temperatures drop and return to shallow water in spring and summer. Mature females spawn during the summer months, individually releasing several batches of eggs in bottom habitats of all substrate types.

Major spawning grounds include the southern Georges Bank, coastal Gulf of Maine, and waters south of Rhode Island.

Rising to the surface, the pelagic eggs drift with the currents, hatching in as few as two days (depending on water temperature). For the first two months, the fry feed pelagically. When they reach 17 to 20 millimetres in length, they descend to the bottom as demersal juveniles.

The fast-growing silver hake usually reach sexual maturity by year 2, when they may be 22 to 32 centimetres long. Males can reach 34 centimetres in length at 6 years of age. Females almost double those numbers, reaching a maximum of 64 centimetres at 12 years. Rarely, silver hake can attain lengths of 78 centimetres and weigh over 2 kilograms.

FISHERY STATUS

Because of their former abundance and availability, silver hake once supported important Canadian, American, and overseas fisheries. Landings have decreased substantially since 1977, however, and are currently at a historical low. Sustained and significant mortality of juvenile silver hake occurs when they are taken as bycatch in large- and small-mesh otter-trawl fisheries and in the northern shrimp fishery.

An annual American biomass index survey shows population declines every year since 1998. In Canada, COSEWIC has not yet assessed the status of the species. Silver hake is, however, on the Group 1 Candidate List, which is the highest priority for assessment.

Did You Know . . .

- Silver hake is commonly known as "frostfish" because, on winter nights, these fish sometimes beach themselves — exactly *why* is not known. One theory is that they accidently run aground while pursuing prey.
- Hake are the main predators of young hake. They account for 70 per cent of first-year and 60 per cent of second-year deaths.

Identifying silver hake

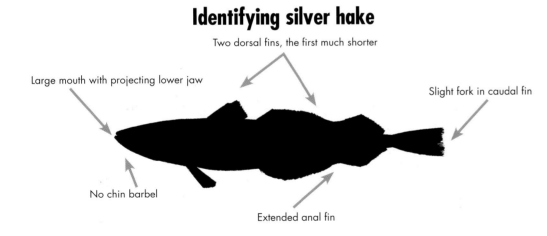

Two dorsal fins, the first much shorter

Large mouth with projecting lower jaw

Slight fork in caudal fin

No chin barbel

Extended anal fin

OTHER CHARACTERISTIC FEATURES
- Two or more rows of sharp curved teeth (may not be visible in silhouette)
- Pectoral fins extend to start of anal fin
- Straight lateral line from head to caudal peduncle
- Pelvic fins lack feelers common to other hake species

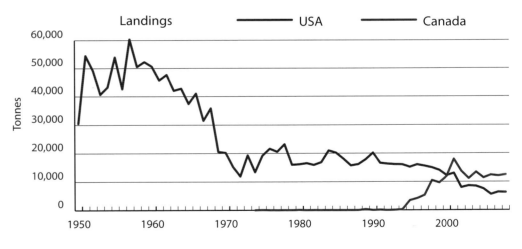

Landings — USA — Canada

} 300 to 600 m

White hake

Urophycis tenuis

Hake, ling, mud hake, *merluche blanche*

The white hake—which is actually mud brown in colour—is often compared to the Atlantic cod. A northwest Atlantic species, it ranges from the Gulf of St. Lawrence to the Middle Atlantic Bight, and from estuaries and nearshore waters to the deep canyons of the upper continental slope and the even deeper basins of the Gulf of Maine. The areas of highest concentration for this species include the southern edge of the Grand Banks, the Scotian Shelf, the Gulf of St. Lawrence, the Gulf of Maine, and Georges Bank.

HABITAT AND APPEARANCE

The white hake has a small barbel on its chin below a large mouth that hinges beneath large eyes. The gill covering has a dusky blotch. The body is elongated and the pelvic fins have thread-like rays that extend beyond the pectoral fin tips.

White hake have two dorsal fins: the anterior is triangular with a thread-like ray. The other, low and even, extends from immediately behind the first dorsal fin to the caudal peduncle. The anal fin, also low, is about two-thirds its length and extends from the vent to the caudal peduncle. The caudal fin is slightly rounded or truncate. The pelvic fins are reduced to filaments, which white hake use to feel the bottom for food.

White hake are usually mud-coloured or purple-brown on the back. The sides have a bronze or golden tinge, the yellowish white belly is stippled with tiny black spots. Female white hake are generally larger than males.

Mature white hake migrate inshore in summer, disperse to deeper water in fall, and migrate to the deepest areas of their range in winter. White hake eggs, larvae, and juveniles less than 8 centimetres are pelagic. Older juveniles and mature fish are demersal.

Eelgrass is an important habitat for demersal juveniles. Younger fish seek shallow areas and habitat away from older year-classes—

an essential survival instinct since mature white hake are cannibalistic. In southwestern Nova Scotia's coastal and nearshore habitats, older juveniles collected in an otter-trawl survey were associated with warm, less saline water and sandy bottoms.

Demersal juveniles and adults likely feed in the dark using their pelvic-fin feelers and barbels to find prey. The younger fish feed on marine worms, shrimp, and small crustaceans. Older white hake eat large quantities of shrimp and krill, and some fish. As they mature, white hake increase the amount and type of finfish they eat, including Atlantic herring, cod, haddock, redfish, Atlantic mackerel, northern sand lance, winter flounder, and younger white hake.

Research off the coast of Maine indicates that Atlantic puffin and Arctic tern prey on pelagic juvenile white hake. Smaller juveniles are eaten by adults of their own and other species. Predation by grey seals may contribute to white hake's dangerously high mortality rate in the southern Gulf of St. Lawrence, where the population continues to decline.

LIFE HISTORY
The northern white hake stock (in the southern Gulf of St. Lawrence and on the Scotian Shelf) spawns from July to September. The southern stock spawns during April and May in deep waters south of Georges Bank and the Middle Atlantic Bight. Few white hake spawn in the Gulf of Maine.

White hake spawn in the water column, releasing several million buoyant eggs annually. The larvae emerge during the spring and summer, remaining in the upper water column as they develop. At about 8 centimetres they become juvenile white hake and seek out demersal habitat.

The abundance of age groups of white hake on the Grand Banks and elsewhere varies significantly. Some scientists believe ocean currents influence the numbers.

In the Gulf of Maine, pelagic juveniles are present in May and June. In the fall, demersal young of the year are most often seen on the southern Grand Banks at 50 to 80 metres, in the same general areas as pelagic juveniles (8 to 15 centimetres). Juveniles of 15-plus centimetres are found with larger fish as they migrate southwest toward the shelf edge to overwinter. By thefollowing spring, 1-year-olds up to 30 centimetres long are integrated into the schools of white hake on the outer Banks.

FISHERY STATUS
The white hake, exploited throughout its range, has been a targeted species in Canadian waters since 1988 and taken as bycatch for much longer. Historically, it was one of the five most important ground fisheries in the southern Gulf of St. Lawrence, where fishers on inshore vessels landed their quotas in summer and fall. Today, white hake fisheries are primarily pursued on the Scotian Shelf and off southern Newfoundland. The white hake population is now under serious—some would argue unsustainable—pressure in parts of its range, however. Since 1995, a fishing moratorium has protected the southern Gulf of St. Lawrence stock.

Near-surface ocean currents are a natural mechanism that may help improve survival rates: eggs, larvae, and young-of-the-year remain in them for months, concentrating individuals in early life stages in specific locations. The size of the large 1998 and very large 1999 year-classes may be due to their having settled onto the shallow part of the Grand Banks, where temperatures are warmest. White hake reach a commercially harvestable size in less than three years, but it takes longer for a good year-class to mature and replenish a population's adult component. The large 1999 year-class spurred a steep population increase, with good survival over the next

two years. From 2002 to 2005, Division 3NOP's population was low but similar to 1996 to 1998 numbers.

Very little recruitment, however, has occurred since then. Despite low numbers, heavy fishing pressure in the NAFO Regulation Area in 2002 and 2003 led to allowable but unsustainable catches (averaging 5,771 tonnes per year). According to one 2005 survey, abundance was approximately 2 per cent of the 2000 estimate. If true, the decline is so enormous that COSEWIC could give white hake Endangered status, should an assessment be completed and the report made public.

Some researchers criticize the existing NAFO quota—8,500 tonnes, more than the unsustainable combined American and Canadian catch since 1995—as too high to support a recovery or even sustain the stock at its current low numbers, particularly given the recent lack of significant recruitment.

Identifying white hake

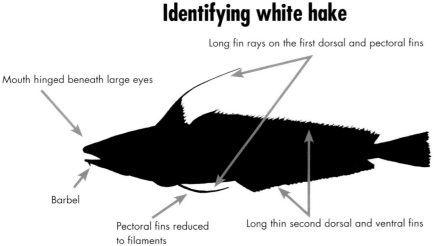

Mouth hinged beneath large eyes

Long fin rays on the first dorsal and pectoral fins

Barbel

Pectoral fins reduced to filaments

Long thin second dorsal and ventral fins

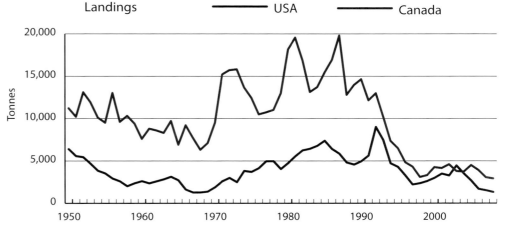

Landings — USA — Canada

Tonnes

20,000
15,000
10,000
5,000
0

1950   1960   1970   1980   1990   2000

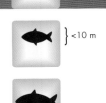

} <10 m

Cunner

Tautogolabrus adspersus

Bergall, blue perch, conner, perch, sea perch

The cunner lives year-round in the nearshore ecosystem and can be abundant in the sheltered habitats it prefers. Restricted to the northwest Atlantic, it is found only from Labrador to New Jersey and, rarely, as far south as the coast of Virginia. The cunner is most common around the coast of Newfoundland and into the Gulf of St. Lawrence, with significant populations in favourable environments all the way to Chesapeake Bay.

HABITAT AND APPEARANCE

Though it is thin from side to side, the cunner's body is deep from top to bottom, sloping quickly to a narrow caudal peduncle. Cunner usually weigh less than 1 kilogram. The pointed snout has a small mouth that, like the pharynx, has several rows of uneven, cone-shaped crushing teeth. These enable the cunner to break and grind hard-shelled prey.

The dorsal profile from the lip to the base of the dorsal fin is relatively straight. The front of the single long dorsal fin is spiny; the rest is soft-rayed. The front of the anal fin (three stout spines and nine rays) begins just under or behind the soft part of the dorsal fin. The caudal fin is slightly convex with rounded corners. Pelvic fins originate directly beneath the pectoral fins. The cunner's back is mottled red to blue-brown. The colour fades on the sides and is palest on the belly. Distinguishing marks include a band of pigment over the gut and a pair of spots between the anus and the caudal fin.

Mainly an inshore fish, the cunner is active by day and inactive at night, when it seeks shelter around piers and breakwaters and in eelgrass beds. Although most of the cunner population is found within a dozen kilometres of shore, larger individuals are also found in small numbers on offshore banks to depths of 130 metres.

These small omnivorous fish eat continuously. They browse among seaweed and stones and on dock pilings—nipping off barnacles and small blue mussels. Amphipods, shrimp, young lobster, small crab, and other small crustaceans of all kinds also figure significantly in their diet, as do annelid worms and eelgrass. Cunner sometimes eat small sea urchins and occasionally small silversides, sticklebacks, mummichogs, and the fry of larger species. They also eat fish eggs and are known to feed on animal refuse.

LIFE HISTORY

The cunner is a non-migratory inshore species. It remains in shallow inshore waters, living on or near the bottom, all year long. It does not school, but will congregate in large groups around wharves and wrecks and even in seaweed.

Male cunner defend their territories throughout the reproductive season (May to November). Females initiate spawning activity with territorial males and then, after a brief but elaborate courtship, spawn daily for six weeks. Female cunner have a very low rate of egg production. They spawn mainly in late spring through early summer, releasing round transparent eggs.

The larvae have taken on adult form by the time they reach 15 millimetres and by 25 millimetres have adult coloration. The predominance of male fish increases in older year-classes, which suggests that females have a higher mortality rate.

Cunner feed actively during the day and rest in groups at night, when the skin that is most exposed to view takes on a camouflaging pattern. Their activity slows in the fall until the water temperatures reach 7° or 8°C. In preparation for their seasonally dormant period, they seek out the shelter of crevices and rock overhangs, stop feeding, and grow torpid. Within three weeks the larger fish, and then the smaller ones, become dormant for the winter.

FISHERY STATUS

Cunner was a favourite frying fish during the late 19th and early 20th centuries. Its tough skin and musky flavour, however, make it an acquired taste today. As a result the cunner is no longer regarded as a commercial or sport species. But it is a significant part of the catch for children fishing from wharves and those who fish for bait along the shore. This fishery is unregulated.

Did You Know . . .

- Cunner can change body colour. They camouflage themselves nightly and during seasonal dormant periods.
- Cunner are sometimes so abundant in rocky pier habitats that they exceed the biomass (fish density) found in some tropical reef systems.

Identifying cunner

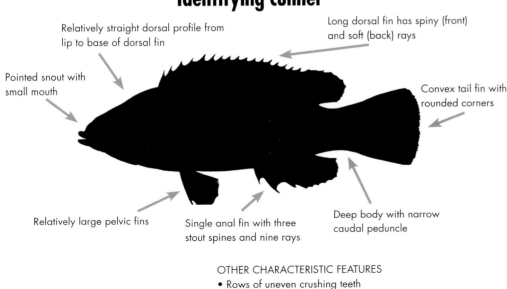

Relatively straight dorsal profile from lip to base of dorsal fin

Long dorsal fin has spiny (front) and soft (back) rays

Pointed snout with small mouth

Convex tail fin with rounded corners

Relatively large pelvic fins

Single anal fin with three stout spines and nine rays

Deep body with narrow caudal peduncle

OTHER CHARACTERISTIC FEATURES
- Rows of uneven crushing teeth

} NDA

Endangered
(COSEWIC, 2004)

Porbeagle shark

Lamna nasus
Atlantic mackerel shark, Beaumaris shark,
bottle-nosed shark, *requin-taupe commun*

With a vast ocean and coastal range, this large shark is the only member of its genus in the North Atlantic. One of the most cold-tolerant pelagic shark species, it prefers water temperatures lower than 18°C. The range of the northwest Atlantic porbeagle population—which is a separate stock from the South Atlantic population—straddles the Canadian and American offshore economic zones. It is found off the coasts of Greenland, Canada, the United States, and Bermuda. In Canadian waters, it is found off the island of Newfoundland, in the Gulf of St. Lawrence, along the Scotian Shelf, and into the Bay of Fundy.

HABITAT AND APPEARANCE

The porbeagle shark's heavy, spindle-shaped body is deepest at the dorsal fin. The snout is moderately long and conical. The eyes and gill slits are large. The mouth is moderately sized with conspicuous, blade-like teeth flanked by lateral mini-teeth, or cusplets.

The large first dorsal fin has a white rear edge, which distinguishes the porbeagle from the salmon shark (mako) and the white shark. The second dorsal and anal fins can pivot on their vertical axes. The caudal peduncle is strongly keeled on the upper edge, with short secondary keels along the lower. The caudal fin is heterocercal. The sides and underside of the body—including the first dorsal fin, abdomen, and head—are blue-grey.

Opportunistic feeders, porbeagle prey primarily on pelagic fish such as herring and mackerel, in spring and summer. In the fall, their diet is primarily groundfish—sand lance, flounder, hake, and cod—with squid as the second-most-common prey. There are no records of attacks on humans. Little is known about the porbeagle's marine predators but adults are large and swift enough to discourage attack.

The porbeagle's circulatory system has a "counter-current heat exchanger," a mechanism that transfers body heat from warm arterial blood to colder blood flowing back to the heart, warming it before it reaches the body core. This adaptation allows the porbeagle to keep its body 5° to 10°C warmer than the surrounding water, which enables it to hunt in deeper water for longer than other sharks and to swim farther north for food.

LIFE HISTORY

The porbeagle shark of the northwest Atlantic is believed to mate annually from September to November. During mating, males bite females on the back and dorsal fins. The scars help scientists determine if a female has recently mated.

The porbeagle is ovoviviparous: the embryos have no placental or other direct connection to the uterus during their eight- to nine-month gestation. In the later stages, once the yolk sac is exhausted, embryos obtain nutrients by devouring unfertilized eggs ovulated by the mother. A litter of one to five pups is born offshore in late spring or early summer, from the banks of Newfoundland south to the Sargasso Sea.

As juveniles, both sexes grow at a similar rate: 16 to 20 centimetres annually. The species is slow to reach maturity. Males are considered adults at 8 years, females by 12 to 13 years.

The porbeagle shark's extensive north/south migrations are most likely driven by water temperature. Individuals from the northwestern Atlantic population travel each year between southern Newfoundland and Gulf of St. Lawrence waters and waters off Massachusetts.

Catch statistics indicate that these sharks school by size and sex: large mature females remain separate from mature males and juveniles for part of the annual cycle. This separation may serve both to limit breeding to a specific season and possibly to prevent adult males from cannibalizing newborn pups.

FISHERY STATUS

The porbeagle shark fishery began in 1961 off Newfoundland and New England. Within three years, Norwegian longliners were harvesting 9,000 tonnes annually. |This was unsustainable. Within six years the stocks collapsed. By 1967, annual landings had dropped below 1,000 tonnes. They declined even further in the 1970s and 1980s.

Despite reduced harvesting, population recovery was limited: porbeagle numbers stalled at 30 per cent of their original abundance. But the fishery geared up again in the early 1990s. Catches several times higher than the estimated sustainable limit again led to a sudden, steep decline to a new record low. Bycatch continued in the swordfishery.

By 1994, the population of porbeagle in the northwest Atlantic was less than one-third of pre-1961 numbers. Nevertheless, three Canadian fishing vessels began to target it that year. Annual catches of 1,000 to 2,000 tonnes during the 1990s took the porbeagle to an unprecedented low.

In 2001, porbeagle shark biomass was calculated to be at 11 per cent of the pre-1961 population, but a stock assessment report by the Canadian Department of Fisheries and Oceans advised that "an annual catch of 200 to 250 tonnes would allow population growth." Based on that, the Canadian quota was reduced to 250 tonnes for 2002 to 2007. The downward population trend continued, however, despite both the reduced TAC and tighter restrictions that included limits on licences and bycatch, a

ban on de-finning, and restrictions on gear, area, and seasons.

With the porbeagle population now estimated to be as low as 10 per cent of pre-1961 numbers, COSEWIC disputed the findings of the DFO stock assessment and, in 2004, noted that the quotas set for 2002–07 were unsustainable. And, even if the porbeagle can survive these harvest targets, the rate of recovery cannot be calculated given the population's low number of mature individuals. COSEWIC designated the porbeagle Endangered in 2004.

In addition to the current limited commercial fishery, sport fishers in the United Kingdom, Canada, and the United States enjoy the strong fight put up by the porbeagle in hook-and-line fishing, even though this shark does not jump out of the water as the related shortfin mako does.

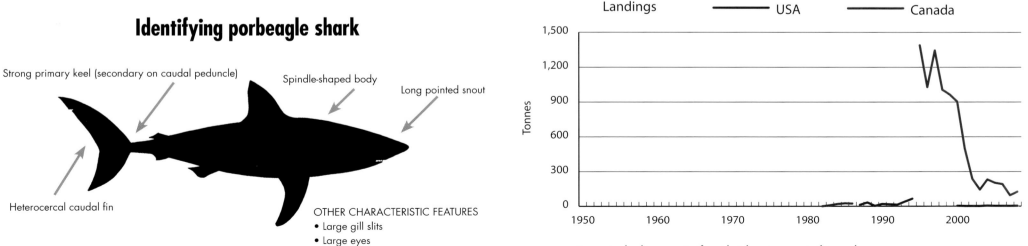

Identifying porbeagle shark

Strong primary keel (secondary on caudal peduncle)

Spindle-shaped body

Long pointed snout

Heterocercal caudal fin

OTHER CHARACTERISTIC FEATURES
• Large gill slits
• Large eyes

Landings — USA — Canada

Tonnes

1,500
1,200
900
600
300
0

1950   1960   1970   1980   1990   2000

Norwegian landings are significant but do not appear in this graph.

Monkfish

Lophius americanus

Allmouth, American goosefish, angler fish, bellyfish, fishing frog, frogfish, goosefish, large-headed angler, monk-tail, sea devil, *baudroie*

} 0 to 320 m

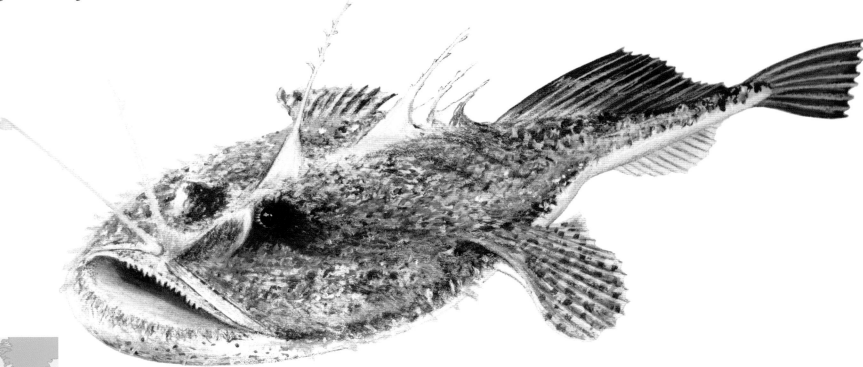

O ften described as "a mouth with a tail attached," monkfish are found in the western Atlantic Ocean from the Labrador Shelf to northern Florida. In Canadian waters, monkfish are most often encountered on the southern Grand Banks, in the Gulf of St. Lawrence, on the Scotian Shelf, and in the Bay of Fundy. The species inhabits warm slope regions with a variety of sediment types. It is most often found at depths from 0 to 320 metres but has been recorded at depths of more than 650 metres in some environments. Monkfish tolerate a wide variation in water temperature.

HABITAT AND APPEARANCE

The monkfish is a large and languid bottom-dwelling fish with a flat, tapered body well adapted to partially submerging itself in the bottom substrate. Its large head has an enormous mouth, and both jaws are lined with inward-pointing canine-like teeth. The lower jaw, the head, and the sides of the monkfish have a distinctive fringe of fleshy flaps.

Large flattened pectoral fins at the body's midpoint have small gill slits just behind them. Monkfish use the pectorals, which resemble small arms, to move along the bottom. Much smaller pelvic fins are located ahead of the pectorals. On the back, in addition to two dorsal fins, are several slender spines. The first spine serves as a modified fishing lure, which the monkfish uses to attract unsuspecting prey within range of its mouth. The anal fin tip extends beyond the caudal peduncle.

Monkfish are usually dark brown, fading to light tan toward the abdomen. The pelvic fins are red and pectoral fins have dark tips.

Voracious predators, monkfish with their large mouths will consume fish almost as large as themselves. They eat herring, sand lance, smelt, cod, haddock, mackerel, striped bass, sculpin, sea raven, flounder, skate, crab, starfish, marine worms, and any other organism they can get their teeth on.

Young monkfish are on the menu for a number of predatory marine fish. While the size of larger monkfish gives them some protection, the remains of adult monkfish have been found in swordfish stomachs.

LIFE HISTORY

Monkfish seek out warm slope regions from the low-tide line to approximately 650 metres. Studies indicate monkfish have a limited seasonal migration on the Grand Banks, occupying shallower water in summer and returning to deeper water for the colder months.

Despite a relatively short lifespan—just 11 years—the monkfish takes between four and seven years to reach sexual maturity. Early rapid growth is similar for both sexes (to 11 centimetres within the first year). By age 7 they can reach 76 centimetres; by age 10 they may measure 102 centimetres or more and weigh as much as 27 kilograms.

Monkfish spawn between June and September in Canadian waters, laying up to 1 million spherical eggs at the surface in large, pink, ribbon-shaped mucous veils. They are the only fish known to employ this method of spawning. The newly hatched larvae float on the surface and feed pelagically for several months before settling into a sedentary but voracious life on the bottom.

FISHERY STATUS

In 2010, Greenpeace added monkfish to its Red List, indicating that the fish in grocery stores most likely comes from an unsustainable fishery. Initially, monkfish was taken as a bycatch only in 3LNOPs. They have been captured on pelagic longlines set for swordfish/tuna. A related species is heavily fished off southern Europe.

The decline of other marine resources in the late 1980s and 1990s led to the creation of a directed trawl fishery in 1991, followed by an experimental gill-net fishery in 1993–94. Since then, there has been a limited gill-net monkfish fishery. Landings remained low until 2002–03, when an expanding demand in the Asian market spurred the fishery to take 2,795 tonnes—more than six times the amount taken in the previous five years. There are currently no quota restrictions on the monkfish fishery.

Did You Know . . .

- To catch prey, monkfish often hide themselves in sea-bottom mud. They use the "fishing lure" on the top of their head to attract prey, which are quickly captured by their huge jaws.
- Occasionally, anglers using live bait can catch a monkfish. Handling these fish calls for extra care because their teeth are very sharp and they bite—hard.
- The monkfish is called "the poor man's lobster" because of the flesh's firm texture and lack of bones, which for many people make it a culinary treat.

Identifying monkfish

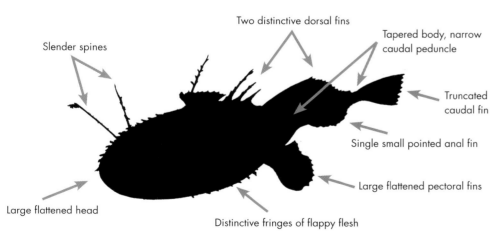

Slender spines

Two distinctive dorsal fins

Tapered body, narrow caudal peduncle

Truncated caudal fin

Single small pointed anal fin

Large flattened pectoral fins

Distinctive fringes of flappy flesh

Large flattened head

OTHER CHARACTERISTIC FEATURES
- Gill slits immediately behind pectoral fins
- Sharp inward-pointing teeth
- Enormous mouth
- Smaller pelvic fins in front of pectorals

Marlin-spike grenadier

Nezumia bairdii
Common grenadier, common rattail, *grenadier du Grand Banc*

500 to 800 m

The marlin-spike grenadier is rarely seen except by those engaged in deepwater fisheries from the Grand Banks of Newfoundland south to Cape Hatteras. This slope-dwelling species is most common at moderate depths of 500 to 800 metres. Relatively small, members of this species are likely to slip through the mesh of commercial trawls.

HABITAT AND APPEARANCE

The pointed snout and large eyes of the marlin-spike grenadier are characteristic of the Macrouridae family, as is a chin barbel, so the serrated spine of the first dorsal fin is a good diagnostic feature for identifying this species. The mouth is armed with several rows of small curved teeth. The scales on the head and body have sharp, densely packed little spines.

The marlin-spike grenadier's slender body, flattened beyond the vent, tapers quickly to a point. The two dorsal fins are distinctly different. The first begins just behind the gill opening and is twice as high as it is long. Its front edge has 14 or more slender serrations that point upward. The second dorsal fin, separated from the first by a distance equal to the height of the first, extends right to the tip of the tail but is so low that it is barely discernible. The anal fin is more than twice as wide as the second dorsal fin and much longer, but it has fewer rays. On the triangular pelvic fins a single ray extends as a long filament. Directly above and a little forward of these fins are the pectoral fins, which have a rounded tip.

Although grey overall, the marlin-spike grenadier has several touches of colour, including pink on the underside of the snout, large dark blue eyes, and a deep purple throat. The first dorsal fin is pink with blackish spines.

Marlin-spike grenadier are bottom fish, usually found over soft mud. They prefer water temperature within a few degrees ±5.5°C and when they select habitat exhibit a depth pattern called "tropical submergence": the farther south they go within their range (from Newfoundland south to the Straits of Florida), the deeper the water in which they live. Their diet includes amphipods, various worms, and krill. Because of the great depths at which the marlin-spike grenadier lives, few species other than swordfish prey on them.

LIFE HISTORY

As with most species of grenadier, neither the eggs of the marlin-spike grenadier nor its larvae have ever been seen. This simple fact highlights how little is known for certain about the species' life cycle. What is known has been pieced together from limited research data, information about other closely related grenadier species, and the knowledge of fishers. It suggests that the marlin-spike grenadier's life history may follow a seasonal and age-related migration.

A very poor swimmer, marlin-spike grenadier migrate seasonally to deeper water. Mature fish occur at greater depths than immature fish. They likely spawn near the bottom in summer and fall, releasing buoyant eggs that rise through the water column as far as the plankton-rich transition layer between colder deep water and warmer surface water. There the larvae likely feed until they reach the juvenile stage, around January of their second winter, when they descend to the bottom and first appear in bottom trawls.

FISHERY STATUS

From 1971 to 1978, marlin-spike grenadier numbers were low. Abundance and percentage occurrence gradually increased until 1987 and remained relatively high until the early 1990s. Over the next decade, their overall abundance dropped by 60 per cent.

Since the early 1990s, despite this overall decline, there has been an increase in smaller and presumably immature marlin-spike grenadier—both in absolute numbers and as a percentage of the total catch. This could be taken as an encouraging sign. It is offset, however, by the fact that marlin-spike grenadier measuring more than 30 centimetres, once captured regularly, are now relatively rare. Officially, the status of the species remains unassessed.

Did You Know . . .

- Lacking a true caudal fin, the marlin-spike grenadier—like other "rattail" species—is not a strong swimmer.
- Marlin-spike grenadier can produce a downward-directed light from a bioluminescent organ located on their ventral surface.
- Like many deep-sea fish, this species illustrates the "bigger-deeper" phenomenon: the larger individuals live deeper in the water column than do the smaller ones.

Identifying marlin-spike grenadier

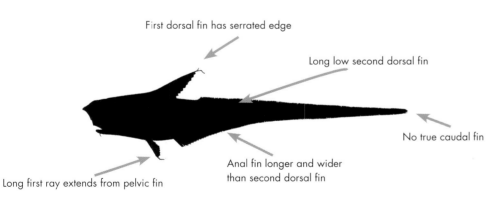

First dorsal fin has serrated edge

Long low second dorsal fin

No true caudal fin

Anal fin longer and wider than second dorsal fin

Long first ray extends from pelvic fin

OTHER CHARACTERISTIC FEATURES
- Pectoral fins slightly forward of first dorsal fin

300 to 500 m

Special Concern

(COSEWIC, 2007)

Roughhead grenadier

Macrourus berglax

Grenadier berglax, onion-eye, smooth-spined rattail, *ingminniset*

The roughhead grenadier is found in deep water off the Davis Strait and southward along the continental slope of North America to the deep channel separating Georges and Browns banks. It is also found in the deep gullies that interrupt the Scotian Shelf.

In the northeast Atlantic, the roughhead grenadier has been identified in the Barents Sea south to Norway, the Faroe Islands, and the Irish Atlantic slope.

HABITAT AND APPEARANCE

Up to 1 metre in length, this deep-sea fish has a moderately slender body that tapers evenly to a pointed tail. Its broad ridged head accounts for one-quarter of its body length. The mouth is moderate in size, and the lower jaw is inferior. The upper jaw has an enlarged outer row and two to four irregular inner rows of pointed teeth. In the lower jaw, teeth are confined to one or two irregular rows.

The short chin barbel is about half the diameter of the eye in length. Large scales on the head and "shoulder" are armed with either a longitudinal row of spines or up to four radiating ridges of spines. The scales farther back each have a single spine. Together, the spines form longitudinal ridges along the tail end of the fish. Unlike some other species in its family, the roughhead grenadier has no light organ.

The roughhead grenadier is ash grey, darker toward the belly. The rear edge of the scales toward the tail is slightly darker. The anal fin, immediately behind the anus, also has a narrow dark edge. The first dorsal fin and the pectoral fins are a sooty colour.

LIFE HISTORY

Very little is known about the life history of the roughhead grenadier. Research suggests a prolonged reproductive period with batch spawning taking place from late winter to early summer (timing varies by region). No complete picture of total egg production has been developed, but captured females 70.5 centimetres long yielded 25,000 eggs.

FISHERY STATUS

The roughhead grenadier is one of two grenadier species occasionally targeted by fishers in the North Atlantic. Catch statistics for the species, however, are not separated from those of the roundnose grenadier. As the abundance of roundnose grenadier has declined, the relative importance of roughhead in the landings has grown. But the fishery is unregulated. Most landings currently are as bycatch in the Greenland halibut fishery.

Roughhead grenadier landings in the North Atlantic have declined steadily since a high in 1972 of more than 83,000 tonnes, less than a decade after the fishery began. Based on life history characteristics and apparent population declines, COSEWIC listed the roughhead grenadier as a Species of Special Concern in 2007.

Identifying roughhead grenadier

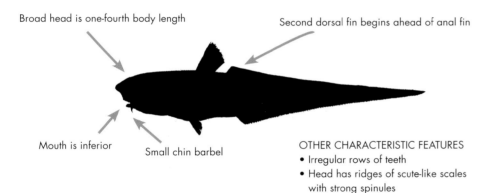

Broad head is one-fourth body length

Second dorsal fin begins ahead of anal fin

Mouth is inferior

Small chin barbel

OTHER CHARACTERISTIC FEATURES
- Irregular rows of teeth
- Head has ridges of scute-like scales with strong spinules

} 400 to
1,200 m

Endangered

(COSEWIC, 2008)

Roundnose grenadier

Coryphaenoides rupestris

Black grenadier, rattail, rock grenadier, *grenadier, grenadier de roche*

Despite the enormous range of the roundnose grenadier in the North Atlantic, this species is Endangered. It occurs from Baffin Island and Greenland in the western Atlantic south to the deep waters off the coast of the District of Columbia in the United States. In the east, the roundnose grenadier inhabits the depths off Iceland and Norway and south to North Africa. It does not occur outside the Atlantic Ocean.

Although the fishery for the roundnose grenadier only began in the mid-1960s, the species has been dangerously over-exploited. Fishing activity is mainly by factory trawlers that fish to depths of 1.3 kilometres.

HABITAT AND APPEARANCE

The head of the roundnose grenadier is short—just 15 per cent of its total body length—and relatively broad. The rounded snout has a large, blunt, tubercular scute at the tip and a small barbel on the chin. The large inferior mouth has a cleft that extends behind the eye.

The body of the roundnose grenadier tapers to the "rattail" that is characteristic of this family of fish. Scales on the body and tail are large and detach easily. Scales on the head are smaller and adhere more strongly. Adult roundnose range in colour from medium brown to grey. Fins may be black or brown-grey.

A demersal species, the roundnose grenadier commonly makes excursions into pelagic regions. It feeds on a variety of fish and invertebrates but primarily on crustaceans such as shrimp and amphipods. Cephalopods and lantern fish make up a small fraction of the diet. Its main predators include at least two species of redfish and blue ling.

LIFE HISTORY

The roundnose grenadier is long-lived, slow-growing, and late to mature. It takes 17 years for one generation to produce enough offspring to replace itself. Such a slow rate of reproduction makes the species susceptible to over-exploitation.

The roundnose grenadier moves to deeper waters in the summer. It returns to shallower waters in the winter. Current research suggests that the species forms large schools in late summer and early fall for an annual spawning migration. Unfortunately for the species, this is the period when the fishery is most intensive.

FISHERY STATUS

The roundnose grenadier was assessed as Endangered by COSEWIC in 2008, given the unprecedented decline in its abundance. It was estimated that populations were reduced by more than 95 per cent over the previous decade. The directed commercial harvest ceased in Canadian waters in 1974, but fisheries outside Canadian waters remain largely unregulated. Surveys show a continuing decline for this long-lived, slow-maturing species.

Did You Know . . .

• Roundnose grenadier can migrate 1 kilometre or more up the water table every day. They rise from the bottom to reach prey in the upper levels of the ocean and return at nightfall to the depths.

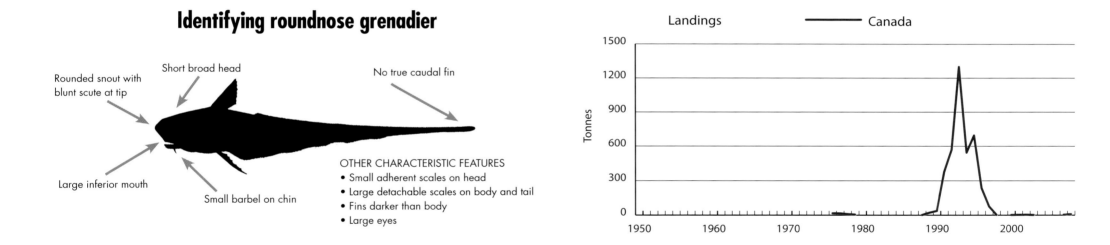

Identifying roundnose grenadier

Rounded snout with blunt scute at tip

Short broad head

No true caudal fin

Large inferior mouth

Small barbel on chin

OTHER CHARACTERISTIC FEATURES
• Small adherent scales on head
• Large detachable scales on body and tail
• Fins darker than body
• Large eyes

Landings — Canada

Tonnes

1500
1200
900
600
300
0

1950   1960   1970   1980   1990   2000

} 125 to 400 m

Atlantic hagfish

Myxine glutinosa

Borer, common hag, hagfish, northern hagfish, slime eel, *myxine, myxine du nord*

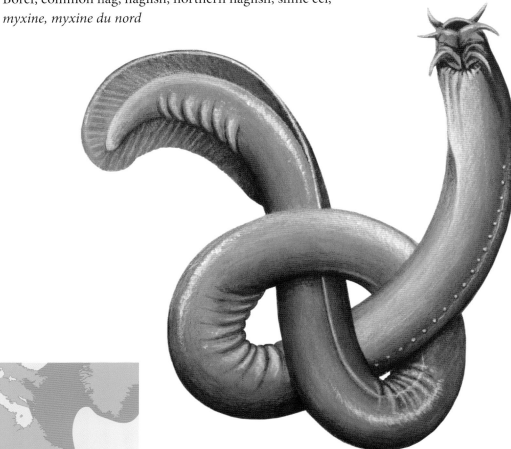

Found only in the North Atlantic Ocean, the Atlantic hagfish is widely distributed in Arctic waters and south on both the European and the North American sides of the ocean. One of more than 60 species of hagfish around the world, it is the planet's only remaining descendant of the first creatures to develop a skull to protect the brain. Over the more than 500 million years since, its evolutionary path has been separate from that of vertebrates.

HABITAT AND APPEARANCE

The Atlantic hagfish has an eel-like body. A single finfold runs along its back, around the tail, and along the belly. It can secrete several litres of stringy slime in seconds from a row of pores along each side. Its jawless and lip-less mouth has horn-like teeth—even on the tongue. It has a barbel on each side of the mouth and four around the single nostril. A pair of gill openings behind the head lack a covering skin fold.

This species has no scales, soft skin, and a skeleton of cartilage. Coloration varies with the ocean bottom. Most often Atlantic hagfish are brown, red-brown, purple-brown, or grey, and generally paler on the belly. The primitive circulatory system links a systemic heart—the main pump—to three branchial hearts (accessory pumps).

The Atlantic hagfish lives in dense colonies at depths of 20 to 1,800 metres throughout Atlantic Canada in waters where there is a muddy ocean floor, constant salinity, slow currents, and relatively warm temperatures. Its limited home range can be as small as 2 square kilometres. Hagfish burrow into the sediment until only the head is visible.

An active nocturnal hunter, it eats marine worms and other burrowing invertebrates, molluscs, northern shrimp, lobster, hagfish eggs, bird and mammal remains, and various finfish including cod, haddock, mackerel, porbeagle, and dogfish. It is also a scavenger. Using the rasp-like teeth on its tongue, it attaches itself to dead and dying fish and other creatures that have sunk to the bottom and burrows in to hide from predators while it eats the carcass from the inside out.

The jawless hagfish can tear off pieces of flesh from their prey. It knots its long body and, with teeth embedded in a carcass, pulls its head through the knot, which strips off the meat.

Atlantic cod, white hake, and Atlantic halibut prey on hagfish eggs and young but these predators avoid larger hagfish because, when threatened, hagfish secrete litres of stringy slime. The slime blocks the predators' gills and can suffocate them. The presence of hagfish in the stomachs of dolphins and seals suggests that the slime is not an effective defence against mammals.

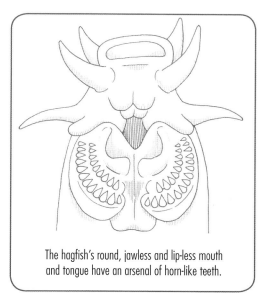

The hagfish's round, jawless and lip-less mouth and tongue have an arsenal of horn-like teeth.

LIFE HISTORY

In the mid-1800s, the Royal Danish Academy of Sciences and Letters offered a reward to anyone who could discover how hagfish reproduce. As of 2012, no one had claimed the prize. All that *is* known is that adults do not guard their offspring and that juvenile fish—though not hermaphrodites—possess both ovaries and testes; as they mature they become either female or male.

Apparently, individuals can also switch gender from season to season. During a research fishery in Newfoundland's offshore waters that began in 2004, 99 females were found for every male caught. The reason for the gender disparity is unclear—it may be natural or it may be related to the use of baited traps instead of nets.

Researchers believe hagfish may spawn year-round because catches include females with ripe eggs year-round. Atlantic hagfish produce fewer than 48 eggs a year (body length may be a factor). Fertilized eggs have large yolks and are enclosed in a horny shell with anchor-tipped filaments at each end. Such eggs require a great deal of energy to produce but improve chances of survival.

Newly hatched hagfish emerge as fully formed fry. The smallest juvenile fish captured off Newfoundland weigh between 0.9 and 2 grams and range from 98 to 100 millimetres long. With no known way to determine hagfish age, the species' rate of growth, age at maturity, and lifespan remain a mystery. We do know that, in the waters around Newfoundland, Atlantic hagfish are shorter and heavier than in more southern waters, such as the Gulf of Maine.

FISHERY STATUS

The slimy hagfish is an unwanted bycatch in most commercial fisheries. In Southeast Asia, however, it has a ready market. South Koreans consume more than 2,250 tonnes of hagfish annually. Its strong but pliable skin is marketed as eelskin and used in everything from handbags to boots.

Today, the Asian hagfish is considered a threatened species and the market has turned to the North Atlantic. In Atlantic Canada, the hagfish fishery is primarily an emerging industry. A targeted fishery off Nova Scotia began in the late 1980s, but by 2012 there were still fewer than 10 licensed fishers. Exploratory fishing in the Newfoundland and Labrador region has been ongoing since the 1990s.

There is no fisheries management plan. A research fishery undertaken in 2004 to determine sustainable yields caused concern among government scientists that the species is susceptible to overfishing. The study postulated that once an area was depopulated—given the small number of eggs females produce—it likely would take a long time (if ever) for the species to rebuild.

There is currently no scientific basis for determining a sustainable harvest level. Without careful management, the Atlantic hagfish population could go the way of its Pacific cousin.

Did You Know . . .

- Like other hagfish species, the Atlantic hagfish has a limited ability to regulate its cells' internal pressure. To survive, it requires stable salinity in its environment.
- The microscopic fibres reinforcing Atlantic hagfish slime are as strong as Kevlar (the material used to make bulletproof vests).
- To clear slime from its nasal opening, it sneezes, a phenomenon that may be unique to this species.
- Hagfish eat netted fish and can significantly reduce the take of a single haul.

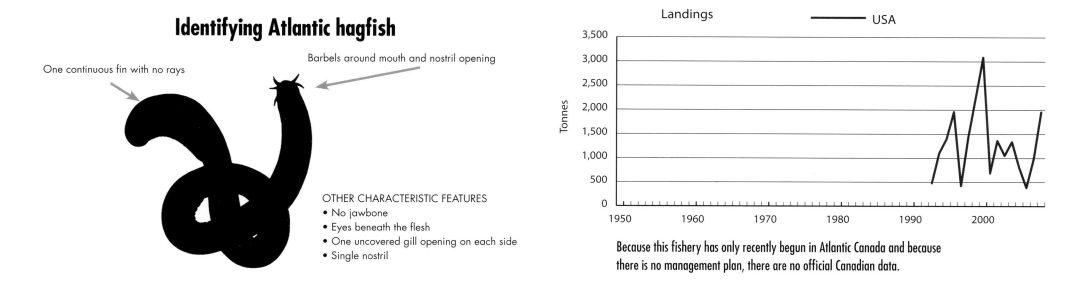

Identifying Atlantic hagfish

One continuous fin with no rays

Barbels around mouth and nostril opening

OTHER CHARACTERISTIC FEATURES
- No jawbone
- Eyes beneath the flesh
- One uncovered gill opening on each side
- Single nostril

Landings ———— USA

Because this fishery has only recently begun in Atlantic Canada and because there is no management plan, there are no official Canadian data.

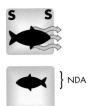

} NDA

**Prioritized
Candidate List**
(COSEWIC, GROUP 2)

Capelin

Mallotus villosus
Caplin, white fish, *capelan, capelan atlantique*

Capelin school throughout Arctic and sub-Arctic waters. In the northwest Atlantic, they range from west Greenland and Hudson Bay south to Maine. They are most numerous around the island of Newfoundland. The capelin in some stocks spend most of their lives offshore but migrate inshore to spawn on beaches.

In the early 1990s, concurrent with cooling ocean trends, the capelin population declined dramatically. More recently, they have been observed farther south than their historic range: in the southern Gulf of St. Lawrence and on the Scotian Shelf (where historic reports are rare but not unknown). They have even been reported in Cape Cod and Passamaquoddy Bay in the Gulf of Maine.

HABITAT AND APPEARANCE

Small and elongated, the capelin has a pointed snout and a slightly protruding lower jaw. The dorsal fin is relatively large; an adipose fin is located closer to the forked caudal fin. The body is olive green above the lateral line and silver below it. The belly is silver white. Scales and teeth are tiny. Mature capelin grow 13 to 20 centimetres in length. The longest male found in Newfoundland waters was 25 centimetres.

During the early summer spawning season, the head and back of males darken and their pectoral, pelvic, and anal fins become more pronounced. Males also develop a row of elongated scales (spawning ridges) along their sides, above the lateral line. Capelin feed most intensely in late winter and early spring, then stop feeding until several weeks after spawning is over.

Capelin are a major forage fish for other species. They eat planktonic shrimp and other microscopic organisms, making that energy available to a long list of predators. So crucial to the diet of Atlantic cod are they that, unless the species once again becomes abundant in northern waters, the growth, condition, and fecundity of northern cod is not likely to improve. Other predators include dogfish, flounder, haddock, halibut, herring, and salmon, marine mammals, and seabirds.

Capelin eggs are also a food source. For example, demersal eggs make up 59 per cent of the food (by weight) of small winter flounder (14 to 34 centimetres long).

LIFE HISTORY

Capelin live in sub-Arctic water and exploit its rich planktonic food resources, but water temperatures below their tolerance drive enormous schools south in search of relatively warmer waters. During this migration, capelin travel along coastal profiles on both sides of the North Atlantic. In the northeast Atlantic, they spawn in water up to 280 metres deep, where water temperatures are 2° to 7°C.

In the northwest Atlantic, mature capelin move inshore in large schools. They begin to spawn anywhere from mid-April to early July, choosing gravel or sandy sites. With the high tide, and usually at night, the males roll in with the waves to reach the beaches first. When the females roll in, the males clasp them with their fins. Together they use rapid tail movements to clear a shallow depression in the sand or gravel, quickly deposit sticky red eggs and milt, then ride the tidal surge back out to deeper water. After the spawning run, the waters and strand of coastal beaches are littered with dead capelin.

Female mortality during spawning can reach 90 per cent, though some females will live to spawn for two or three more years. For males, however, mortality is closer to 100 per cent, due to injuries sustained during repeated mating.

Fertilized eggs are red and can be buried up to 15 centimetres deep. They incubate for two weeks. Newly hatched larvae remain in the sand for several days, absorbing the yolk sac. When they emerge, the tide carries them to the sea.

FISHERY STATUS

On the island of Newfoundland, capelin were traditionally harvested from spawning beaches for food, bait, and fertilizer. The annual take could reach 25,000 tonnes. In the early 1970s, the fishery moved offshore, foreign fleets targeted the species, and the harvest increased exponentially. A peak offshore catch—250,000 tonnes—was taken in 1976. This fishery was closed in Division 3L in 1979 but persisted in divisions 2J3K until 1992.

During the late 1970s, an inshore fishery for roe-bearing female capelin began in Atlantic Canada and persisted through the 1980s. It began in the middle of June off the south coast of Newfoundland and finished in mid-July off the north coast. Since the early 1990s, this fishery has operated mainly in July and early August in Division 3K. Inshore landings peaked from 1988 to the early 1990s. Interest in the northwest Atlantic capelin fishery has grown steadily since 2004, following the closure of the unsustainable Barents Sea capelin fishery. Landings from 2006 to 2008 have been at, or slightly higher than, the current Canadian Total Allowable Catch.

The capelin biomass densities increased in 2007 and 2008, especially in northern areas of Division 3L. But the overall picture is troubling, as these recent increases bring the population to numbers comparable with the very low counts of the 1990s.

The cod collapse meant fewer capelin predators, so their numbers should have increased in the 1990s. But anticipated increases did not occur. Instead there was a dramatic downturn—in the number of capelin, their size and age at maturity, and even in the timing and length of the spawning season. Colder, harsher water conditions may have played a role: capelin was extirpated along sections of the Labrador coast at this time, as populations moved to the northern Grand Banks. But overfishing was the primary factor in the population collapse.

Identifying capelin

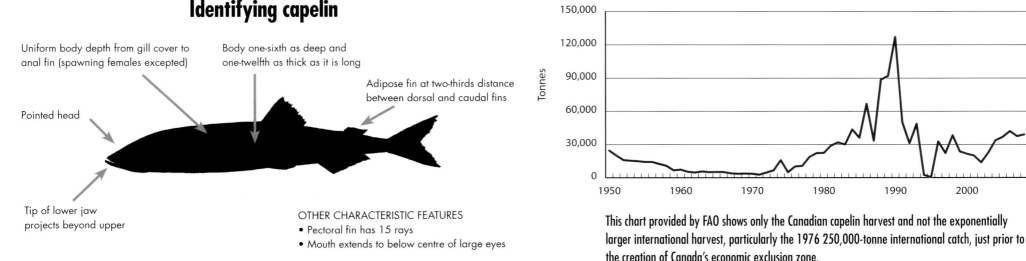

Uniform body depth from gill cover to anal fin (spawning females excepted)

Pointed head

Tip of lower jaw projects beyond upper

Body one-sixth as deep and one-twelfth as thick as it is long

Adipose fin at two-thirds distance between dorsal and caudal fins

OTHER CHARACTERISTIC FEATURES
- Pectoral fin has 15 rays
- Mouth extends to below centre of large eyes

Landings — Canada

Tonnes

150,000
120,000
90,000
60,000
30,000
0

1950   1960   1970   1980   1990   2000

This chart provided by FAO shows only the Canadian capelin harvest and not the exponentially larger international harvest, particularly the 1976 250,000-tonne international catch, just prior to the creation of Canada's economic exclusion zone.

Rainbow smelt

Osmerus mordax

American smelt, bay capelin, freshwater smelt, ice fish, leefish, outside capelin, smelt, white fish, *éperlan arc-en-ciel, éperlan du nord*

Rainbow smelt occupy waters along the east coast of North America from the Labrador coast to the Gulf of St. Lawrence and south to the Delaware River. It is also native to lakes and ponds in New Brunswick, Nova Scotia, Newfoundland and Labrador, Quebec, and eastern Ontario. Though naturally anadromous, smelt readily adapt to landlocked conditions and are important forage fish in northern lakes.

The North American range of smelt significantly expanded in the 1900s when it was introduced into the Great Lakes. Beginning in 1906 there were several failed attempts to introduce the species into rivers and lakes that fed into Lake Michigan, to be a forage species for Atlantic salmon populations. The smelt introduced in 1921, however, did much better than expected and spread throughout the Great Lakes, especially Lake Erie. They became the basis for an inland smelt fishery that, at times, exceeded the total volume and dollar value of the east coast fishery. Unexplained population crashes, however, undermined that fishery. Inland stocks have not recovered from the crash of 1979.

HABITAT AND APPEARANCE

A pelagic schooling species, the rainbow smelt inhabits nearshore coastal regions and mid-water depths of large freshwater lakes. Extremely sensitive to light and temperature, mature smelt concentrate in schools near the bottom during daylight hours. Short and slender, they are generally silver though their backs are pale green or olive green, with a purple, blue, or pink iridescence.

Their large scales are easily detached. During the spawning

season males develop tiny, button-like "nuptial" tubercles on the scales.

The rainbow smelt's lower jaw protrudes beyond the upper; the mouth extends back to mid-eye. The tongue tip has a few large prominent teeth. About halfway along the back is a large dorsal fin followed by a small adipose fin.

Smelt larvae eat small zooplankton. The adult diet includes shrimp and shrimp-like organisms and other larger zooplankton, aquatic worms, and juvenile herring, juvenile smelt, and other small fish. In the marine environment, smelt are prey to cod, salmon, seals, cormorants, and mergansers. Freshwater fish species prey on smelt—lake trout, brook trout, salmon, walleye, and yellow perch—as do gulls, and crows. Smelt eggs are a primary food for mummichog.

LIFE HISTORY

Female smelt grow faster and bigger and live longer than males do. Both marine and landlocked adult smelt migrate upstream to their natal rivers to spawn in the spring. On average, two-thirds of the smelt that spawn in a given year are 2 years old, slightly less than one-third are 3 years, and the remaining smelt (about 4 per cent) are 4, 5, or 6 years old.

Within five to ten days after spawning, most of the males perish. The surviving adults migrate downstream and spend the summer in an estuary or in coastal waters (within 2 kilometres of shore), in depths less than 6 metres. In the fall, ocean-going adults return to the estuary to overwinter.

Females spawn at night, attended by two or more males, where water flows in rapid currents over a gravel bottom. Individual males may milt for up to eight consecutive nights; females spawn over three or four nights. The eggs adhere loosely to gravel, sand, and submerged vegetation by a "stem" that enables the eggs to flutter in the current for better aeration.

Within three weeks, slender and nearly transparent larvae emerge and, where not landlocked, drift downstream to a tidal estuary. Like adults, larvae remain near the bottom in the day and rise at night to feed near the surface. At about 19 millimetres they begin to school, seeking shallow water after dark and returning to deeper channels by day. They reach 20 to 40 millimetres in length within a month and 66 to 82 millimetres after a year. As temperatures cool in the fall, juveniles move into upper estuary channels to join multi-generation schools.

FISHERY STATUS

The rainbow smelt is most important today as a winter recreational fishery for one very important reason: they are tasty.

No comprehensive management plan has yet been developed for commercial smelt fisheries. Growth and natural-mortality rates for given populations are not fully understood, and regulation is a patchwork of provincial restrictions on location, gear, and timing. There are no estimates of population size, so an annual harvest for a sustainable fishery cannot be calculated with any certainty.

On the Atlantic coast, smelt are caught mainly during the winter through holes in the ice, using a variety of gear (most popular is the double-ender box net). In the Great Lakes, smelt are fished commercially by trawls. At market, the smelt caught on the Atlantic coast fetches two to three times the price of the landlocked smelt.

Identifying rainbow smelt

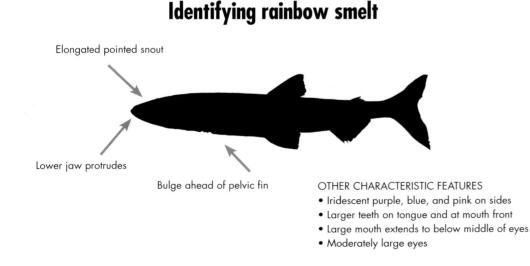

Elongated pointed snout

Lower jaw protrudes

Bulge ahead of pelvic fin

OTHER CHARACTERISTIC FEATURES
- Iridescent purple, blue, and pink on sides
- Larger teeth on tongue and at mouth front
- Large mouth extends to below middle of eyes
- Moderately large eyes

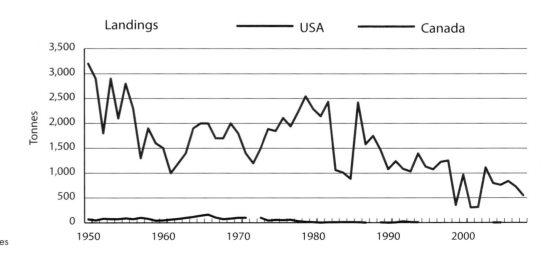

Landings — USA — Canada

90 to
250 m

Threatened
(COSEWIC, 2009)

American plaice

Hippoglossoides platessoides
American dab, blackback, Canadian plaice, flounder, long rough dab, plaice, rough dab, sand dab, sole, *faux flétan*, *plie*

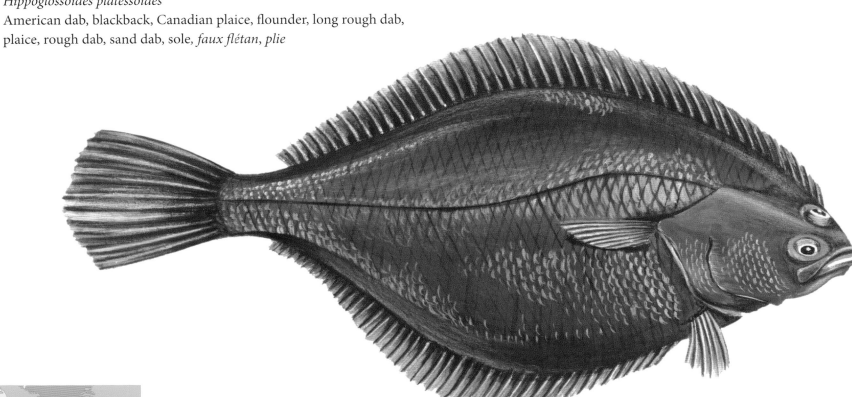

The American plaice is an Arctic flounder that inhabits both sides of the North Atlantic over the continental shelves of northeastern North America and northern Europe. In the western Atlantic, the species is common from the coast of Labrador, south from Hamilton Inlet, around the island of Newfoundland to the Grand Banks, in the Gulf of St. Lawrence, and west and south to Cape Cod.

HABITAT AND APPEARANCE

As plaice mature, the left eye migrates to the right side of the body. At the same time, the fish re-orients itself to swim right side up and left side down.

The colour of the right (upper) side of the body ranges from reddish to greyish brown. The left (under) side is white. Both sides are covered in small scales. The dorsal fin (on the mature fish's left side) and the anal fin (on the mature fish's right) are continuous. The tail fin is rounded. The lateral line curves slightly just behind the gill openings. The mouth is large, extending beyond the eyes.

Larval plaice feed on plankton near the surface. As the fish grow and settle to the bottom, they adapt their diet to feed on invertebrates such as the sand dollar, brittle star, and marine worms. At night they forage higher up in the water column for capelin, sand lance, and other fish.

Greenland shark, cod, halibut, monkfish, and spiny dogfish are the primary predators of American plaice, except along the Scotian Shelf and in the Gulf of St. Lawrence, where grey seals are the main predators.

LIFE HISTORY

American plaice has no specific spawning ground, but in the northwest Atlantic it spawns as early as the first of April on the Flemish Cap and the southern half of the Grand Banks, and as late as May or early June off Labrador.

Female plaice begin spawning at different ages, depending on their location. Some may start as early as 8 or 9 years of age, when they are about 30 centimetres long. Most, however, do not spawn until they reach 40 to 45 centimetres, usually in year 11. Males mature within three years, when they are just 15 to 20 centimetres

long; all males are mature by their sixth year, regardless of location.

A newly mature female produces 250,000 eggs; older females (70 centimetres or more) may produce up to 1.5 million. Plaice spawn and fertilize their eggs near the ocean floor. Once fertilized, the eggs are buoyant and rise to the surface layer, where currents distribute them throughout the northwest Atlantic before they hatch. The time between fertilization and hatching varies according to surface-water temperature. Developing eggs and larvae can be carried great distances before young fish swim to the bottom.

When plaice hatch, they swim like most other fish and have an eye on each side of the head. Migration of the left eye begins when larvae are approximately 20 millimetres long. It is usually complete by the time larvae reach 30 to 40 millimetres.

American plaice are relatively sedentary in the adult phase. Tagging results indicate only minor migration. Most tagged fish have been recovered less than 48 kilometres from the tagging site eight years later.

FISHERY STATUS

Once one of the most abundant of the small flatfish in the northwest Atlantic, American plaice is one of the major commercially exploited groundfish species inside Canada's economic exclusion zone, and both stocks in Atlantic Canadian waters are listed as Threatened.

There is currently a moratorium (no directed fishery) in NAFO areas 3LNO and 3M. The most recent assessments (2008 and 2009) concluded that the stock biomass of American plaice in 3M is very low, with no sign of recovery (though it has been increasing steadily since 1995). NAFO's

Scientific Council recommends no directed fishing of American plaice, and also that bycatch in other fisheries be restricted to the lowest possible level: "unavoidable." Much of the plaice's habitat is inside Canadian waters, however, and the federal Department of Fisheries and Oceans describes the species as "abundant" and permits a fishery. The American plaice accounts for 50 per cent of all flatfish species harvested.

Identifying American plaice

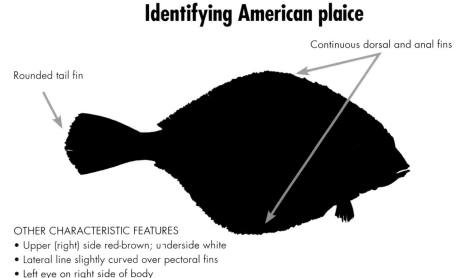

Rounded tail fin

Continuous dorsal and anal fins

OTHER CHARACTERISTIC FEATURES
• Upper (right) side red-brown; underside white
• Lateral line slightly curved over pectoral fins
• Left eye on right side of body
• Mouth extends beyond eyes

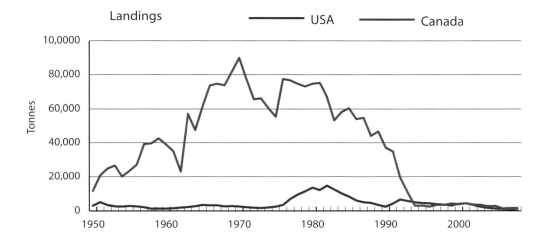

} NDA

Not at Risk
(COSEWIC, 2011)

Atlantic halibut

Hippoglossus hippoglossus
Cherry bellies, common halibut, halibut, giant halibut,
greys, *flétan, flétan atlantique*

Atlantic halibut is a target species actively sought in commercial quantities from the outer edge of Labrador's continental shelf to the Flemish Cap, on the southern part of the Grand Banks, off Newfoundland's west coast, throughout the Gulf of St. Lawrence to the Scotian Shelf, and south to Georges Bank, parts of the Gulf of Maine, and into the Nantucket Shoals. Rarely, they have also been taken off New Jersey and New York.

Some Atlantic halibut can be found in the area of the Labrador Current—but likely at depths where the water is slightly warmer, since this species prefers temperatures greater than 2.5°C.

HABITAT AND APPEARANCE

The Atlantic halibut is by far the largest member of the family Pleuronectidae. Size alone is enough to distinguish mature individuals from all other flatfish species. Immature halibut, however, can be identified by body shape, which is not as wide but relatively much thicker than other members of the flatfish family. The concave caudal fin and a strongly curved lateral line above the pectoral fin also aid in distinguishing the Atlantic halibut.

Atlantic halibut fry swim like other fish: they have eyes on each side of the head. Over the first year of life, the left eye migrates toward the right side of the head, creating a blind left side. As fish mature, they reorient their bodies to swim with the right side facing up and the blind side down.

The mouth of an Atlantic halibut is large—it opens as far back as the eyes—and has sharp curved teeth. The upper (right) pectoral fin is obliquely pointed and the lower (left) is rounded. The long dorsal fin begins at the eye and runs the length of the fish, broadening then abruptly narrowing near the caudal peduncle. The anal fin is similar to the dorsal, but shorter. Like other Atlantic flatfish, halibut are scaly and coated in mucus.

Adult Atlantic halibut colour ranges from uniform chocolate brown to olive brown or slate brown or even black on the upper (right) side. The lighter under (left) side may be grey. Juvenile Atlantic halibut have the adult's mottled colouring on the right side but are white on the underside.

Atlantic halibut have several feeding phases. Up to 30 centimetres, they eat worms and small shrimp. Between 30 and 80 centimetres, they feed on crustaceans and small fish. Mature adults prefer large fish such as cod, haddock, herring, and even smaller halibut. Mainly bottom-feeders, Atlantic halibut also seek food in the water column, rising after sunset to feed then returning to the bottom at dawn.

Juvenile halibut are a preferred food of seals and cod, but the size and strength of adult halibut exclude it from the diet of most predators except killer whales and Greenland sharks.

Preferring water that ranges between 3° and 9°C, halibut seek out areas with sandy soft bottoms in which they can bury themselves. In the winter, they move to water 500 or more metres deep, migrating to shallower water in the warmer seasons.

LIFE HISTORY

Like other female flatfish, mature female Atlantic halibut are capable of producing several million eggs a year, depending on their age and size. When first released near the bottom, the unfertilized eggs are large, round, and pink. After fertilization they become transparent and buoyant, rising to drift suspended in the water column until the larvae hatch. Larvae live off the yolk sac for up to five weeks before they begin feeding on plankton.

Newly hatched Atlantic halibut larvae swim belly down and drift in mid-level water for several months. When they reach 16 to 20 millimetres, the left eye starts its gradual migration over the top of the head to the right side. The transition continues for several months. By the time the fish reach 44 millimetres, both eyes are on the pigmented right side.

At 50-plus millimetres, juveniles begin to swim right side upward and slowly migrate toward the bottom of deeper ocean channels. They grow rapidly, sometimes doubling in length to more than 1 metre at sexual maturity. Females grow faster than males. The overall rate of growth after maturity is slow but varies according to population density and competition for available food. This characteristic—as well as late-onset maturity—renders halibut populations extremely vulnerable to overfishing.

Tagging has shown that Atlantic halibut can migrate 2,500 kilometres or more, from the east coast of Canada to the west coast of Iceland. Generally, however, they seem to prefer to remain in the waters where they hatched.

FISHERY STATUS

In the earliest days of the Atlantic fishery, the Atlantic halibut was regarded as more of a nuisance than a food fish. In the 19th century, however, people came to appreciate its firm and tasty flesh, and so the fishery grew. Strong demand for this slow-growing species eventually pushed the

fishery to unsustainable levels. After the 1970s, the abundance of halibut on the Grand Banks and Labrador Shelf decreased until 2002, when the trend reversed. On the Scotian Shelf and in the Gulf of St. Lawrence, the population has been increasing since the 1990s.

Targeted and bycatch fisheries were unrestricted until the 1980s, when catch limits and size restrictions were intro-duced in some areas. In 2011, analysis of the Scotian Shelf and southern Grand Banks population indicated there were enough fish for a sustainable fishery and the total catch was within the limits to maintain the population.

Identifying Atlantic halibut

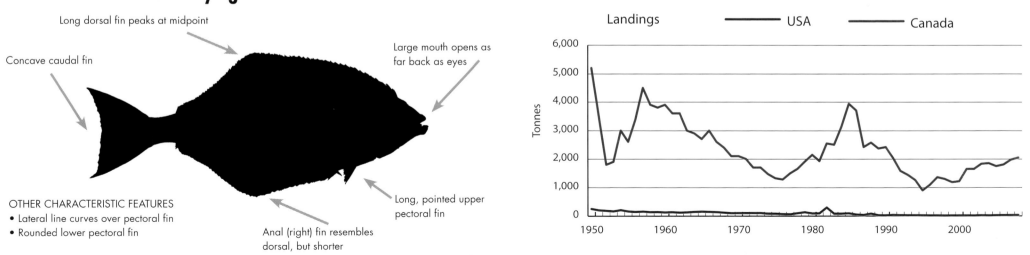

Long dorsal fin peaks at midpoint

Concave caudal fin

Large mouth opens as far back as eyes

OTHER CHARACTERISTIC FEATURES
• Lateral line curves over pectoral fin
• Rounded lower pectoral fin

Anal (right) fin resembles dorsal, but shorter

Long, pointed upper pectoral fin

Landings — USA — Canada

Tonnes

6,000
5,000
4,000
3,000
2,000
1,000
0

1950   1960   1970   1980   1990   2000

}200 to
800 m

Greenland halibut

Reinhardtius hippoglossoides
Black halibut, Greenland flounder, Greenland turbot, lesser halibut, turbot

This deepwater fish occurs in the cold waters of the western North Atlantic and well into the Arctic Ocean. Able to tolerate sub-zero temperatures, it can also be found in the eastern Atlantic and the eastern North Pacific. In the northwest Atlantic, Greenland halibut distribution is more or less continuous along the continental slope from western Greenland south through the waters of Newfoundland and Labrador, into the Gulf of St. Lawrence and as far south as New England.

HABITAT AND APPEARANCE

Greenland halibut is a right-sided flatfish. When mature, its left eye is positioned only as far as the dorsal ridge of the right forehead, which both distinguishes it from other flatfish and gives this species wider peripheral vision.

Greenland halibut are black or brown on the upper (right) side and paler on the relatively blind (left) underside. The caudal fin is concave; pelvic fins are symmetrical. The dorsal fin (left) is longer and has a different shape than the anal fin. The lateral line is straight above the pectoral fin. The elongated body has equally developed swimming muscles on both sides. This suggests that these flatfish swim more "upright" than other species (though this behaviour may be rare) and spend relatively more time actively swimming and feeding in the water column (evidenced by harvesting success with both trawls and surface drift nets).

Greenland halibut mainly consume pelagic or bathypelagic crustaceans such as deep-sea prawns. The species also eats bottom-dwelling invertebrates. The fish in the Greenland halibut diet include eelpout, capelin, and redfish.

Larvae are eaten by cod, salmon, and younger, bottom-dwelling fish; medium-sized juveniles are eaten by cod and by larger Greenland halibut. The most significant predator, however, is the Greenland shark, which thrives at the same depths inhabited by this species.

Historically, periodic disappearances of Greenland halibut have usually coincided with increased sightings of beluga whales. New whale invasions into Greenland's fjords are now recognized as an indicator of the imminent collapse of the halibut fishery. Additional predators include seals and narwhals.

LIFE HISTORY

Juvenile Greenland halibut of both sexes are equal in number and have similar growth rates. Once fish reach 45 centimetres (at age 6 to 7 years), male growth decreases and mortality increases: energy previously used for growth is diverted to the gonads. All Greenland halibut longer than 90 centimetres are female.

Greenland halibut migrate between spawning and feeding areas over distances of more than 100 kilometres. They appear to have a peak and a secondary spawning period—and some individuals are in spawning condition during both seasons. During the main spawning season (December to April), Greenland halibut are most abundant in the Davis Strait. However, some members of the species may spawn at any time of year in waters remote from traditional spawning grounds.

Ocean currents carry fertilized eggs and larvae—which remain pelagic for several months—from Davis Strait to at least two nursery areas. The West Greenland Current sweeps one portion of the larvae north to Baffin Island, and the Labrador Current carries another south to Labrador and Newfoundland. The newly hatched larvae—6 millimetres long—remain in the water column until they reach 70 millimetres. Then, as juveniles, they descend to depths more typical of mature Greenland halibut.

FISHERY STATUS

Like many other deepwater species, Greenland halibut have come to be heavily fished as shallower-living populations of other species have been depleted. Increasing exploitation of the species is reinforcing the need for accurate data on stock structure. Since 2003, Greenland halibut has been in the Group 3 (low priority) category of COSEWIC's candidates-for-assessment list. It is recognized that the Greenland halibut is overfished and exploited at a rate that is not sustainable.

Did You Know . . .

- Greenland halibut are marketed fresh as "turbot" in Canada. They are commonly sold smoked in Europe.
- Because its left eye migrates only just past the dorsal ridge, the Greenland halibut is the flatfish with the greatest relative distance between its eyes.

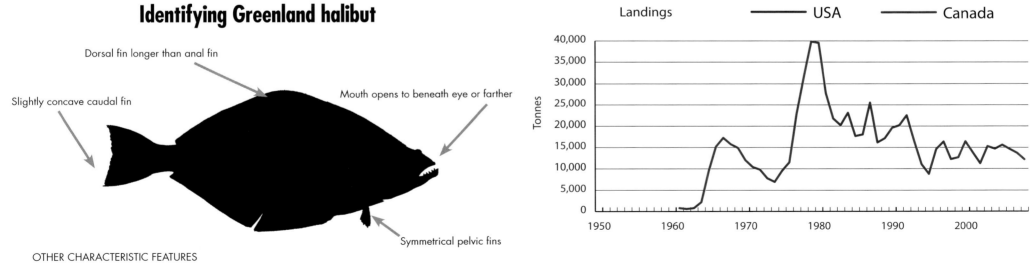

Identifying Greenland halibut

Dorsal fin longer than anal fin

Slightly concave caudal fin

Mouth opens to beneath eye or farther

Symmetrical pelvic fins

OTHER CHARACTERISTIC FEATURES
- Left eye on dorsal ridge

Landings — USA — Canada

Tonnes

3.5 to
10 m

Smooth flounder

Pleuronectes putnami
Christmas flounder, eelback, foolfish,
smoothback flounder, *plie lisse*

The smooth flounder is an estuarine flatfish that, although taken occasionally by fishers, is smaller than the more commercially valuable winter flounder. The northern limit for this species is Ungava Bay. From there it ranges south along the coast of Labrador to the Strait of Belle Isle, where it is the most plentiful flatfish year-round. Juvenile smooth flounder are common in the shallow pools of Pistolet Bay on the Newfoundland side of the Strait. Smooth flounder is also found on both sides of the Gulf of St. Lawrence, off the Cape Breton coast, around the Magdalen Islands and Prince Edward Island, and all the way into the Gulf of Maine and Massachusetts Bay.

HABITAT AND APPEARANCE

Relatively small by flatfish standards, the smooth flounder is a right-sided small-mouthed fish that resembles winter flounder, yellowtail, and witch flounder. Between its eyes the skin is smooth and without scales. Females' skin is smooth on both sides.

The smooth flounder has relatively long pectoral fins for a flounder, especially on the right side. This upper pectoral fin is significantly longer on males (80 per cent of the head length) than on females.

This flounder varies in colour on the upper (right) side from grey to a dark slate brown to almost black. The dorsal, anal, and caudal fins are similar in colour but often mottled. The blind underside is white. The prominent lateral line is straight, as is the dorsal (left) profile of the head. The long dorsal fin and shorter anal fin are widest at their midpoints and taper at both ends.

The smooth flounder has a remarkable tolerance for the seasonal changes in water temperature to which it is exposed in the nearshore locations it inhabits (from the tide line to a maximum depth of 28 metres).

The smooth flounder is found in greatest abundance in areas with smooth muddy bottoms, such as estuaries, river mouths, and sheltered bays and harbours. Intertidal mudflats are important nursery grounds. With a small mouth, young fry 70 to 100 millimetres feed on tiny crabs, shrimp, and a range of other crustaceans, as well as polychaete worms. This flounder's diet also includes very small amounts of sand shrimp (never more than 5 per cent by mass). Mature smooth flounder eat the worms, crustaceans, and molluscs found in shallow water. The species is prey to cod, spiny dogfish, monkfish, winter skate and other large flounder, harbour seals, and seabirds.

LIFE HISTORY

Little is known about smooth flounder egg production, spawning activity, or larval development. There is evidence that this species spawns in winter, as early as December until mid- to late March.

Spawning probably takes place on the bottom, in shallow water. The demersal eggs drift freely near the bottom. When the larvae hatch, they begin to swim singly and in groups near the shore.

During spring and summer, smooth flounder are found in upstream areas of estuaries. They migrate to the lower estuary during late autumn and winter. In nearshore locations, where water is less than 1.5 metres deep, the smooth flounder population includes fish less than 10 centimetres long. During the fall and winter, these populations move to deeper waters. Larger flounder (more than 15 centimetres long) occupy deeper offshore waters.

Half of the year-class is mature by the time males reach 9.6 centimetres and females are 13.4 centimetres. Feeding activity is highest during June and July; it declines during October and November and stops altogether during spawning.

FISHERY STATUS

A highly edible table fish for its size, the smooth flounder is not sufficiently large, plentiful, or widely distributed to be of any great commercial value. There is no directed fishery nor regulations, and the status of the species has not been assessed. At one time there was a small Canadian fishery for smooth flounder (in the Miramichi River); the catch was sold mainly to fox farms.

Identifying smooth flounder

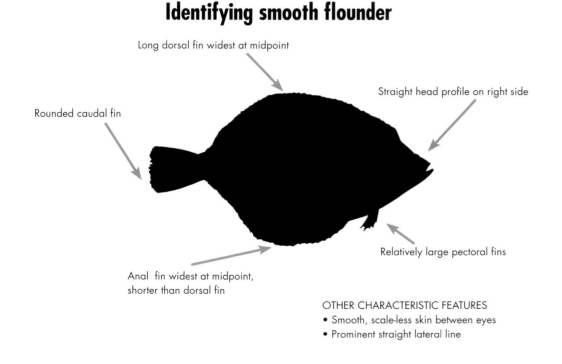

Long dorsal fin widest at midpoint

Straight head profile on right side

Rounded caudal fin

Relatively large pectoral fins

Anal fin widest at midpoint, shorter than dorsal fin

OTHER CHARACTERISTIC FEATURES
- Smooth, scale-less skin between eyes
- Prominent straight lateral line

} sub-tidal to 37 m

Winter flounder

Pseudopleuronectes americanus

Black flounder, blackback flounder, dab, flounder,
Georges Bank flounder, lemon sole, mud dab,
rough flounder, sole, *carrelet, limande, plie rouge*

T he winter flounder is the most common shallow-water
flounder on the northeast coast of North America. It seeks
out waters with sandy and muddy bottoms, where it can
bury itself, concealing all but its eyes.

The winter flounder's range extends south from Ungava Bay
along the north Labrador coast. It becomes more numerous in the
Strait of Belle Isle, along the north shore of the Gulf of St. Lawrence,
and on the south and southeast coasts of Newfoundland, as far west
as the southern part of the Grand Banks, and south to Chesapeake
Bay. It is occasionally found as far south as North Carolina.

HABITAT AND APPEARANCE

The winter flounder's profile is almost oval. The caudal peduncle
and tail are wider than those of other small flatfish, and the lateral

line is straight or slightly bowed. The dorsal (left) profile of the
head is slightly concave. A right-sided flatfish, the winter flounder
has relatively wide-set eyes. The nose is blunt and the mouth is
small with thick fleshy lips. The dorsal (left) jaw is usually toothless. The lower (right) jaw has close-set incisor teeth.

The long dorsal fin of the winter flounder has 60 to 76 rays.
It originates near the eye and tapers very little. The anal fin (45 to
58 rays) is widest about midway and is preceded by a short, sharp
spine. Both the dorsal and anal fins are less tapered than those of
other small flatfish. Identical pelvic fins are separated from the anal
fin by a large gap.

Sometimes spotted or mottled, the right side colour varies from
a muddy red to almost black. These fish change colour to camouflage
their presence. The blind side is white, often tinged with yellow.

Scales are rough on the upper side and smooth on the blind side.

An opportunistic feeder, the winter flounder eats crustaceans, sea urchins, snails, crabs, shrimp, annelid worms, molluscs, and seaweed. Adults occasionally eat small fish and squid.

Larvae and juvenile winter flounder are on the menus of a variety of fish including summer flounder. The main predators of adult winter flounder include cod, spiny dogfish, monkfish, and winter skate. Additional predators include grey, harp, and harbour seals and a variety of seabirds.

LIFE HISTORY

Generally, the northwest Atlantic winter flounder population consists of localized stocks in coastal bays and estuaries. Winter flounder seek out deeper channels during summer and shallower water in the fall. They return to deeper water in winter and migrate inshore again in the spring. Despite this seasonal movement, winter flounder is considered non-migratory, as it inhabits the same local area for its entire life.

To breed, reproductively isolated adult populations typically seek out specific estuaries or coves and bays in early spring, where spawning takes place. Batch spawners, they choose shallow water, usually over sandy bottoms or weed beds. The larvae and juvenile winter flounder remain inshore for their first two years then move offshore.

Habitat varies by life stage and affects the species' distribution. The preferred depth ranges from the sub-tidal zone to 37 metres. Inshore, they prefer muddy bottoms broken by patches of eelgrass but are also found over sand, clay, or pebble substrates. Winter flounder remain near the bottom, where they lie motionless during low tide and scatter on the flood in search of food. Though they spend much of their time hidden, winter flounder can strike quickly.

Just before spawning, winter flounder stop feeding. Females spawn with an astonishing fecundity for such a relatively small fish, releasing up to 1.5 million demersal eggs in batches on sandy bottoms, often in very shallow water, where they remain in densely massed clumps.

Within 14 days of hatching, larvae grow to 5 millimetres in length and absorb the yolk sac. Between weeks six and ten, they reach 8 millimetres, the left eye is visible on the right side, and fins are fully formed. When the fish reach 9 millimetres, the left eye has migrated to the right side and the tiny fry rest and swim as adults do.

FISHERY STATUS

Traditionally, winter flounder was a bycatch in the cod, white hake, and American plaice fisheries. It was taken for lobster bait and for limited food markets. When the cod fishery was shut down, winter flounder become a directed fishery.

Winter flounder stocks support local commercial fisheries in vessels of less than 13.7 metres. Otter trawls account for up to 75 per cent of winter flounder landed over the last 40 years; in most years since 1986, however, modified gill nets (tangle nets), normally set over beds of herring eggs, have accounted for up to 25 per cent of landings, mainly in the southeastern Gulf and near the Magdalen Islands (NAFO Divisions 4TG and 4Tf).

Between 1997 and 2001, landings of winter flounder averaged 600 tonnes; in 2004 they bottomed out at 381 tonnes—the lowest harvest recorded since 1960 (during that period, landings averaged 1,671 tonnes a year).

Directed fishing declined in the 1990s, which partially explains recent declines in landings. A TAC of 1,000 tonnes, introduced in 1996, was exceeded only in 1997 (when 1,129 tonnes were landed). Several changes in Canadian regulations may have also have contributed to the reduced landing statistics since the mid-1990s. These include a requirement to identify species caught, better dockside monitoring, and the introduction of fixed-gear logbooks.

Identifying winter flounder

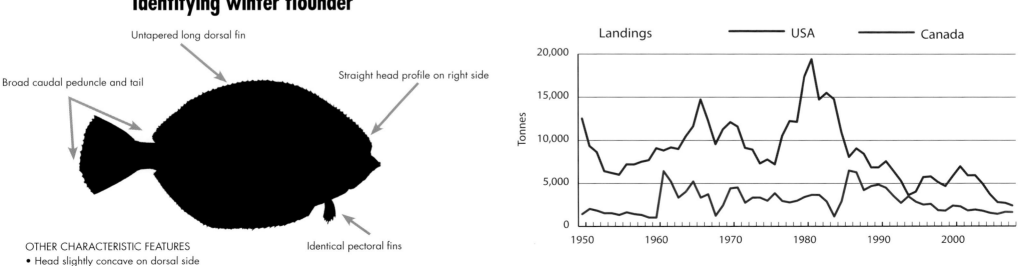

Untapered long dorsal fin

Broad caudal peduncle and tail

Straight head profile on right side

OTHER CHARACTERISTIC FEATURES
- Head slightly concave on dorsal side

Identical pectoral fins

Landings — USA — Canada

45 to
500 m

Witch flounder

Glyptocephalus cynoglossus
Grey sole, pale flounder, pole flounder, sole, Torbay sole,
white sole, witch, *plie, plie cynoglosse*

The witch flounder is found in the northwest Atlantic from Labrador's Hamilton Inlet south to Cape Hatteras, usually offshore in moderately deep water. The species prefers the muddy bottoms typical of the continental slope that borders the offshore banks of Newfoundland and Labrador.

Witch flounder is often taken as bycatch in offshore cod and plaice fisheries; a small inshore fishery targets it in the deepwater bays of Newfoundland. Populations in the Gulf of St. Lawrence and the Gulf of Maine are also fished commercially.

HABITAT AND APPEARANCE

A right-eyed, small-mouthed flatfish, the witch flounder is adapted for life in deep offshore waters, on the soft-bottomed floor of the North Atlantic. The narrow temperature range in which the species is found suggests temperature may be more important than depth in regulating habitat choices.

Three times as long as it is wide, witch flounder has an elongated body and a small head (just one-fifth as long as the entire body). The dorsal (left) side of the head is convex. The mouth has small incisor teeth arranged in a single row.

The dorsal and anal fins, uniform in width, taper only slightly at head and tail. The pectoral and pelvic fins on both sides are identical. The caudal fin, though rounded like those of other North Atlantic flounder species, is much smaller relative to body size.

The lateral line is straight or slightly arched near the pectoral fin. The entire body and head—except for the tip of the snout and the lower jaw—is covered in rough scales.

Less variable in colour than other flatfish, witch flounder are uniformly brown or grey on the upper side; they may have dark transverse bars with plain or spotted pectoral fins tinged with purple. The end of the upper pectoral fin is black—a distinguishing feature of witch flounder. The blind side is white speckled with tiny black spots. Witch flounder that are pigmented on both sides have occasionally been caught.

Adult witch flounder feed largely (three-quarters of their diet) on benthic polychaete worms that are associated with soft bottoms. Crustaceans, molluscs, and echinoderms are also important. For juveniles of 20 centimetres or less, however, crustaceans make up three-quarters of the diet and polychaetes account for less than one-fifth of stomach contents.

A range of pelagic predators eats witch flounder eggs and larvae. The demersal juveniles and adults are prey to monkfish, spiny dogfish, halibut, cod, and harp seal.

LIFE HISTORY

As with many deepwater fish, much of what we know about the life cycle of the witch flounder has been pieced together from occasional field observations. Some dedicated research has also yielded results. Relative to other flatfish in the northwest Atlantic, the witch flounder is considered slow growing, late maturing, and long lived—usually a sign that a commercial fishery is a threat to sustainable stock management.

Witch flounder in Canadian waters are believed to stop feeding in winter. There is also some evidence of seasonal movement, though no migration has actually been observed. For example, juvenile witch flounder in the Bay of Fundy are caught only from November to May. Adults are caught there only from June to October. On the Scotian Shelf, however, more adults are found in shallower depths during the spring and summer spawning season than in winter.

The witch flounder has a long spawning season—and ripe fish have been taken year-round. Spawning peaks vary by location. In Labrador, peak spawning occurs from March through May, but in the Gulf of Maine spawning peaks in July and August.

Females release their eggs near the bottom, in batches; fertilized, the buoyant eggs rise to the surface. The pelagic larvae inhabit the top metre of water, feeding at temperatures of 10°C or warmer.

It takes four to twelve months for the left eye of witch flounder to migrate to the right side—a long time compared with other flounder species. Once the metamorphosis is complete (when juveniles are 20 to 68 millimetres), fish settle to the bottom. Just prior to maturing, the larger juveniles (up to 37 centimetres for males and 44 centimetres for females) join the schooling adults.

In winter and spring, witch flounder can be found in spawning concentrations along the continental shelf of the St. Pierre Bank and in particular in the "Halibut Channel." Offshore commercial fisheries have focused their efforts to coincide with these spawning concentrations.

FISHERY STATUS

Witch flounder numbers in all year-classes have been substantially reduced since the early 1990s. Fish older than 13 years are rarely observed in commercial or survey catches.

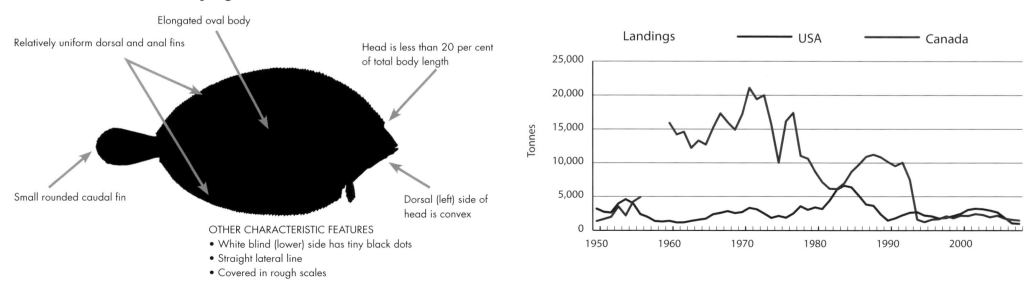

Identifying witch flounder

Relatively uniform dorsal and anal fins

Elongated oval body

Head is less than 20 per cent of total body length

Small rounded caudal fin

Dorsal (left) side of head is convex

OTHER CHARACTERISTIC FEATURES
- White blind (lower) side has tiny black dots
- Straight lateral line
- Covered in rough scales

Landings — USA — Canada

Tonnes

25,000

20,000

15,000

10,000

5,000

0

1950 1960 1970 1980 1990 2000

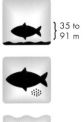

35 to 91 m

Yellowtail flounder

Limanda ferruginea
Dab, lemon sole, mud dab, rusty dab, rusty flounder,
sand dab, sole, *plie, sériole*

The yellowtail flounder grows faster and matures earlier than most other flatfish. It occurs along the northeastern coast of North America from the Labrador side of the Strait of Belle Isle, across northern Newfoundland, on the Newfoundland Grand Banks, along the North Shore of the Gulf of St. Lawrence, and south to Chesapeake Bay.

HABITAT AND APPEARANCE

Yellowtail flounder is a right-sided, small-mouthed flatfish. The dorsal fin usually has 76 to 85 rays. The anal fin, similar in outline but shorter than the dorsal, has 56 to 63 fin rays and it is preceded by a short, forward-pointing spine.

A pointed snout and thin body, a lateral line that arches above the pectoral fin, and more numerous fin rays distinguish yellowtail from the winter flounder. The concave dorsal profile of its head and the scales between its eyes—as well as the arched lateral line and fewer fin rays—distinguish it from the smooth flounder. And the lateral line, fewer fin rays, concave dorsal profile of the head, and absence of mucous pits on the blind side of the head distinguish it from the witch flounder.

The upper side of the yellowtail flounder is brown to olive green with many rust-coloured spots. It has a whitish belly and—not surprisingly—a yellow tail.

Like the other flounder, the yellowtail prefers sandy to muddy bottoms, where it preys primarily on polychaete worms and amphipods, shrimp, isopods and other crustaceans, and occasionally on small fish such as capelin and sand lance. The makeup of its diet varies with age. Adults primarily eat crustaceans and the juveniles' diet is mainly polychaetes.

The yellowtail flounder is prey for cod, Atlantic halibut, bluefish, smooth skate, spiny dogfish, winter skate, sea raven, and silver hake.

LIFE HISTORY

The recent use of data-storage tags on this species has helped dispel the belief that the yellowtail flounder is sedentary. Analysis of mark-and-recapture data suggests that this species makes both daily (off-bottom) and seasonal (moving to warmer and deeper waters in winter) migrations.

Batch spawners, yellowtail release their eggs at or near the bottom. Once fertilized, the eggs become buoyant and rise in the water column. Larvae emerge within two weeks and feed pelagically until they reach lengths greater than 14 millimetres. They then settle to the bottom to begin the demersal phase of their lives.

For the first two years, male and female yellowtails have a comparable rate of growth. After that, the females' rate accelerates. Both genders are sexually mature by year 2 or 3. Females, however, generally mature later (at a larger size) and live longer than males.

FISHERY STATUS

Survey biomass data are variable but generally indicate high biomass in the late 1970s and early 1980s, followed by a decline in the late 1980s, a rapid increase in the late 1990s, record levels in 2001, and a decline since then. The age structure of the yellowtail flounder population has shifted as the stock has declined, leaving a very low proportion of fish aged 5 years or older.

On Georges Bank, an area where Canadian and American waters overlap, the yellowtail flounder stock is only 47 per cent of the target level set in New England. In fact, throughout New England waters the yellowtail flounder is overharvested and not rebounding. The Southern New England/Middle Atlantic stock has declined to a troubling 13 per cent of the target level; and the Cape Cod/Gulf of Maine stock is just one-quarter of the target level.

The news is not all declines, however. Estimates from Canadian and Spanish surveys on the Grand Banks indicate that between 1994 and 2007 the yellowtail population has slowly increased throughout much of its range.

This "success" may have nothing to do with management but rather with the species' dietary characteristics. Small flatfish

such as yellowtail, which feed on worms and crustaceans, may be better able to tolerate habitat destruction caused by otter trawls, since the trawlers rake and re-rake the bottom, stirring up prey and encouraging the growth of worms. While the yellowtail's diet consists mainly of worms and crustaceans, it can survive this activity and may even profit from it. But it may be a short-term benefit: when individuals grow large enough to require more fish in their diet, they become vulnerable. This may help explain why, despite their apparent increasing abundance, yellowtail flounder older than 4 years are now rare.

Identifying yellowtail flounder

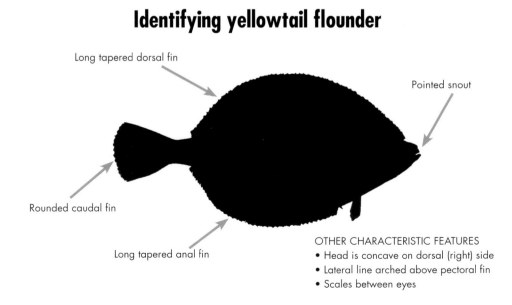

Long tapered dorsal fin

Pointed snout

Rounded caudal fin

Long tapered anal fin

OTHER CHARACTERISTIC FEATURES
• Head is concave on dorsal (right) side
• Lateral line arched above pectoral fin
• Scales between eyes

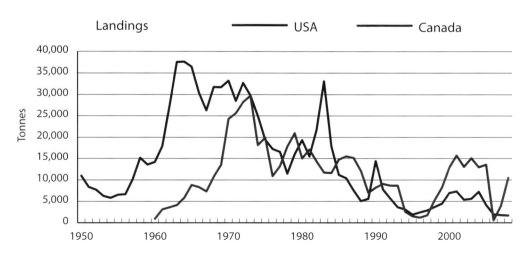

Landings — USA — Canada

Tonnes

} 0 to 180 m

Not at Risk
(COSEWIC, 2010)

Barndoor skate

Dipturus laevis
Barndoor winter skate, *grande raie*

Barndoor skate was once a common bycatch in shallow-water trawl fisheries, but it appears to have been extirpated from virtually its entire historic northwest Atlantic range: Labrador to the Newfoundland Grand Banks, the Gulf of St. Lawrence and outer coast of Nova Scotia, and the Scotian Shelf to Cape Hatteras.

Analysis of data from Canadian surveys and commercial fisheries, however, indicates that its overall distribution may actually extend to deeper and more northerly waters than originally thought. Barndoor skate have been taken as far north as the Labrador Shelf and from depths of more than 1,500 metres, with significantly higher catch rates from deeper than 450 metres. These findings add fuel to the debate about the accuracy of low estimates and the predictions of extinction that were issued in the late 1990s, and about actual status of the stock today.

HABITAT AND APPEARANCE

The smooth-skinned barndoor skate has a pointed snout with a blunt tip. Its flattened body and pectoral fins form a broad disk with steeply angled corners. The front edge is concave and the back edges are rounded. The moderately short tail has three rows of spines and two small dorsal fins near its tip.

The barndoor skate has thorns on the snout and along the front edges of the pectoral fins. The male has a patch of erectile hooks on the outer part of each pectoral fin. The two dorsal fins are separated by a short space with one or more spines.

The female's teeth are close-set and have rounded cusps; the adult male's teeth are widely spaced and arranged in rows with sharply pointed cusps.

The dorsal (upper) side of the barndoor skate is brown with a distinct red tint and darker blotches of varying size. At the base of each pectoral fin is a large oval spot. The body's underside is grey or white, graduating from darkest at the snout to lighter at the tail end. The mucous pores are very noticeable.

Bottom-dwelling fish, barndoor skate are strong and active swimmers, preferring smooth sea bottoms. They frequent water as shallow as the intertidal zone but also depths greater than 450 metres.

Barndoor skate prey on benthic species including squid, crustaceans, bivalves, worms, and gastropods. Larger individuals can take bigger and more active prey such as spiny dogfish, alewives, herring, menhaden, butterfish, sand lance, cunner, tautog, sculpin, silver hake, hake, various species of flatfish, and cod. The pigmented belly suggests that this species may depend less on bottom-dwelling prey than other (white-bellied) skates.

Because of their large size, adult barndoor skate have few predators, with the possible exception of large sharks and killer whales.

LIFE HISTORY

The barndoor skate is one of the most vulnerable of all skates. Its slow growth rate, late maturity, large size, and low rate of reproduction make this species extremely susceptible to overfishing.

Females produce relatively few eggs—between 42 and 115 a year. Females taken in January in Nova Scotian waters contained fully formed egg capsules, evidence that skate eggs are laid in winter. Each fertilized egg is enclosed in a leathery yellowish or greenish capsule called, colloquially, a mermaid's or a devil's purse. Rectangular and 124 to 132 millimetres long and 68 to 72 millimetres wide, the capsules have a short horn at each corner. Their edges are lined with slender filaments and they are much larger and have shorter horns than those of other skates in the region.

Barndoor skate lay their capsules in sandy or muddy flats. The eggs and larvae develop over 6 to 16 months. Juvenile skate, 19 centimetres long, emerge fully formed.

FISHERY STATUS

Intensive trawling by otter trawls and scallop draggers threatens the survival of the barndoor skate, since it is taken as bycatch in multi-species fisheries.

Populations in shallow waters are targeted as more valuable, with resultant overfishing.

Studies by the U.S. National Marine Fisheries Service show the abundance of barndoor skate peaking in the early 1960s. From the mid-1960s to the 1990s, numbers declined by an alarming 99 per cent. In the 1990s, the fishing effort declined in shallow areas and juveniles began to increase in number in no-take zones on Georges Bank, the southern New England shelf, and adjacent areas to the north and south.

The barndoor skate is currently a prohibited species in American waters and the biomass appears to be slowly recovering; nevertheless, the IUCN has listed the species as Endangered, a sharp contrast to COSEWIC's Not at Risk designation.

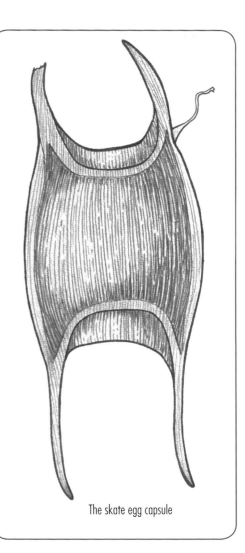

The skate egg capsule

Identifying barndoor skate

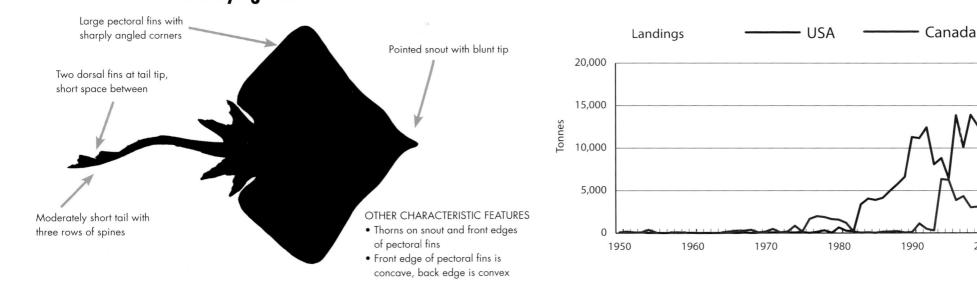

Large pectoral fins with sharply angled corners

Two dorsal fins at tail tip, short space between

Moderately short tail with three rows of spines

Pointed snout with blunt tip

OTHER CHARACTERISTIC FEATURES
• Thorns on snout and front edges of pectoral fins
• Front edge of pectoral fins is concave, back edge is convex

Landings — USA — Canada

Tonnes

20,000

15,000

10,000

5,000

0

1950   1960   1970   1980   1990   2000

} 0 to 90 m

Little skate

Leucoraja erinacea
Hedgehog skate, little common skate,
summer skate, tobacco box, *raie hérisson*

**Prioritized
Candidate List**

(COSEWIC, GROUP 2)

Regarded as a shallow-water species, the little skate is found occasionally on the Grand Banks and in northeastern Newfoundland waters but more commonly from the southern half of the Gulf of St. Lawrence and the Scotian Shelf south to Cape Hatteras, North Carolina. Its highest population densities are in American waters.

The little skate is one of the fastest growing species of skate in the northwest Atlantic: it matures at a small size and an early age and has a short lifespan. Reports about population size conflict. Some research indicates the numbers are trending downward throughout the range, while other research indicates the population is increasing slightly.

HABITAT AND APPEARANCE

Juvenile little skate, particularly females, are easily mistaken for immature winter skate. The similarities decrease as the little skate matures. It has a rounded snout with a blunt nose. The jaw plates hold 38 to 66 rows of rounded teeth with transverse cutting edges, an impressive collection that the little skate uses to grind its food.

Even though it has five gill slits on its belly, little skate will partially bury themselves in the bottom substrate. Like other skate they can pull clean water in through two spiracles that open on the top of the head and circulate it over the gills to breathe.

Little skate are wider than they are long: on an adult fish, the width of the disk from wingtip to wingtip is 1.2 times its length.

The two dorsal fins near the end of the tail are joined at the base. The skin on the terminal two-thirds of the tail may have lateral folds or ridges. The caudal fin is small. Overlapped by the pectoral fins, the pelvic fins are divided into front and rear lobes. In newly hatched young, the tail is slightly longer than the body. As little skate mature, the ratio decreases to 0.9 times the body length.

Young little skate have thorny spines along the midline of the back. These are lost as they mature. Males and females both have spines on the tail and shoulders, on each side of the dorsal ridge, and on the belly. The overall pattern of these thorns, however, differs between the sexes. On females, the spines are distributed all over the back and are most prominent on the snout, head, shoulders, and sides of the tail. The males usually have fewer spines, and they shed them from the inner side of the pectorals as well as from the mid-dorsal ridge.

Coloration ranges from grey through cloudy light brown to very dark brown with small round darker spots on the back. The edges of the pectoral fins are pale. The ventral side is white or grey except for the tail, which has different-sized grey blotches or an overall dark grey appearance.

Mainly inactive in daylight, little skate hunt crabs, shrimp, worms, amphipods, sea squirts, molluscs, squid, and sand lance. Predators of juvenile and adult skate include sharks, other skate, cod, monkfish, sea raven, longhorn sculpin, bluefish, summer flounder, grey seal, and rock crab. Sea urchins and whelks prey on the egg cases.

LIFE HISTORY

As with the other skate species, very little is known about the little skate's life history. It does migrate over relatively short distances, shifting to shallower water in summer and deeper water in late fall or early winter, but this movement is believed to be related more to seasonal temperature than to reproduction.

Female little skate spawn year-round, depositing egg capsules on sandy or muddy bottoms or attaching them to seaweed. Spawning activity peaks in the late fall, early winter, and early summer. The oblong egg capsules are amber or deep yellow when first deposited. Like other skate capsules, they have four rigid horns— one at each corner.

The nutrient-rich yolk within each capsule must sustain the embryo for six months or more. Young skate emerge through a crossways slit in the side of the capsule. Empty black capsules can often be found in seaweed washed ashore.

For the first few days of life, the young skate has an abdomen swollen with yolk and a whiplash-like extension on the tail. Both disappear within a few days of hatching.

FISHERY STATUS

The little skate is a frequent bycatch in otter trawls, traps, and weirs. The species is not considered to be valuable commercially, but it is used as bait in lobster and eel traps and in the manufacture of fish meal. Processors tried marketing little skate wings as imitation scallop but production was too labour-intensive. The species is also used in laboratories in biochemical and physiological studies.

The little skate has not been assessed by COSEWIC but it has been on the Candidate List since 2003. It is listed as "near threatened" by the IUCN. While there is no specific management plan in place for little skate, the United States does have a framework that could impose restrictions on its fishery if biomass levels fall below threshold levels. In Canada, on the eastern Scotian Shelf, the little skate population appears to be increasing. This may be an opportunistic response to the decline in the numbers of competitive winter skate, which share the same waters.

Identifying little skate

Disk 1.2 times as wide as it is long

Rounded snout with blunt nose

Small caudal fin

Two joined dorsal fins near tail end

OTHER CHARACTERISTIC FEATURES
- 38 to 66 rows of rounded teeth with transverse cutting edges on jaw plates
- Spiracles
- Spines on tail and shoulders and along dorsal ridge
- Lateral folds on skin of anterior two-thirds of tail

} 300 to 800 m

Prioritized Candidate List

(COSEWIC, GROUP 2)

Round skate

Rajella fyllae
Round ray, *raie ronde*

In the northwest Atlantic, the round skate ranges from Davis Strait off west Greenland south to the slopes off Nova Scotia and Georges Bank. Captures of this species in Canadian Atlantic waters, however, are rarely reported. It is more frequently found in the northeast Atlantic, from Iceland and the Barents Sea to waters off Norway and Denmark.

HABITAT AND APPEARANCE

The round skate closely resembles the winter skate, from which it can be distinguished by its proportionally longer, broader, and plain-coloured tail, especially in the young (which have a tail 1.3 to 1.6 times the body length). Round skate also have fewer teeth and those they do have are blunt, conical, cusped, and arranged in 30 to 38 rows in the upper jaw.

Round skate have a curved snout that ends in a small point with three to five thorns. The body disk (body and pectoral fins) is distinctly spade-shaped and has rounded outer corners. The dorsal fins are connected directly to each other—there is no intervening thorn. A triangular area of 20 to 30 large thorns is prominent around the "shoulder" and continues as three to five parallel mid-dorsal rows of claw-like thorns.

Broad, prickly thorn patches also run along the front edges of the disk. On its dorsal (upper) side, this thorny skate is covered with small, densely packed spinules—it has no bare areas. By contrast, the ventral (under) side is bare. The pelvic fins are bi-lobed; the front fins resemble fingers.

Preferring the deeper shelf and slope waters up to 2 kilometres beneath the surface, round skate are most often found in water ranging from 3° to 5.5°C. Bottom fish, they prey on invertebrates such as copepods, amphipods, and mysids. Research into predators is not plentiful. It is likely that, since this species occupies the same ecosystems as witch flounder, it also shares some of the same predators, such as monkfish, spiny dogfish, halibut, Atlantic cod, and harp seal.

LIFE HISTORY

Little is known about the life history of the round skate. As with other skate species in the northwest Atlantic, it is no longer considered to be sedentary. Migration patterns have been identified, and the size and depth of the known range have been extended. Adults are found over the deep shelves and slopes.

The round skate has a distinct pairing with embrace when mating. The egg capsules of the round skate can be 36 to 42 millimetres long and 24 to 26 millimetres wide. These oblong capsules, which have stiff pointed horns at the corners, are deposited in sandy or muddy flats. When the young first emerge from the capsules, they tend to follow large objects, such as their mother.

FISHERY STATUS

The round skate is a rare species in the northwest Atlantic. Captures in Canadian Atlantic waters are seldom reported. It is occasionally taken as bycatch in some areas, but round skate is not an economically significant species.

Did You Know . . .

• Despite this skate's extensive range, its life cycle remains a mystery to scientists and fishers alike.

Identifying round skate

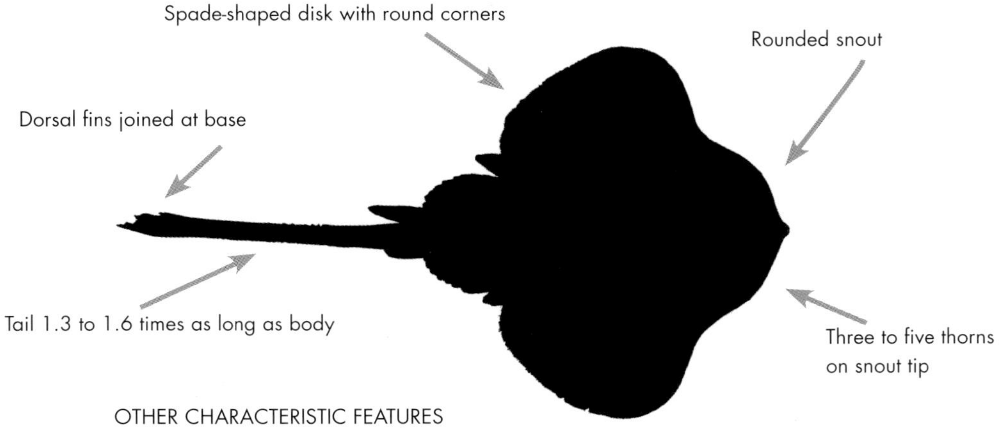

Spade-shaped disk with round corners

Rounded snout

Dorsal fins joined at base

Tail 1.3 to 1.6 times as long as body

Three to five thorns on snout tip

OTHER CHARACTERISTIC FEATURES
• Irregular dark spots in rough symmetry
• Pale areas flanking snout, between eyes, and in mid-disk
• Dorsal side covered in spinules
• Three rows of thorns along tail

} 20 to 120 m

Special Concern
(COSEWIC, 2012)

Thorny skate

Amblyraja radiata
Starry skate, prickly skate, *raie épineuse*

The thorny skate was one of the most abundant skate species in the Gulf of St. Lawrence, off northeastern and south-eastern Nova Scotia, and in the Gulf of Maine. In the last half of the 20th century, it was the most frequently caught skate on the Grand Banks, making up 90 per cent of skate captured in research survey trawls. And it also accounted for 80 per cent of all skates taken in commercial offshore fisheries on the northeastern shelf and on the Grand Banks during the 1980s and '90s.

Thorny skate range widely in the North Atlantic, from eastern waters off Greenland and Iceland to the English Channel, in northern sections of the North Sea, and in the western part of the Baltic. In the western Atlantic, the thorny skate's range includes Greenland and Hudson Bay, southern Baffin Bay, the Gulf of St. Lawrence and St. Lawrence estuary, and south through the Gulf of Maine to the Scotian Shelf's Middle Atlantic Bight.

HABITAT AND APPEARANCE

A mid-sized skate species, adult thorny skate generally measure less than 100 centimetres long by about 50 centimetres wide. The underside is smooth, but the upper side—as its name suggests—is roughened by many small thorns. In addition, 13 to 17 large thorns form a line from the back of the head to end of the tail. There are also smaller, star-shaped thorns on the pectoral fins. Adult males have two rows of hooked, erectile thorns near the outer corners of the pectoral fins.

The snout tip is blunt with somewhat bulging edges. There are

36 to 46 rows of teeth in each jaw of the mature male; the number varies in females and juveniles. Two dorsal fins near the tail tip are either joined at the base or separated by a short space (with no intervening thorns).

On the upper side, the thorny skate is uniformly brown, somewhat mottled, or spotted with a darker brown, particularly smaller fish. Occasionally, there are white spots beside each eye, on either side of the nape, and on each side of the disk. The underside is white but may have irregular sooty or brown blotches.

An opportunistic bottom-feeder, the thorny skate preys on fish and invertebrates, including worms, whelk, crab, and other crustaceans. Larger adults eat sand lance, juvenile haddock, redfish, and sculpin. Thorny skate also eat fish offal. Major predators include seals, sharks, and halibut.

LIFE HISTORY

Information about the life history of the thorny skate is limited, although fish biomass surveys suggest that the species does migrate to deeper water in winter.

Studies to determine age and growth characteristics of the thorny skate show the species to be slow growing, late maturing, and long lived—all factors that render it vulnerable to over-exploitation. Recent evidence suggests that this species grows more slowly and lives longer than previously reported. It can reach a maximum age of 28 years or more—the oldest proven age of any skate species.

In northeast and northern Atlantic waters, thorny skate mature at smaller sizes than their counterparts in the northwest. Even within a given area, great variability exists in the rate and size at which individuals mature. Females lay a limited number of capsules annually, each with a single embryo. Spawning females have been found during every month of the year, but peak spawning often occurs in the fall and winter. In the Gulf of Maine, peak reproductive activity and egg-case deposition occurs in October. However, on the eastern Scotian Shelf spawning peaks in May and again in October.

The larger the female, the larger the egg capsules it produces. Embryos may take up to 30 months to develop. When they finally break out of their leathery shell, juveniles are 11 centimetres long.

FISHERY STATUS

Since the 1960s, regular fall surveys of biomass indices show that thorny skate have declined to what are now historic lows—10 per cent of the peaks observed in the late 1960s—and that the species is overfished throughout its range. It is one

of two species of skate from which the wings are harvested for human consumption (the other is the winter skate).

Survey evidence on the Grand Banks from the mid-1990s to early 2000s indicated that thorny skate numbers were, at best, stable at historically low levels or, at worst, so reduced in range that the species is more vulnerable than ever to extirpation in commercial fishing areas. However, since three-quarters of the catch in some areas is taken outside Canada's 370-kilometre limit, the fishery is largely unregulated.

Identifying thorny skate

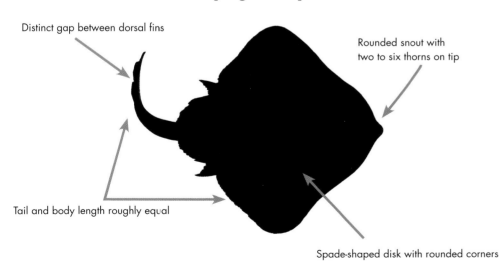

Distinct gap between dorsal fins

Rounded snout with two to six thorns on tip

Tail and body length roughly equal

Spade-shaped disk with rounded corners

} 0 to 90 m

Endangered
(COSEWIC, 2005)

Winter skate

Leucoraja ocellata
Big skate, eyed skate, winter big skate, *raie tachetée*

The winter skate is native to the northwest Atlantic. About half of its range is in American waters, the other half in Canadian. It occurs from the Gulf of St. Lawrence and southern Newfoundland to off Cape Hatteras, North Carolina.

This species occupies a relatively narrow band of the continental shelf. Variations in size and age at maturity among fish indicate that there are four distinct isolated stocks. Winter skate is most abundant on Georges Bank (where the population is listed by COSEWIC as of Special Concern), the eastern Scotian Shelf (Threatened), southern Gulf of St. Lawrence (Endangered), and Northern Gulf–Newfoundland (undesignated).

HABITAT AND APPEARANCE

As with all skate species, the head, body, and greatly enlarged pectoral fins of the winter skate form a roughly circular disk. Although its five gill openings and mouth are on the ventral (under) side, winter skate have adapted to settling into the bottom substrate by developing two spiracles just behind the eyes on the dorsal (upper) side, through which the skate takes in clean water and passes it over the gills. The teeth of juveniles and females have a blunt cusp.

The long compressed tail has lateral folds along its length and one or two small caudal fins near the tip. The tail also has two small dorsal fins, roughly equal in size and shape. The pelvic fins form two separate limb-like structures (depending on the sex of the individual): on females these fins are fan-like, while on males they are modified to form claspers, used for the embrace during mating.

The upper side is usually light to dark brown, with large white eye spots near the rear corner of each pectoral fin. The white belly is marked with irregular pale brown patches toward and along the tail.

Winter skate can be distinguished from many other skate species (little skate excepted) by its round blunt snout, long midline, three or more rows of thorns (the central row disappears over time), round dark spots on the upper side, and one to four "eye spots" near the pectoral fins.

Juveniles smaller than 35 centimetres have no spots and closely resemble the little skate species. The teeth of mature male winter skate are widely spaced and have high conical cusps with blunt tips. All winter skate have more upper tooth rows than little skate (the number varies with age) and more spines (usually 21-plus) on the tail's midline. Other characteristic features include a dense prickling on the tail's underside (except at the tip), and no spines behind the shoulders.

In northern areas, the winter skate prefers sand and gravel bottoms in shallow water. Bottom type appears to be more important than water depth for habitat selection.

This species is most active at night, hunting rock crab, squid, worms, shrimp, razor clams, and small fish such as sand lance and members of the herring family. Winter skate predators include sharks, other rays, and grey seals.

LIFE HISTORY

Much of the life history of the winter skate is undetermined, but it is known that they are slow growing and produce few eggs per year.

Reproduction occurs year-round but peaks offshore in the summer. During the mating period, pairing includes an embrace. Mature females deposit 6 to 50 egg cases (or "purses") on the bottom in offshore waters. Each has stiff pointed horns at the corners and a single embryo. After 18 to 22 months of gestation, juvenile winter skate emerge. They resemble adults in shape and have an instinct to follow large objects.

The migration patterns of the four winter skate stocks vary somewhat but all

migrate seasonally, suggesting a preference for cool temperatures. They leave shallow water in early summer and move onto the banks, dispersing as the water there warms. They reappear in shallow water in early autumn. In winter, they prefer deeper water and their distribution is more concentrated.

FISHERY STATUS

The North American skate fishery dates to the late 1800s. Landings did not exceed more than a few hundred tonnes until the advent of the industrial fishery of the 1950s and the increase in foreign fleets of the 1960s. Today there is a directed American fishery for winter skate in New England and a small Canadian fishery on the eastern Scotian Shelf, the latter regulated by catch quotas. The bulk of the American skate harvest is taken as bycatch in the ground-fish, monkfish, and scallop fisheries.

The large and relatively thick pectoral fins are a delicacy in some cultures. Most of the skate wings harvested in the United States are exported to France, Greece, and Korea. North American demand is limited mainly to processed skate wings for high-end restaurants. Skate is also harvested for fish meal and lobster bait.

Biomass surveys in American waters show a population peak in the mid-1980s and decline through the early 1990s. Numbers have stabilized somewhat but scientists believe the species is overfished. In 2010, more than 17,000 tonnes of skate were harvested in the United States, where the National Oceanic and Atmospheric Administration (NOAA) categorized the fishery as sustainable. In October 2011, NOAA increased the quota by 55 per cent,

to 21,773 tonnes, a decision based on 2008 to 2010 trawl survey data that showed significant improvement in the total skate population, and on NOAA-funded research on the survival of discarded skate, which found that more fish survived than was previously assumed.

In contrast to the population growth reported by American authorities, the species appears to be under threat in Canadian waters. Juvenile winter skate numbers increased in the 1970s, stabilized in the 1980s, and subsequently dropped rapidly. Based on catch rates, it is estimated that the mature winter skate population has declined by more than 90 per cent since then.

Contributing to the decline is bycatch in some ground fisheries (Grand Banks, southern Gulf of St. Lawrence, and Gulf of Maine) and in the offshore scallop and clam fisheries. Skate egg cases, which remain on the bottom for up to two years before hatching, are vulnerable to damage from bottom trawling, dredging, and other bottom disturbances. The natural mortality of adults also increased over this period as seal populations grew. According to Canadian sources, no recovery is expected for the now Endangered winter skate in Canadian waters, even if directed and bycatch rates could somehow be reduced to zero.

Identifying winter skate

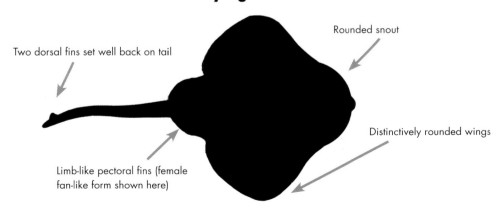

Two dorsal fins set well back on tail

Rounded snout

Limb-like pectoral fins (female fan-like form shown here)

Distinctively rounded wings

OTHER CHARACTERISTIC FEATURES
• Two or more rows of spines flank midline (shoulder to first dorsal fin)
• "Ocelli" (eye spots) on wings

30 to 70 m

Arctic char

Salvelinus alpinus

Breeder, char, sea trout, *iqaluk*, *tariungmiutaq*

The arctic char is found throughout the Canadian Arctic. An anadromous species, it spends most of its life in the ocean—but significant numbers spend their entire lives landlocked in northern lakes and rivers, never entering salt water. Important landlocked populations have staked out habitat in Maine and in northern New England. The now-extinct Sunapee trout (of the same species) was found in southern New Hampshire; the red trout of Quebec is also an arctic char.

In Atlantic Canada, the species spawns in rivers and lakes on the north coast of Labrador.

HABITAT AND APPEARANCE

The arctic char has an elongated and streamlined trout-like body and can be distinguished by its small, delicate head. Scales are very small. Char from different stocks vary considerably in body form and coloration, depending on location, time of year, and degree of sexual development. Sea-run char reach adult sizes of 2.1 to 4.5 kilograms; lake dwellers are smaller, ranging in weight from 0.2 to 2.3 kilograms.

The arctic char's snout is short. The upper jaw extends to the back edge of the eye. The dorsal fin has 8 to 11 rays. A small dorsal adipose fin is located about four-fifths of the distance between the dorsal fin and the caudal peduncle. The caudal fin is slightly forked. Distinguishing features include a series of large round spots—generally violet-pink—scattered along the sides. The largest spots are usually bigger than the eye pupil. Brook trout, which are similar in appearance, have red spots with blue haloes.

In sea-run adults, the back is dark brown and sometimes has a green cast. The sides are lighter and the belly pale. Both sides and back have several pink or red spots. Fins are pale in young fish but, in adults, the dorsal and caudal fins are dark. Spawning adults, especially males, are brilliant orange-red to bright red on the ventral side and on pectoral, pelvic, and anal fins. Young have about 11 dark bars ("parr marks") on each side, which provide camouflage.

Juvenile arctic char feed on freshwater shrimp and the waterborne larvae of some insects. Adults feed on small fish and bottom organisms including snails, clams, and insect larvae. At sea, arctic char eat other fish such as sculpin, arctic cod, sand lance, smaller arctic char, and invertebrates. Char stop feeding when they migrate into fresh water to spawn.

LIFE HISTORY

Anadromous arctic char migrate to sea between the ages of 2 and 5 years, when they are 14 to 25 centimetres long. To make the transition from fresh to salt water, they haunt the brackish river estuaries, building tolerance to ocean water, then enter nearshore waters and spend five to eight weeks of the summer feeding on the abundant marine life there.

Ocean migrations are limited. Most char can be found within 100 kilometres of their rivers of origin. Anadromous arctic char, bigger and faster than freshwater char of the same year-class, return to fresh water in the fall to overwinter—though not necessarily to their home river (this is particularly true in years when they are not spawning). Downstream migration takes place from ice breakup to mid-July. Upstream migration usually occurs from mid-August to mid-September.

Anadromous char first spawn at age 4 to 10 years. Landlocked char spawn earlier, between ages 2 and 5 years. Every four to five years during their adult lives, sea-run adult char, usually measuring between 30 and 50 centimetres, return to spawn. Males migrate to the spawning grounds first. They defend territories at the bottom of lakes and rivers, in water of 3 to 6 metres over gravel beds. There they court returning females, which scour a round nest (redd) in the gravel. When the redd is completed, the fish release eggs and milt and swim out of the excavation. They repeat the process up to five times before the female covers the eggs with gravel by fanning her tail.

Over several days, a female mates successively with two or more males before all her eggs are deposited. Males often mate with more than one partner as they continue to aggressively defend their territory. When there are no more breeding females, they finally abandon the area.

The eggs incubate for six months. Arctic char larvae, about 22 millimetres long, emerge in mid-spring.

After spawning, adult char behaviour varies according to the water body. If it is a river that freezes, the arctic char migrate to either the estuary or back into the marine environment. However, in rivers deep enough to remain mainly unfrozen, the arctic char may winter in fresh water, shedding 30 to 40 per cent of their body weight before they return to the sea, in diminished health, on the spring flood. At least three to four years pass before they spawn again. The rigours of this over-wintering may explain why most anadro-mous arctic char usually spawn only once or twice in their lives and live an average of 15 years. Some arctic char, however, manage to spawn as many as five times.

FISHERY STATUS

In northern Labrador, arctic char have been exploited commercially for more than a century. Most of the catch comes from a 225-kilometre section of the coast from Hebron Fjord south to Voisey's Bay. Significant (but uncounted) quantities of char are also harvested by subsistence and recreational fishers. The fisheries management data for arctic char are based on catch rates, as there are no regular surveys or direct indices of abundance.

Identifying arctic char

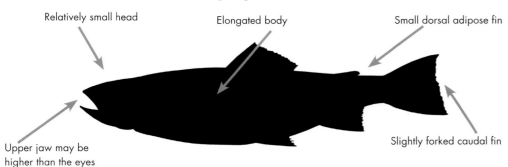

Relatively small head

Elongated body

Small dorsal adipose fin

Upper jaw may be higher than the eyes

Slightly forked caudal fin

} 1 to 10 m

Endangered
(VARIES BY STOCK)

Atlantic salmon

Salmo salar

Black salmon, Kennebec salmon, salmon, Sebago salmon, *salmon*

Landlocked salmon: greyling, *ouananiche*
Post-spawning: black salmon, kelt, slink
Year-old spawning: grilse
Juveniles: parr, salmon peel, smolt

Big cool rivers with extensive gravelly bottom headwaters are essential habitat during the first two years of an Atlantic salmon's life. The species' native range includes such streams in Russia, Portugal, Iceland, and Greenland. In North America, spawning rivers occur along the coast from Labrador to Connecticut. Landlocked Atlantic salmon persist in some North American lakes, particularly in Quebec and in Newfoundland and Labrador. The historic Great Lakes stocks no longer exist.

HABITAT AND APPEARANCE

The Atlantic salmon's overall shape, length of head, and depth of body vary with each stage of sexual maturity. In adults, the body deepens from its pointed snout to the dorsal fin then tapers to a slender caudal peduncle. The caudal fin is forked.

Sea-run Atlantic salmon grow faster and larger than landlocked salmon of the same year-class, and range in weight from 2.3 to 9.1 kilograms. Colour varies with age. Young parr (at 6.5 centimetres) develop up to 11 marks on their sides and a single row of red spots along the lateral line.

As they mature into silver-sided smolt, salmon lose the parr marks. The back takes on brown, green, and blue hues with black spots. Both males and females turn bronze-purple during spawning season; on males the head also grows longer and the lower jaw develops a distinct curvature (the "kype").

In fresh water, juvenile Atlantic salmon eat aquatic insect larvae, blackflies, mayflies, and other insect species drifting on the surface. They also eat invertebrates, amphipods, and smaller fish. At sea, smolt eat marine zooplankton, crustaceans, and eggs. Adults feed on squid, shrimp, and fish such as herring, smelt, capelin, mackerel, and sand lance.

Salmon fry are prey to water beetles and predatory fish. Parr are prime food for eel, northern pike, other trout, and birds. At sea, particularly when under 0.33 kilograms, preditors include grey and harbour seals, Greenland shark, skate, cod, and halibut.

LIFE HISTORY

Atlantic salmon spawn from October to November. Before reaching their natal river, mature salmon have stopped eating.

They remain in brackish water while adapting to fresh water.

After migrating upriver, females choose gravel nesting sites. They fan away silt with their caudal fin to clear a nest (redd) 16 to 34 centimetres wide. A male then swims close to the female, chasing away competitors while encouraging the release of eggs and sperm.

Of all salmonids, Atlantic salmon vary the most in size at maturity within distinct populations, possibly because two male types coexist on most spawning grounds. The first has the gene for large anadromous males that take three to four years— including a sea-run phase—to mature. The second (grilse) has the gene for smaller males that mature, often in fresh water, usually by the second summer. The small fish adopt a guerrilla approach to fertilization, evading the big protective males to fertilize up to 90 per cent of the eggs in a nest.

Females deposit 1,400 to 1,600 pale orange eggs per kilogram of body weight, in five to seven batches over several days. The eggs adhere to the bottom long enough for females to cover them with gravel. When their egg supply is exhausted, some females die.

The remaining fish return to the ocean or drift downriver to large pools and rest for a few weeks before leaving. Others overwinter in fresh water, rejoining the sea on the spring flood. These salmon all return once more to spawn, but few salmon spawn three times.

The eggs hatch in April. The larvae (alevins) remain in the gravel until the yolk sac is absorbed. In May or June they emerge as 2.5-centimetre-long salmon fry. For the next year (or up to three), territorial young salmon feed by day in the river system, hiding under stones and in vegetation, gradually growing to12 to 15 centimetres in length, when they are ready to enter the marine ecosystem.

Triggered by spring runoff, young smolt form schools and migrate by night to the sea, a downstream journey that imprints their "home" river's characteristics and guides them back as spawning adults. Once at sea, they migrate to feeding grounds off western Greenland and growth accelerates. Little else is known about their life in the ocean. Archival tagging techniques may soon provide the data needed to better understand this phase of the salmon life cycle.

FISHERY STATUS

From 1971 to 1985, the number of North American Atlantic salmon at 1 sea winter (1SW) of age fluctuated between 0.8 and 1.7 million. After that, a population crash continued to a point where, between 1995 and 2006, the estimated annual number of 1SW salmon was just 0.4 to 0.7 million.

These declining salmon numbers underlined our inability to manage salmon stocks despite conservations measures, which can be traced to the closure of selected commercial fisheries in 1972. In 1984, closures were expanded to all commercial fisheries in the Maritimes and parts of Quebec. The same year, mandatory catch-and-release was enforced in recreational fisheries in the Maritimes and on the island of Newfoundland. When stocks failed to rebuild, commercial salmon fishing was suspended entirely: in 1992 (Newfoundland), 1998 (Labrador), and 2000 (all of eastern Canada).

Data indicate that the sea-survival rate of returning populations is still dwindling. The most severe declines are to the rivers of the Bay of Fundy. Returning New England populations have also declined sharply. In fact, Atlantic salmon are now found in only a few Maine rivers and nowhere else in the

United States. In 2010, COSEWIC gave the 16 identified stocks of Atlantic salmon in Canada at-risk designations that ranged from Extinct (Great Lakes) to Not at Risk (for four stocks). Most are At Risk, Threatened, or Endangered.

Despite extensive research and the drastic reduction of commercial fishing, we are no closer to understanding the source of this problem. Canada's Department of Fisheries and Oceans has identified acid rain in Nova Scotia's southern upland rivers and illegal fishing in marine and fresh waters in Newfoundland and Labrador as contributing factors. The extensive aquaculture of salmon in the Maritimes and now on the south coast of Newfoundland may also negatively affect returning wild stocks. Nevertheless, salmon aquaculture is a rapidly growing industry in Atlantic Canada.

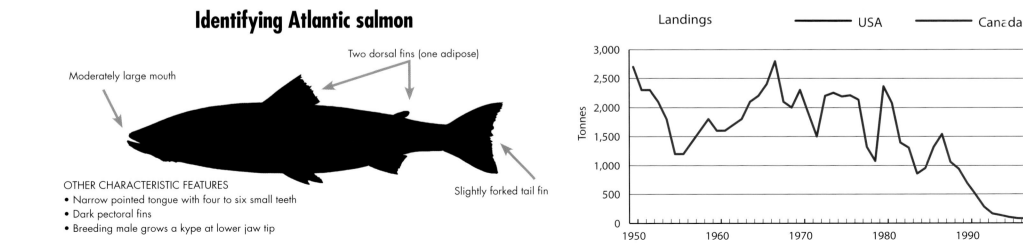

Identifying Atlantic salmon

Moderately large mouth

Two dorsal fins (one adipose)

Slightly forked tail fin

OTHER CHARACTERISTIC FEATURES
• Narrow pointed tongue with four to six small teeth
• Dark pectoral fins
• Breeding male grows a kype at lower jaw tip

Landings — USA — Canada

Tonnes

3,000
2,500
2,000
1,500
1,000
500
0

1950   1960   1970   1980   1990   2000

F S

15 to
30 m

Brook char

Salvelinus fontinalis

Baiser, breeder trout, brook trout, brookie, char, coaster, eastern brook, harness, mountain trout, mud, native trout, salter, sea trout, slob, speck, speckled, whitefin, *truite de mer, truite mouchetée, iqaluk*

The spectacularly coloured and voracious brook char is native to northeastern North America. It requires clear, pure, oxygenated fresh water within a narrow pH range. It is found in eastern Canada from the western side of Hudson Bay south to Newfoundland; its range extends into the St. Lawrence, the Great Lakes, and in the United States in the Mississippi River basin to Minnesota and northern Georgia. Extremely sensitive to environmental effects, the brook char has been extirpated in many areas.

HABITAT AND APPEARANCE

These streamlined fish grow to an average adult length of 25 to 35 centimetres. The mouth is large; breeding males develop a kype on the lower jaw. Brook char are deepest just in front of the dorsal fin. Like all salmonids, they have a small adipose fin on the back, about four-fifths of the distance from the dorsal fin to the slightly forked caudal fin.

The brook char's coloration—one of its outstanding features—is largely determined by environment. Fish of a light metallic blue are usually salters (sea-run) or coasters (inhabitants of large, deep, clear lakes). Those with dark brown and yellowish bodies are likely landlocked behind beaver dams or in mountain ponds. Colour intensifies during spawning and is most pronounced in males. In all fish, the belly is silver white.

There are three ways to use colour to tell brook char from brown or rainbow trout or other char: look for white piping on the outer edges of the anal, pelvic, and pectoral fins, a narrow black stripe on the inside of the white stripe, and wavy lines (vermiculations) on the back and head—a feature unique to brook char.

The latter also show up as tiger stripes on the dorsal, adipose, and caudal fins.

Compared to other char, salmon, and trout, the brook char is a generalist in its habitat demands—as long as the pH and oxygen levels of the water meet its needs. That means, as long as those conditions are within the narrow range required by this species, it can adapt to a wide range of northern habitats including rivulets, small brooks, creeks, larger streams, big rivers, ponds, and lakes. In addition, a unique organ in its kidneys (the glomerulus) allows it to be anadromous—these fish can migrate into riverine estuaries and brackish streams fed by ocean tides and even move into the marine environment. If they do reach the sea, they usually spend three months or less there—when they may be taken as bycatch in other marine fisheries—before migrating back upstream to spawn.

The brook char eats just about everything that crosses its path, including aquatic insect larvae, worms, leeches, crustaceans, terrestrial insects, spiders, molluscs, other fish, amphibians, snakes, and even small mammals. While larger individuals eat more fish than the juveniles, insects—particularly mayflies and the larvae of dragonflies—are very important in the brook char's diet.

Predators include eels, white perch, yellow perch, smallmouth bass, chain pickerel, as well as eastern belted kingfisher and American merganser. Limited cannibalism occurs in spring and during spawning.

LIFE HISTORY

In its native range, brook char move upstream in early spring, summer, and late fall. They migrate downstream in late spring and early fall. Some brook char—the "salters"—enter the ocean in the spring as river temperatures rise. Though they may remain there up to three months, they never travel more than a few kilometres from the home river's mouth.

Mature brook char spawn once a year. Their size at first maturity depends on whether they are sea-run or the smaller freshwater char, availability of food, and other environmental factors. Females create 10- to 30-centimetre-wide redds by turning on their sides and rapidly fanning their tail fins to sweep away silt and detritus. They deposit 40 to 60 eggs; usually just one male fertilizes the eggs, but occasionally others will take advantage of the opportunity. Unlike salmon and arctic char, the larger males are generally more successful breeders.

Males jockey for spawning rights and position by nipping at and displaying themselves to competitors. During fertilization, a male fish pins the female against the floor of the redd. Once in this position, both fish vibrate, discharging eggs and milt at the same time. Afterwards, females cover the eggs by refilling the redd with loose gravel.

Depending on the water temperature, 44 to 165 days pass before the alevins emerge. They remain in the gravel until the yolk sac is absorbed, then at about 13 to 15 millimetres they emerge as fry. At this size they must hide under banks and among vegetation. As they grow, some brook char venture into other cold bodies of water—swiftly running streams or beaver ponds, for example, returning to the river when mature to spawn. Others move downstream to the marine environment

but also return as mature fish to the freshwater river. They may swim many kilometres upstream before spawning.

FISHERY STATUS

An aquatic equivalent of the canary in the coal mine, the wild population of brook char is susceptible to the effects of human development and deforestation in surrounding aquatic ecosystems. The species has been extirpated from a significant portion of its original native range but the population has not been assessed by COSEWIC.

Brook char is farmed to a certain extent and has been exported live to other countries.

Identifying brook char

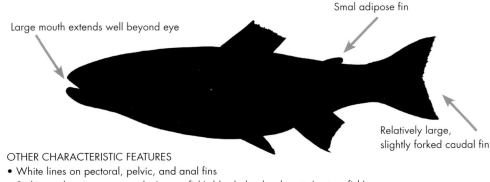

Large mouth extends well beyond eye

Smal adipose fin

Relatively large, slightly forked caudal fin

OTHER CHARACTERISTIC FEATURES
• White lines on pectoral, pelvic, and anal fins
• Striking coloration: parr marks (young fish), blue-haloed red spots (mature fish)

Atlantic mackerel

Scomber scombrus

Boston mackerel, common mackerel, tacks, tinker (juvenile), *maquereau, maquereau bleu*

Mackerel stocks span the Atlantic. They are found from the Mediterranean and Black seas north to Portugal, around the British Isles and farther north still to the waters off Iceland and Norway, and from there west across the ocean to the banks off Newfoundland and Labrador, into the inshore waters and south to Cape Hatteras, North Carolina.

HABITAT AND APPEARANCE

With an extremely hydrodynamic body, larger specimens of Atlantic mackerel can reach speeds of 35 kilometres an hour or more. The mouth is large but the eyes are relatively small. Live fish are irides-cent blue-green above the lateral line, with a silvery white belly.

Down the back are 20 to 33 distinctive black wavy lines, from the pectoral fins to the caudal fin. The two dorsal fins are relatively large and the caudal peduncle is narrow. Pectoral fins are black at the base; the deeply forked caudal fin is grey. There are five finlets between the second dorsal fin and the caudal fin and another five between the anal and caudal fins.

Mature Atlantic mackerel are 25 to 40 centimetres long. Average weight varies from 0.2 to 0.7 kilograms and individuals more than 0.65 kilograms are considered large. Male and female Atlantic mackerel grow at about the same rate and can live to 20 years of age.

This species feeds at night. It is suspected that it filter-feeds, but the gill rakers are not fine enough to retain smaller zooplankton. The dietary list includes shrimp and shrimp-like crustaceans, crab larvae, small squid, fish eggs, and some small fish including capelin, smelt, and juvenile herring and mackerel.

The Atlantic mackerel is a forage fish for many predators, including whales, dolphins, porpoises, harbour seals, Atlantic bonito, Atlantic cod, Atlantic bluefin tuna, blue shark, bluefish, dogfish, monkfish, mako and thresher sharks, porbeagle, red, silver, and white hake, sea lamprey, and swordfish.

LIFE HISTORY

The northern and southern components of the northwest Atlantic mackerel population follow a migratory pattern that brings them close to shore in warmer months and takes them offshore in fall and winter. Enormous schools of the species, grouped by age, occupy the relatively shallow waters of the continental shelf around Newfoundland and Labrador, on the Atlantic coast of Nova Scotia, and in the Gulf of St. Lawrence and the Gulf of Maine. Atlantic mackerel enter the Bay of Fundy less frequently.

The northern and southern components both overwinter at the edge of the continental shelf, from Cape Sable off Nova Scotia to North Carolina's Cape Hatteras. In the spring, the southern stock migrates inshore and north to spawn in the Scotian Shelf's Middle Atlantic Bight. The stock then moves farther north, reaching the Gulf of Maine during the summer months. The northern stock reaches southern New England waters in mid-spring and continues north to the Gulf of St. Lawrence. There they spawn in early to mid-summer. Both groups migrate south to the continental shelf in the fall, where they remain until the following spring.

The Atlantic mackerel spawns in batches of 50,000 or more eggs, five to seven times during the spawning season. This usually occurs within 10 and 200 metres of the surface. The buoyant eggs soon hatch at the depth they are laid. Feeding pelagically, rapid-growing juveniles reach 20 centimetres in length by November—a growth rate of 67 times the larval length (0.3 millimetres) in just five months. These "tinkers," common in inshore waters and estuaries, are a popular fish for young anglers.

FISHERY STATUS

The spawning biomass of the Atlantic mackerel reached a low of 1.7 million tonnes in 1972 and did not increase again until 1978. Growth was so good in the late 1980s and early 1990s, however, that by 2004 it had reached a record high of 2.3 million tonnes—well above the target level of 644,000 tonnes.

Canadian landings remained stable from the 1960s to 2000 at 21,000 tonnes, as the chart shows, and have increased significantly since then. This reflects the increases in the stock—as does the fact that older fish have become rare in current landings, which are instead dominated by juveniles and young adults.

Did You Know . . .

- In Atlantic mackerel schools, all fish are of the same year-class (cohorts) and roughly the same size.
- All fish in a school also have the same top cruising speed, which allows the school to stay together even as it migrates over very long distances.
- Mackerel can feed both by filtering prey and by direct pursuit and capture.

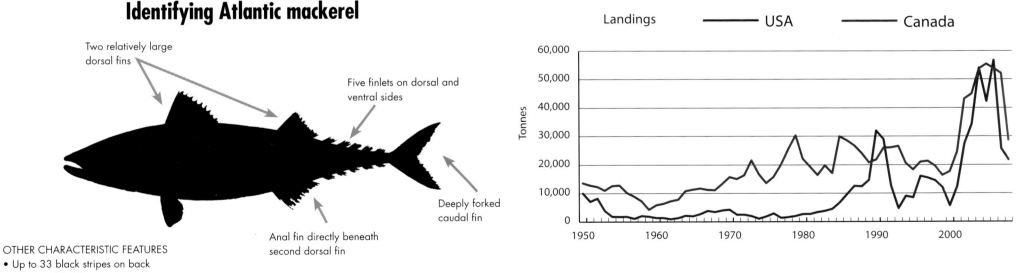

Identifying Atlantic mackerel

Two relatively large dorsal fins

Five finlets on dorsal and ventral sides

Deeply forked caudal fin

Anal fin directly beneath second dorsal fin

OTHER CHARACTERISTIC FEATURES
- Up to 33 black stripes on back
- No swim bladder

Landings — USA — Canada

Tonnes

1950   1960   1970   1980   1990   2000

Endangered
(COSEWIC, 2011)

Bluefin tuna

Thunnus thynnus
Atlantic bluefin tuna, bluefin tunny, giant bluefin, horse mackerel,
northern bluefin tuna, squid hound, tunny, *thon rouge*

The Atlantic bluefin tuna is one of the few large pelagic species that occurs regularly in temperate inshore Atlantic waters. One of the largest of all bony fish (and the largest in the northwest Atlantic), it is also the biggest tuna species: the current record-holding bluefin weighed 679 kilograms.

In the eastern Atlantic, this species ranges from Norway to the Canary Islands and into the Mediterranean and Black seas. In the western Atlantic, it is found from the island of Newfoundland south to the Caribbean and into the coastal waters of Venezuela and Brazil.

HABITAT AND APPEARANCE

The bluefin tuna has a powerful spindle-shaped body. Deepest below the middle of the first dorsal fin, it tapers to a narrow caudal peduncle. The conical head has a pointed snout with a slightly projecting lower jaw. The eyes are flush with the body surface.

The first dorsal fin can collapse into a groove in the body, as can the small pelvic fins. Seven to ten yellow finlets follow down the back from the second dorsal fin to the lunate caudal fin. The anal fin mirrors the second dorsal fin in size and shape. It may be followed by up to nine finlets.

Atlantic bluefin tuna have a dark metallic blue back. The colour fades to silver near the lateral line. The belly has iridescent bands and spots of white, grey, and silver. The first dorsal fin is yellow or blue—a key feature for identifying these fish at sea. The second dorsal fin is red-brown. Dusky ventral fins have lighter shades of white, grey, and silver. Anal fins sometimes have a yellow hue. The dorsal finlets along the caudal peduncle are yellow;

the ventral finlets are dusky yellow. The dorsal fin colour, number of gill rakers on the first arch, and short pectoral fins distinguish the bluefin. Adults average 3 metres in length but can reach 4 metres or more and weigh 130 to 680 kilograms (large fish are now rare). In Canadian waters, bluefin tuna range between 1.5 and 3 metres long.

A tuna holds its body rigid when it swims, rapidly flicking its large tail back and forth, transferring a great amount of energy into forward motion. These fish can reach speeds in excess of 70 kilometres an hour.

The Atlantic bluefin tuna prefers waters up to 500 metres deep. It can maintain a stable internal body temperature in cold and warm water.

Atlantic bluefin larvae feed primarily on copepods and other zooplankton. Juveniles feed on crustaceans, cephalopods, and fish. Adults mainly eat fish (capelin, herring, lantern fish, mackerel, menhaden, sand lance, squid, and white hake).

Predators include marine mammals such as killer and pilot whales, mako shark, and large predatory fish. Bluefish and seabirds prey on the smaller juveniles.

LIFE HISTORY

There are two separate populations of bluefin tuna. Juvenile and adult feeding and migratory habits bring them into the same areas along the North American coast, but they spawn in widely separate locations. The smaller western Atlantic population spawns in the Gulf of Mexico and the Straits of Florida. The larger eastern Atlantic population spawns in the Mediterranean Sea.

Bluefin tuna are highly migratory. This—plus their speed—makes them difficult to follow, but tagging technology is now changing what we know. Individual tuna have been tracked crossing between North American and European waters in less than 60 days, several times a year.

At just under 5 kilograms, 1-year-old schooling Atlantic bluefin tuna appear sporadically in the summer off the North American east coast. Between ages 2 and 4, schools of fish (of up to 36 kilograms) regularly visit North American feeding grounds, migrating farther north each summer as they grow. They return south in the fall. Exact coastal migration patterns vary with the presence of forage fish. The schools that migrate to Canadian waters

have 50 or fewer individuals.

In the western Atlantic, bluefin tuna aged 7 or 8 years spawn in the Gulf of Mexico from April to June. Females release millions of eggs in batches near the surface, where they are fertilized. Buoyant, they hatch after two days. The transparent larvae quickly reabsorb the yolk sac and begin feeding pelagically.

Larvae generally remain in the Gulf of Mexico until June before migrating to juvenile nursery areas over the continental shelf between Cape Hatteras and Cape Cod. They move farther offshore in winter.

As young fish (36 to 80 kilograms), Atlantic bluefin separate into multi-tuna species schools based on size. Schools may also include albacore, bigeye and frigate tuna, skipjack, and yellowfin. By age 10, bluefin tuna are 2 metres long and weigh up to 150 kilograms; by 20 years they are 3 metres long and weigh 400 kilograms.

FISHERY STATUS

Exploited in the Mediterranean since classical times, bluefin tuna have been exploited heavily by the international fisheries for four decades in the northwest Atlantic with unsustainable results.

Spawning individuals are now at the lowest numbers ever observed.

Overfishing is the main threat to survival, yet efforts over the past three decades to manage the stock have failed and the number of spawning fish has declined by 69 per cent over the past 2.7 generations. There is no evidence this will change any time soon: an international effort is required, migrations cross international borders, and the fish continue to command a high price. Complicating this bleak picture further is 2010's massive Deepwater Horizon oil spill in the Gulf of Mexico, which contaminated a portion of the species' spawning area.

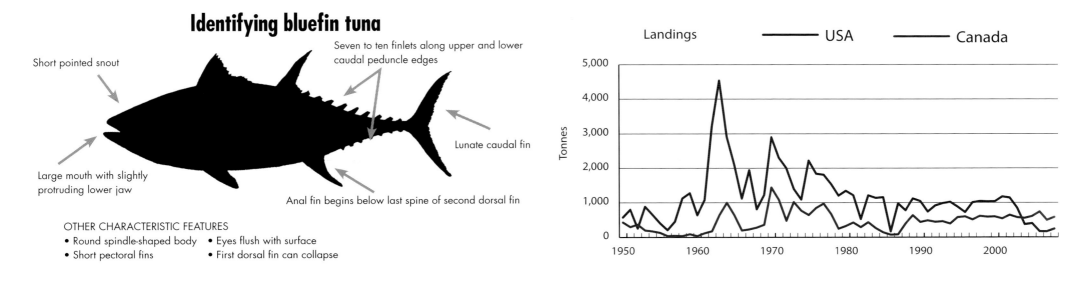

Identifying bluefin tuna

Short pointed snout

Seven to ten finlets along upper and lower caudal peduncle edges

Lunate caudal fin

Large mouth with slightly protruding lower jaw

Anal fin begins below last spine of second dorsal fin

OTHER CHARACTERISTIC FEATURES
- Round spindle-shaped body
- Short pectoral fins
- Eyes flush with surface
- First dorsal fin can collapse

Landings — USA — Canada

Tonnes

1950 1960 1970 1980 1990 2000

150 to
300 m

Threatened
(COSEWIC, 2010)

Acadian redfish

Sebastes fasciatus
Ocean perch, redfish, *sébaste rose, sebastes d'Acadie*

The Acadian redfish is found in the western Atlantic from the Labrador Sea south through the Gulf of St. Lawrence and the Laurentian Channel to the Gulf of Maine and east to the Grand Banks of Newfoundland.

HABITAT AND APPEARANCE

A slow-growing species, the Acadian redfish lives in schools in relatively shallow water with a rocky or clay-silt floor. Like the other two species of redfish in the North Atlantic, it is readily identified by its colour: orange-red, almost scarlet. Similar in appearance to the beaked redfish, it can be distinguished by counting the soft rays

in the anal fin: Acadian redfish have seven or fewer rays, beaked redfish have eight or more. Beyond this marker, reliable identification can only be made by dissection (to examine muscles on the gas bladder) or by genetic analysis.

The Acadian redfish is bright red on the back; the colour fades to whitish on the belly. There are silvery patches near the pectoral fins and on the gill covering. A small bony protrusion on the lower lip is called the "beak." The eyes are large and a fan of spines flanks the gill opening.

Three times as long as it is high, the body has a long two-part dorsal fin that extends from the nape to the narrow caudal peduncle. The first section is spiny-rayed and begins behind the head and extends one-third of the body length. The second section is higher and soft-rayed and ends just before the caudal peduncle. The caudal fin is slightly forked.

This long-lived species bears its young live. Compared with other groundfish it has relatively low fecundity. It does, however, produce more young per individual than the beaked redfish does.

Older juveniles (11 to 20 centimetres) and adults are associated with boulder reefs that have deep crevices and exposed rocks surrounded by dense colonies of anemones. Bottom-dwellers during the day, Acadian redfish migrate toward the surface at night to feed mainly on plankton. Their diet varies depending on age, location, and season.

Predators include cod, pollock, wolffish, monkfish, Greenland halibut, flounder, skate, and swordfish. Seals are also an aggressive and voracious predator of this species.

LIFE HISTORY

The movements of the oceanodromous Acadian redfish are not well understood. Mating likely takes place in the fall, with internal fertilization of the eggs delayed until March or April. Eggs hatch in the oviduct. The larvae develop internally for 45 to 60 days, until most of the yolk sac is consumed. They are then released into the water column at (or rising to within) 10 metres of the surface.

The larvae develop slowly, taking 65 to 100 days to reach 21 millimetres. At 25 millimetres, they transition to fry and can be found as deep as 30 metres (but still in the surface water column). During this early pelagic stage, currents carry very young redfish for hundreds of kilometres. Reaching 42 to 50 millimetres by the early fall of their first year, Acadian redfish then migrate to the bottom.

Generally, the small Acadian redfish occupies shallower waters (75 to 175 metres), where there is available shelter. The Gulf of St. Lawrence off Newfoundland's west coast (including shallow waters and the Esquiman Channel) is a vital area; it has high populations of juvenile Acadian redfish, which appear to occupy coastal habitats and the surrounding deep channels more than beaked redfish do.

Acadian redfish continue to develop at 20 millimetres a year for seven years, then slow to 10 millimetres (females) or 5 millimetres (males) a year. At the end of this period they reach first maturity (22 to 25 centimetres). Females can live up to 58 years and reach a maximum length of 45 to 70 centimetres (males just 40 to 45 centimetres).

Acadian redfish generally live near the bottom; they are considered semi-pelagic because of their nightly vertical migrations to follow prey. The distribution of redfish in the water column also varies by season and over time. Older Acadian redfish tend to settle in deep water and be more sedentary.

FISHERY STATUS

The long-lived and late-maturing Acadian redfish, with strong year-classes only once every decade or so, is highly vulnerable to commercial fishing activity. The number of mature individuals has declined by 99 per cent in areas where the species was most abundant just two generations ago. After this drastic decline bottomed out in the 1990s, there have been no long-term trends of either growth or reduction and population numbers seem to be stable or increasing slightly.

Directed fishing and bycatch are the main threats to the Acadian redfish. Catch statistics are difficult to track for this species, however, because general landing data are not kept regularly for individual redfish species but for unspecified "redfish."

See graph on page 133, with the beaked redfish profile.

The introduction of new trawler technology has helped to reduce bycatch in the shrimp fishery (which reached unsustainable levels in the 1990s), though it is still high enough to set back any potential recovery of the Acadian redfish population. But bycatch in this fishery remains a cause of significant concern. Fisheries are closed in some areas of the range but remain open in others.

Given this situation, the Acadian redfish meets the COSEWIC criteria for Endangered, but it has been designated as Threatened (2010) because of two major factors. First, despite low relative numbers, the species maintains its population over a range so vast that several hundred million mature individuals are necessary to tally even those low numbers. Second, the absence of any demonstrated negative population trends for two decades—with slight increases recorded in some regions—seems to tip the scale toward Threatened.

Identifying Acadian redfish

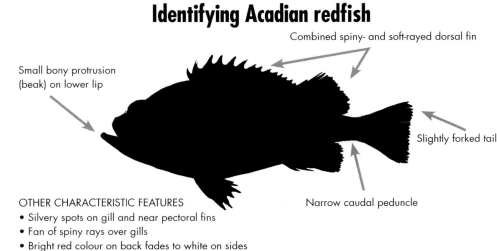

Combined spiny- and soft-rayed dorsal fin

Small bony protrusion (beak) on lower lip

Slightly forked tail

Narrow caudal peduncle

OTHER CHARACTERISTIC FEATURES
• Silvery spots on gill and near pectoral fins
• Fan of spiny rays over gills
• Bright red colour on back fades to white on sides
• Large eyes

} 350 to 500 m

Endangered
(VARIES BY STOCK)

Beaked redfish

Sebastes mentella
Deepwater redfish, deepwater rosefish,
sébaste atlantique

One of the most widespread fish species of the North Atlantic, the beaked redfish is found in a vast swath from the Barents Sea through to the Labrador Sea and from the Grand Banks to the coast of mainland Canada. It became commercially important in the northwest Atlantic only after 1935, though Europeans were eating redfish much earlier. It is harvested by most northern fishing countries.

HABITAT AND APPEARANCE

The beaked redfish makes up more than 90 per cent of the redfish population in Atlantic Canadian waters, particularly in the Gulf of St. Lawrence and the Laurentian Channel in summer and winter.

It is also known as the "deepwater redfish," reflecting its preference for depths of 300 metres or more.

These stout fish have a long dorsal fin; a spiny-rayed section begins behind the head and extends for one-third of the body, then the fin becomes shorter and soft-rayed. The caudal fin is slightly forked. The anal fin has eight or more soft rays—a distinguishing characteristic (Acadian redfish have seven or fewer soft rays in the anal fin). The anal fin spines, in front of the rays, are very strong and well developed, which is true for most redfish species.

Like the Acadian redfish, the beaked redfish has a small bony protrusion on the lower lip—its "beak"—large eyes, and a fan of spines around the gill opening. Its overall colour is bright red on the back fading to whitish on the belly with silvery patches in the area of the pectoral fins and gills.

In the northwest Atlantic, the southern limit of the redfish range is New Jersey waters. The species is normally found in deep water in the Gulf of Maine, on the banks of Nova Scotia, in the Gulf of St. Lawrence, and along the continental slope from the southwest Grand Banks to Hamilton Inlet Bank, and also on the Flemish Cap. It is present but less abundant off the south coast of Baffin Island and off West Greenland. When depths exceed 550 to 600 metres, deepwater redfish become bathypelagic. Very rarely, where the water is cold enough, they are found in shallows near shorelines and around wharves in Newfoundland and in the Bay of Fundy.

Deepwater redfish prefer rocky ocean floors or clay or silt bottoms, as they take shelter among boulders and sea anemones. At night they rise en masse to feed mainly on plankton. Depending on age, location, and season, their diet may also vary. For example, larger individuals eat more fish such as capelin, roundnose grenadier, and Atlantic cod. Where there is an active

fishery, offal displaces natural prey, especially for larger fish.

Predators include cod, pollock, wolffish, monkfish, halibut, flounder, and swordfish. Predation by seals has more than tripled since the 1970s; even as early as 1993, before the current explosion in the seal population, seals may have eaten as many as 72,500 tonnes of beaked redfish a year.

LIFE HISTORY

Despite its commercial importance, the reproduction and life histories of the beaked redfish are poorly understood—in part because of the difficulty of getting significant data about their deepwater habitat, and in part thanks to confusion with closely related species.

Nor are its movements well understood. We do know that some stocks migrate seasonally. For example, the Endangered Gulf of St. Lawrence population, for example, overwinters between Cape Breton and Newfoundland, returning to the Gulf to spawn in the spring and mate in fall through early winter.

After mating, the female can delay internal fertilization of the eggs until February, March, or April. Hatching in the

oviduct, the larvae develop internally until most of the yolk sac is consumed. They are released within 10 metres of the surface—in synchronization with the spring bloom of plankton; this release of live larvae peaks in late May or early June.

The larvae develop slowly, taking 65 to 100 days to triple their birth length to 21 millimetres. At 25 millimetres, they transition to fry and can be found as deep as 30 metres. During this early pelagic stage, ocean currents carry very young beaked redfish hundreds of kilometres. Reaching 42 to 50 millimetres by early fall of their first year, they migrate to the bottom.

Deepwater redfish continue to develop at 20 millimetres a year for seven years, then growth slows to 10 millimetres (females) or 5 millimetres (males) a year. Staying near the bottom during the day, they migrate toward the surface at night to feed, seeking concentrations of their main prey (shrimp-like euphausiids). They reach first maturity at 22 to 25 centimetres. Females will eventually reach 45 to 70 centimetres. Males grow to 40 or 45 centimetres.

FISHERY STATUS

As with all deepwater fisheries, the harvest of beaked redfish did not begin until the 20th century. The various redfish species today are managed as if they were a single species. Redfish stocks are fished in the Gulf of Maine, on the banks of Nova Scotia and Newfoundland, in the Gulf of St. Lawrence, and on continental slopes from the southwest Grand Banks to Hamilton Inlet Bank (with closures in selected areas).

Because of recruitment failures and consistently low levels of detected biomass, the general consensus from fisheries research suggests that there should not be a directed trawl fishery for beaked redfish, area closures should be maintained, and bycatch limits should be as low as possible until the spawning-stock biomass and number of juveniles increase significantly—and the increases have been verified scientifically.

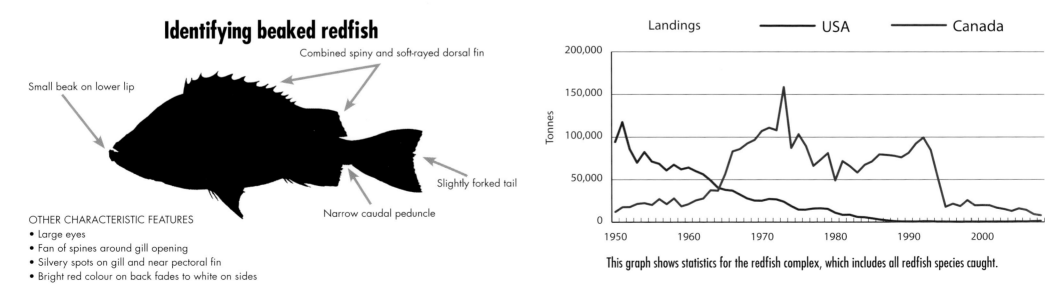

Identifying beaked redfish

Combined spiny and soft-rayed dorsal fin

Small beak on lower lip

Slightly forked tail

Narrow caudal peduncle

OTHER CHARACTERISTIC FEATURES
• Large eyes
• Fan of spines around gill opening
• Silvery spots on gill and near pectoral fin
• Bright red colour on back fades to white on sides

Landings — USA — Canada

Tonnes

This graph shows statistics for the redfish complex, which includes all redfish species caught.

} 0 to 200 m

Special Concern
(COSEWIC, 2010)

Spiny dogfish

Squalus acanthias

Codshark, greyfish, piked dogfish, rock salmon, spotted dogfish, spring dogfish, spurdog, thorndog, white-spotted dogfish, *aiguillat commun*

Distributed widely in temperate ocean conditions, the spiny dogfish is adapted to many habitats. In the northwest Atlantic, it ranges from Labrador to Cape Hatteras. Relatively abundant in Atlantic Canada, it is most often found off southwestern Nova Scotia.

The status of this species is a matter of concern for several reasons, including its extremely low fecundity, the lack of reliable counts of mature female dogfish, and the species' vulnerability to overfishing, whether from targeted fishing or as bycatch.

HABITAT AND APPEARANCE

A small to moderate-sized shark, the spiny dogfish can be identified by its slender body and the heavy spines in front of the dorsal fins. The abdomen width is just 10 per cent of the body length. The head is narrow, the snout pointed, and the eyes large.

Each of the spiny dogfish's two dorsal fins is preceded by a mildly poisonous spine, hence its common name. The front dorsal fin is 1.3 times as high as the length of its base; the second is 0.9 times as high. There is no anal fin. The pale caudal fin is faintly white along the edge with a black blotch at the top of the upper lobe. In juveniles, the anterior edges of both lobes are white. The body is generally deep grey with a few white spots; the belly is off-white.

The spiny dogfish inhabits both inshore waters and offshore continental and insular shelf and upper slope areas. It is common in cold water, usually near rocky bottoms, but it is also found in the mid-level of the water column and at the surface. This species will enter enclosed bays, estuaries, and even fresh water—where it can survive for several hours.

Herring, capelin, and cod are important to its diet, but the spiny dogfish also eats mackerel, sand lance, silver hake, white hake, haddock, pollock, Atlantic salmon, menhaden, winter flounder, and longhorn sculpin, as well as crab, squid, shrimp, polychaete worms, sea anemones, jellyfish, and even algae.

The mature spiny dogfish has few natural predators. Dogfish pups must avoid other sharks and most of the same predatory fish on which they will later feed. Juvenile and adult spiny dogfish are prey for swordfish and grey seals.

LIFE HISTORY

The spiny dogfish also migrates in enormous schools, following cool temperatures. Eggs are fertilized and hatch internally, where the young gestates for 18 to 24 months with no placental connection to the mother—once fetal sharks have exhausted the yolk sac, they eat unfertilized eggs inside the female to survive, a behaviour known as "oophagy." They may even engage in fetal cannibalism. Newborn dogfish pups flee the mother immediately—likely to avoid being eaten.

Several stocks of dogfish that remain largely separate have been identified. They include stocks in the southern Gulf of St. Lawrence, around Newfoundland, on the eastern and central Scotian Shelf, in the Bay of Fundy and southwestern Nova Scotian waters, and off Massachusetts and North Carolina. Seasonal onshore-offshore migrations vary by stock. Some, particularly the more southerly stocks, also migrate north and south.

At least one group—in the southern Gulf of St. Lawrence—is very likely a "sink population." That is, it was colonized abruptly in 1985 and has resided in the region ever since. Individuals are growing larger in size but the group is becoming smaller in number, with no evidence of outside immigration.

In addition, the eastern shelf dogfish population appears to have been resident for many years in NAFO 4VW, but it disappeared in 1992. At around the same time, the Georges Bank population was extirpated. Since these abrupt declines cannot be explained by fishing, researchers assume that these dogfish (whose minimum trawlable biomass was about 300,000 tonnes) migrated elsewhere.

FISHERY STATUS

Spiny dogfish were harvested in the northwest Atlantic before commercial catch statistics were required. Russia (U.S.S.R. at the time) and other European countries dominated in reported landings prior to the extension of Canada's jurisdiction to 370 kilometres (1977). Landings peaked at 25,000 tonnes a year. After 1977, American commercial landings accounted for most of the reported catch, which reached annual rates as high as 27,000 tonnes.

There are still no restrictions on discarding or bycatch in other fisheries and, not surprisingly, the discard rates of spiny dogfish are significant. In recent years, total discards have averaged 2,000 to 3,000 tonnes annually; discards of up to 10,000 tonnes were estimated for some years in the 1990s.

Until 2000, Canadian landings accounted only for a small proportion of the total catch. The introduction of quotas in the United States that year has meant that Canadian landings are now a much larger portion of the take. They average 2,500 tonnes annually, mainly from a directed handline and longline fishery. The primary waters for the Canadian harvest are the Bay of Fundy, off south-west Nova Scotia, and off Halifax. Catches were unrestricted until 2002; since then precautionary directed catch quotas based on past catches were put in place, with varying degrees of success (the 2002 quota of 3,200 tonnes was surpassed by 384 tonnes).

Directed catches after 2002 have remained within the quota: 2,500 tonnes since 2004. However, according to a COSEWIC report, quotas are not based on scientific advice. Since there are no restrictions on spiny dogfish discards and bycatch in other fisheries, the total annual harvest is impossible to estimate with any accuracy. FAO has no Canadian landings statistics for this species.

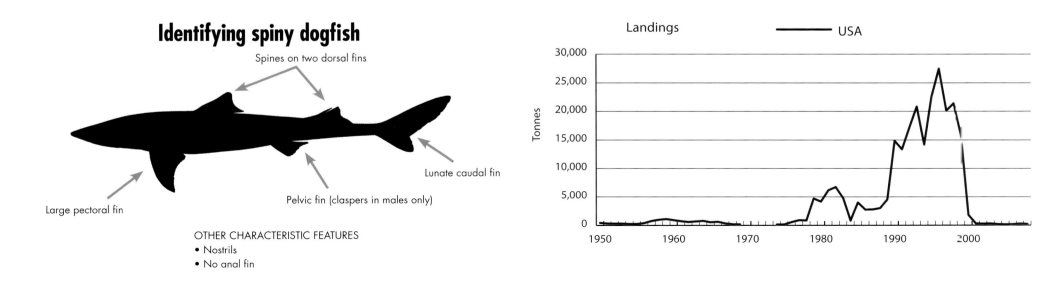

Identifying spiny dogfish

Spines on two dorsal fins

Lunate caudal fin

Pelvic fin (claspers in males only)

Large pectoral fin

OTHER CHARACTERISTIC FEATURES
- Nostrils
- No anal fin

Landings — USA

Swordfish

} 0 to
550 m

Xiphias gladius
Broadbill, broadbill swordfish, *espadon*

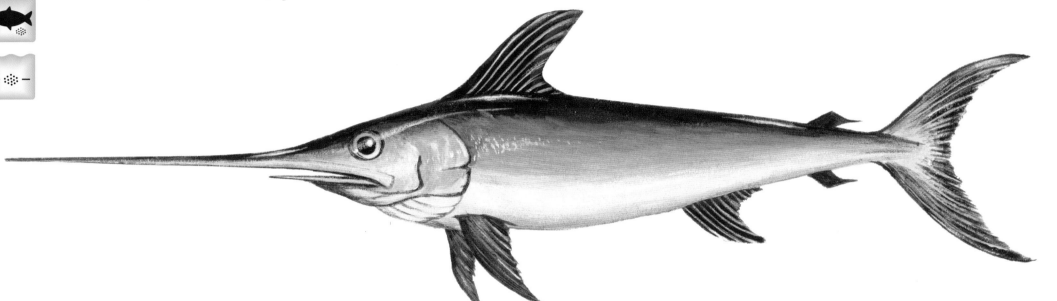

The only member of the family Xiphiidae, the swordfish is a large solitary predator of the open ocean. The species is extremely migratory and found worldwide. It ranges throughout the Atlantic in three separate stocks: northwest, southern, and Mediterranean. In the summer and fall, in Canadian waters, these majestic fish feed within Canadian waters in the fertile waters over the continental slope and shelf. New archival tagging technology is slowly providing insight into what appears to be complex migration and homing patterns.

HABITAT AND APPEARANCE

These ocean "torpedoes" have an elongated cylindrical body that is deepest just behind the gill slits then tapers quickly to a slender but powerful ridged caudal peduncle. The flat, pointed, and sharp upper bill of a mature swordfish can be one-third the length of its body. The lower bill is much smaller but just as pointed. The wide mouth extends to the anterior limit of the distinctive large blue eyes. The gill openings are wide.

Atlantic swordfish fry have snake-like bodies that are covered in spiny scales. Their toothed upper and lower bills are almost the same length, the tail slightly forked. As they mature, juveniles undergo an extreme transformation: they lose their teeth and scales, and their body shape, skin patterns, and the size and shape of the upper bill and fins all change. The two dorsal fins—connected in juveniles—are widely separated in mature fish. The first dorsal fin, with 34 to 49 rays, begins above the gill opening. This rigid fin is taller than it is wide, with a deeply concave rear edge. The second dorsal fin, on the caudal peduncle, is relatively tiny and has four to six rays.

The continuous anal fin of juveniles also devolves into two

separate fins by adulthood. The outline of the first anal fin, with up to 14 rays, is a shorter version of the first dorsal fin (but originates well behind it). The second anal fin is as small as the second dorsal fin and situated below it. Each side of the caudal peduncle has a large keel; there is a deep notch on the keel's dorsal and ventral surfaces. The large but thin caudal fin has a lunate shape. The rigid semicircular pectoral fins (with 16 to 18 rays each) are low on the body. There are no pelvic fins.

Swordfish coloration varies greatly. The back can range from dark brown to grey-blue. The amount of dark shading also varies—from halfway down the sides to covering virtually the entire body. Non-dark areas on the underside are tinged silver white.

Although this species can tolerate cold temperatures better than other billfish can, swordfish are most often found at the surface, where the water temperature is warmer than 13°C. Preferred depth varies by size and sex: the larger the fish, the more it is able to penetrate deeper, colder water. Males show a greater aversion to cooler water than do females.

Larval swordfish feed on copepods but very early in the juvenile stage they switch their diet to fish larvae. Mature swordfish feed throughout the water column, rising to the surface at night and diving as deep as 800 metres during the day. Opportunistic feeders, adult swordfish swallow smaller prey whole—including Atlantic mackerel, silver hake, redfish, herring, deep-sea lantern fish and grenadiers, crustaceans, squid, and diving seabirds.

Juvenile swordfish are prey for sharks and other large predatory fish, but adults are at the top of the food chain. They have few real predators, with the possible exception of some shark species and killer whales.

LIFE HISTORY

Atlantic swordfish have a complex population structure and several inadequately understood migratory pathways. General patterns, however, have been determined. Swordfish make long migrations between relatively hot subtropical waters and the temperate waters of the North Atlantic. Tagging has shown no evidence of movement across the equator, and limited movement between the eastern and western populations.

Swordfish in the northern hemisphere spawn year-round in tropical and subtropical waters, with the most active period of reproduction occurring from early winter to mid-summer (in the Gulf of Mexico, south of the Sargasso Sea, east of the Antilles in the Straits of Florida, and along the southeast coast of the United States). In cooler regions, spawning occurs only in spring and summer. After spring spawning, swordfish migrate north to temperate or cold waters for the summer, returning south for the fall and winter.

During the spawning season, males and females pair up, sometimes in water less than 75 metres deep. Buoyant fertilized eggs hatch in less than three days. At hatching, the tiny newborn swordfish body has no pigment, is covered in prickly scales, and has a short snout. By the time the fry are just 10 millimetres long, they have become voracious pelagic predators, feeding on zooplankton and fish larvae. At 12 millimetres, they bear little resemblance to the mature swordfish but the bill is evident (upper and lower portions are equally long and bear teeth); the upper bill eventually outgrows the lower one and the teeth are shed. At 23 millimetres, a dorsal fin extends along the length of the body. By 52 centimetres, the second dorsal fin is evident; by 150 centimetres, the first dorsal fin has its final adult form.

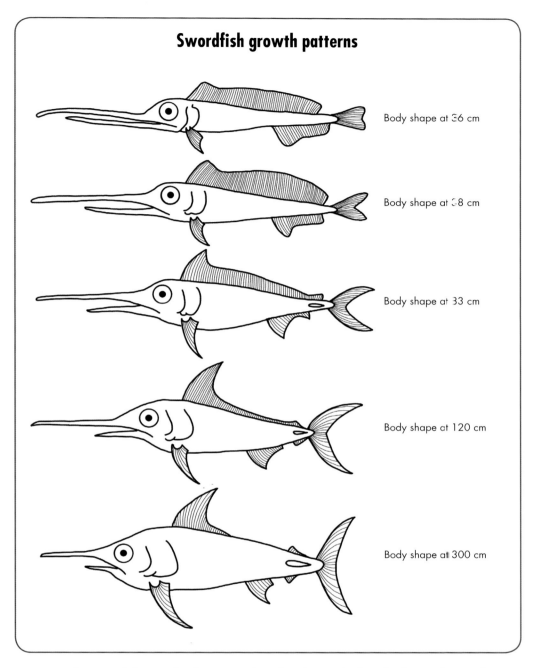

Swordfish growth patterns

Body shape at 6 cm

Body shape at 8 cm

Body shape at 33 cm

Body shape at 120 cm

Body shape at 300 cm

Growth is rapid during the first year of life and then slows. Male swordfish grow more slowly than females and do not reach the same size. Female swordfish grow faster, are proportionally heavier, and live longer than males. Within one year, a female is more than 4 kilograms heavier than her male cohorts. Over the next two years, females triple their body weight, reaching 70 kilograms by their fourth year and 110 kilograms by their fifth (as they prepare to spawn for the first time).

Atlantic swordfish are frequently spotted basking at the surface, which may be how they recover from the demands of the deepwater dives they make in pursuit of prey. This behaviour also makes it possible to harpoon-tag the fish, a faster and less stressful method of attaching archival tags. Atlantic swordfish are powerful swimmers capable of using their speed to make spectacular leaps. Why they do this is a mystery—possibly to dislodge parasites, such as remoras and lampreys, or possibly as a method of surface feeding. Swordfish repeat this leaping action when hooked and can circle a vessel with only the tail in the water, thrashing the surface while propelling its near-vertical body in a frenzied dance to dislodge the hook.

FISHERY STATUS

All three Atlantic swordfish stocks are managed by the International Commission for the Conservation of Atlantic Tunas (ICCAT), which establishes international fishing quotas for its 48 members.

Harpoon-harvested swordfish became popular in North America in the 1940s and remained so until 1971. That year, the U.S. Food and Drug Administration (FDA) found mercury levels higher than 0.5 parts per million (ppm) in swordfish flesh and imposed restrictions that effectively shut down the fishery. The respite for swordfish was brief, however: in 1979, the FDA raised the acceptable mercury level to 1.0 ppm and then "switched" the ban from mercury to methyl mercury levels, reopening the market for northwest Atlantic swordfish.

Swordfish is now largely a longline fishery: a standard "longline" suspends thousands of baited hooks from a buoyed main line that can extend 50 kilometres or more. By 1999, the highest longline swordfish harvests in the North Atlantic belonged to Spain, the United States, Canada, Portugal, and Japan.

In 2003, ICCAT approved a total allowable swordfish catch of 14,000 tonnes—3,600 tonnes more than in 2002. Conservation groups condemned this move. According to research by BigMarineFish.com, 66 per cent of Atlantic swordfish taken by the American fleet are immature fish. Of the females caught commercially, 83 per cent are still immature fish. In addition, ICCAT's minimum size limit is one-quarter of the species' mature weight. Longliners routinely discard up to half of the swordfish they catch, most of which are either dead or dying.

The Marine Stewardship Council (MSC) is an international body that develops standards for sustainable fishing and seafood traceability and for certifying fisheries that meet those criteria. In June 2010, despite international protests by conservation and sustainable fisheries groups, it certified the American swordfishery as sustainable. The designation means that swordfish from the United States can be marketed as being from a "sustainable fishery," a designation that, in this case, seems to defy logic.

Canada has boosted swordfish permits since the early 1990s. The Canadian fleet takes more than 1,400 tonnes of swordfish annually—90 per cent with longlines and 10 per cent with harpoons. The major pelagic longline fishery extends from Georges Bank to the Flemish Cap and

Identifying swordfish

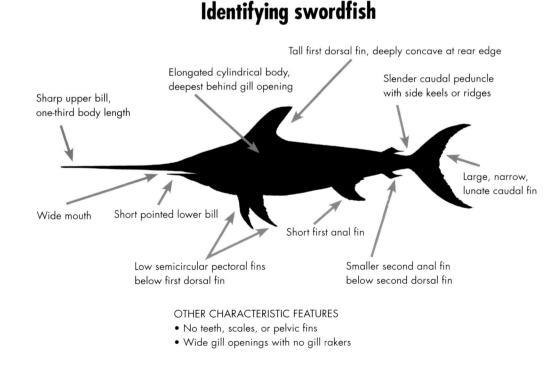

Sharp upper bill, one-third body length

Wide mouth

Short pointed lower bill

Low semicircular pectoral fins below first dorsal fin

Elongated cylindrical body, deepest behind gill opening

Tall first dorsal fin, deeply concave at rear edge

Slender caudal peduncle with side keels or ridges

Large, narrow, lunate caudal fin

Short first anal fin

Smaller second anal fin below second dorsal fin

OTHER CHARACTERISTIC FEATURES
- No teeth, scales, or pelvic fins
- Wide gill openings with no gill rakers

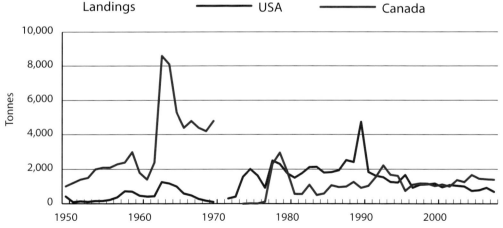

Landings — USA — Canada

A break in the chartline, as here, indicates that no data were reported for the period.

beyond (swordfish migrate into the Canadian Exclusive Economic Zone in the summer and fall). The harpoon fishery targets large female swordfish at the edge of the Georges and Browns banks. Most of the fish caught is exported to the United States.

In 2010, the Canadian longline fishery applied to the MSC for certification as a sustainable fishery. The application is based in part on the assumption that the Atlantic swordfish stock may have achieved a sustainable level after historic lows in 2000. Assessment of the application is ongoing at this writing.

Meanwhile, national and international bodies have filed objections because of the damage this fishery wreaks on both swordfish and other species. In taking the allotted 20,000 swordfish each year, the longliners hook more than 100,000 sharks, of which as many as 35,000 die. More than 80 per cent of the bycatch is blue shark, which COSEWIC listed as a species of Special Concern in 2006. The Threatened

shortfin mako shark and the Endangered porbeagle shark also number significantly in this bycatch—as do sea turtles, which is a cause of great concern for those who fear for the status of these beleaguered reptiles, especially given the mortality rate of 50 per cent after release. Each year, longlines catch 170 or more critically Endangered leatherback turtles, as well as an average of 1,200 Endangered loggerhead turtles. According to some estimates, that's one turtle for every 1,334 hooks used in the Canadian fishery; a single vessel can set a longline of between 48 and 80 kilometres each night, with four or five hooks every 300 metres for a total of between 650 and 1,100 hooks in the water.

In efforts to mitigate its environmental impact, the Canadian pelagic longline fishery has introduced the optional use of circle hooks (illustrated at right) to replace traditional J hooks. Training is also available in turtle disentanglement, which may help to reduce bycatch mortality.

Studies of hooks in the United States show that swordfish fishers can maximize their harvest while minimizing turtle bycatch in two ways: by fishing in water between 12.2° and 18.3°C and by using an 18/0 offset circle hook (shown above) baited with mackerel. Because these circle hooks are more expensive, some fishers will likely continue using the traditional J hooks baited with squid unless regulations or subsidies are introduced.

Species Comparison Tables

FISH COMPARISON TABLE: GENERAL CHARACTERISTICS

FAMILY	COMMON NAME	SCHOOLING	MIGRATION	MATURE LENGTH	MAX. LENGTH	MAX. WEIGHT	PREFERRED DEPTH	DEPTH RANGE	PREFERRED TEMP.	TEMP. RANGE	MAX. LIFE SPAN	SEXUAL MATURITY	AT-RISK STATUS[1]
Acipenseridae	Atlantic sturgeon		F S	190 cm	427 cm	368 kg	10–50 m	NDA	10°–19°C	0°–28°C	60+ years	12 years+ (m) 16 years+ (f)	Threatened 2011
	Shortnose sturgeon		F S	45–55 cm	145 cm	24 kg	NDA	NDA	NDA	NDA	67 years	11 years (m) 13 years (f)	Special Concern 2005
Ammodytidae	American sand lance		NA	8.4 cm (m) 9.0 cm (f)	17 cm	NDA	0–73 m	to 90 m	3°–6°C	0°–11°C	12 years	2 years	Not assessed
	Northern sand lance		NA	8.4 cm (m) 9.0 cm (f)	37 cm	NDA	0–108 m	NDA	3°–6°C	0°–11°C	8–12 years	1–12 years	Not assessed
Anarhichadidae	Atlantic wolffish		NA	60 cm	150 cm	23 kg	150–350 m	to 950 m	1.5°–4°C	-1°–10°C	20 years	8–11 years	Special Concern 2004
	Northern wolffish		NA	>80 cm	146 cm	20+ kg	500–1,000 m	38–1,504 m	2°–5°C	NDA	12 years	4 years	Threatened 2001
	Spotted wolffish		S S	60–70 cm	190 cm	30 kg	100–400 m	25–600 m	1.5°–5°C	NDA	21 years	7–8 years	Threatened 2001
Anguillidae	American eel		F S	65–104 cm	128 cm (f)	7.5 kg	0–35 m	to 350 m	15.4°–19.4°C	0.8°–30°C	43 years	10–25 years size more important	Threatened 2012
Cetorhinidae	Basking shark		S S	4.6–6.1 m	15.2 m	4,000 kg	0–750 m	to 1,250 m	9°–16°C	7°–24°C	12–16 years (m) 16–20 years (f)	NDA	Special Concern 2009

NDA = No data available   NA = Not applicable   [1] COSEWIC status, unless otherwise stated

FAMILY	COMMON NAME	SCHOOLING	MIGRATION	MATURE LENGTH	MAX. LENGTH	MAX. WEIGHT	PREFERRED DEPTH	DEPTH RANGE	PREFERRED TEMP.	TEMP. RANGE	MAX. LIFE SPAN	SEXUAL MATURITY	AT-RISK STATUS[1]
Clupeidae	Alewife	schooling	F S	11 cm	40 cm	0.2 kg	50–150 m	5–200 m	4°C	to 25°C	9 or 10 years	3–4 years (m) 4–5 years (f)	Special Concern, NMFS
	American shad	schooling	F S	40–60 cm	66 cm	5.1 kg	0–120 m	NDA	13°–18°C	NDA	13 years	4 years (m) 5 years (f)	Prioritized Candidate List (Group 2)
	Atlantic herring	schooling	S S	20–25 cm	40 cm	0.5 kg	1–200 m	to 365 m	5°–9°C	1.1–20°C	22 years	3–9 years	Not assessed
Cyclopteridae	Lumpfish	not schooling	S S	33 cm (m) 39 cm (f)	61 cm	9.5 kg	50–150 m	0–870 m	8°C	0°–20°C	13 years	2–4 years (m) 3–5 years (f)	Not assessed
Gadidae	Arctic cod	schooling	S S	20 cm	40 cm	0.94 kg	0–400 m	to 900 m	0°–4°C	-1°–4°C	5–6 years rarely: 7 years	3 years	Not assessed
	Atlantic cod	schooling	S S	31–74 cm	200 cm	96 kg	150–200 m	0–600 m	2°–11°C	-1.5°–20°C	25 years	4–5 years	Endangered (varies by stock)
	Atlantic tomcod	schooling	F S	17 cm	38 cm	0.5 kg	0–6 m	to 69 m	NDA	-1.2°–26°C	7 years	9 months	Not assessed
	Greenland cod	not schooling	NA	27–38 cm	70 cm	NDA	<200 m	to 200 m	NDA	NDA	11 years	3–4 years	Not assessed
	Cusk	not schooling	NA	36–48 cm	100 cm	14 kg	20–549 m	20–1,000 m	2°–12°C	NDA	>14 years	up to 8 years	Threatened 2003
	Haddock	schooling	S S	30 cm	110 cm	3.6 kg	75–200 m	10–450 m	4°–10°C	0°–13°C	20 years	1–4 years (m) 5 years (f)	Prioritized Candidate List (Group 1)
	Pollock	schooling	S S	50–100 cm	130 cm	23 kg	100–125 m	to 200 m	3°–10°C	0°–14°C	25 years	3–6 years	Prioritized Candidate List (Group 2)
	Silver hake	schooling	S S	22–32 cm (m)	34 cm (m) 64 cm (f)	2.0 kg	55–375 m	30–900 m	7°–10°C	2°–17°C	6 years (m) 12–15 years (f)	2–3 years	Prioritized Candidate List (Group 1)
	White hake	schooling	S S	15 cm	50 cm (rare)	0.83 kg	300–600 m	30–1,000 m	10.4°C	5°–14°C	20 years	3 years	Not assessed
Labridae	Cunner	not schooling	NA	7 cm	38 cm	1.2 kg	<10 m	to 130 m	12°–18°C	0°–22°C	6 years	1–2 years	Unregulated
Lamnidae	Porbeagle shark	schooling	S S	196 cm (m) 244 cm (f)	370 cm	230 kg	NDA	0–710 m	5°–10°C	1°–23°C	24–46 years	8 years (m) 12–13 years (f)	Endangered 2004

NDA = No data available   NA = Not applicable   [1] COSEWIC status, unless otherwise stated

FAMILY	COMMON NAME	SCHOOLING	MIGRATION	MATURE LENGTH	MAX. LENGTH	MAX. WEIGHT	PREFERRED DEPTH	DEPTH RANGE	PREFERRED TEMP.	TEMP. RANGE	MAX. LIFE SPAN	SEXUAL MATURITY	AT-RISK STATUS[1]
Lophiidae	Monkfish	(solitary)	S S	30–50 cm (m) 30–60 cm (f)	120 cm	23 kg	0–320 m	to 700 m	6°–10°C	0°–21°C	30 years	4–7 years	Not assessed
Macrouridae	Marlin-spike grenadier	(schooling)	S S	NDA	42 cm	0.5 kg	500–800 m	90–2,500 m	±5.5°C	3.7°–10°C	11 years	2–3 years	Not assessed
	Roughhead grenadier	(solitary)	NA	53.7 cm (m) 42 cm (f)	<100 cm	1.8–2.3 kg	300–500 m	100–2,000 m	2°–5°C	NDA	25 years	NDA	Special Concern 2007
	Roundnose grenadier	(schooling)	S S	40 cm (m) 60 cm (f)	150 cm	1.7 kg	400–1,200 m	180–1,300 m	NDA	NDA	>54 years	NDA	Endangered 2008
Myxinidae	Atlantic hagfish	(schooling)	NA	25 cm	79–81 cm	NDA	125–400 m	20–1,800 m	5.8°–9°C	<12°C	NDA	NDA	Not assessed
Osmeridae	Capelin	(schooling)	S S	13.3 cm	25.2 cm (m) 20 cm (f)	0.52 kg	NDA	0–280 m	6°–10°C	2°–11°C	10 years	2–3 years	Prioritized Candidate List (Group 2)
	Rainbow smelt	(schooling)	S S	20 cm	35.6 cm	NDA	1–150 m	0–450 m	7.2°–15.6°C	NDA	7 years	2–6 years	Not assessed
Pleuronectidae	American plaice	(schooling)	S S	15–20 cm (m) 40–45 cm (f)	83 cm	6.4 kg	90–250 m	10–3,000 m	-0.5°–1.5°C	-1.5°–5°C	24–30 years	3–4 years (m) 6–11 years (f)	Threatened 2009
	Atlantic halibut	(schooling)	NA	135 cm	470 cm	>320 kg	NDA	to 1,000 m	3°–9°C	0.6°–11°C	50 years	8–10 years (m) 10–14 years (f)	Not at Risk 2011
	Greenland halibut	(schooling)	S S	39–62 cm (m) 48–79 cm (f)	80 cm (m) 130 cm (f)	44 kg	200–800 m	1–2,000 m	-0.5°–4°C	-2.1°–6°C	32 years	5–10 years (m) 8–13 years (f)	Prioritized Candidate List (Group 3)
	Smooth flounder	(schooling)	NA	7.3 cm (m) 9.8 cm (f)	32 cm	0.75 kg	3.5–10 m	Tide line–28 m	-1.5°–16°C	NDA	NDA	1 year	Not assessed
	Winter flounder	(schooling)	NA	>24 cm	64 cm	3.6 kg	Sub-tidal–37 m	2–130 m	NDA	-2°–15°C	NDA	3 years	Not assessed
	Witch flounder	(schooling)	NA	28 cm (m) 33 cm (f)	75 cm	2.5 kg	45–500 m	18–1,570 m	2°–6°C	1°–12.5°C	30 years	5 years (m) 9 years (f)	Not assessed
	Yellowtail flounder	(schooling)	S S	26–40 cm	64 cm	1.5 kg	35–91 m	27–364 m	3°–5°C	NDA	12 years	2–3 years	Not assessed

NDA = No data available   NA = Not applicable   [1] COSEWIC status, unless otherwise stated

FAMILY	COMMON NAME	SCHOOLING	MIGRATION	MATURE LENGTH	MAX. LENGTH	MAX. WEIGHT	PREFERRED DEPTH	DEPTH RANGE	PREFERRED TEMP.	TEMP. RANGE	MAX. LIFE SPAN	SEXUAL MATURITY	AT-RISK STATUS[1]
Rajidae	Barndoor skate		NA	106–112 cm (m) 114 cm (f)	153 cm	20 kg	0–180 m	1–1,500 m	1.2°–10.9°C	0.4°–20°C	18 years	9–10 years	Not at Risk 2010
	Little skate		NA	35–44 cm (m) 42 cm (f)	56 cm	1 kg	0–90 m	10–914 m	<15°C	1.2°–21°C	12.5 years	6.5–7 years	Prioritized Candidate List (Group 2)
	Round skate		NA	NDA	55 cm	1.8 kg	300–800 m	170–2,050 m	3°–5.5°C	1°–7°C	NDA	NDA	Prioritized Candidate List (Group 2)
	Thorny skate		NA	36–64 cm (m) 41–77 cm (f)	102 cm	17 kg	20–120 m	18–1,232 m	1°–7°C	-1.4°–10°C	>28 years	5 years	Special Concern 2012
	Winter skate		NA	50–109 cm	150 cm	7 kg	0–90 m	to 400 m	5°–9°C	1.2°–19°C	25 years	11 years (m) 12 years (f)	Endangered 2005
Salmonidae	Arctic char		F S	50 cm (sea-run)	88 cm	15 kg	30–70 m	NDA	4°–16°C	NDA	32 years	4–10 years (anadromous) 2–5 years (landlocked)	Not assessed
	Atlantic salmon		F S	38 cm	152 cm	46.6 kg	1–10 m	0–210 m	2°–9°C	-0.7°–27.8°C	13 years	3–5 years	Endangered (varies by stock)
	Brook char		F S	19–35 cm	86 cm	9.4 kg	15–30 m	1–27 m	1°–18.8°C	1–26°C	4–7 years	2 years	Not assessed
Scombridae	Atlantic mackerel		S S	20–40 cm	66 cm	1.8 kg	1–200 m	to 250 m	9°–12°C	NDA	20 years	3 years	Not assessed
	Bluefin tuna		S S	190 cm	430 cm	680 kg	1–500 m	to 1,000 m	7°–30°C	Varies by size	35–40 years	7–11 years	Endangered 2011
Scorpaenidae	Acadian redfish		S S	18 cm (m) 29 cm (f)	70 cm	11.2 kg	150–300 m	70–550 m	3°–8°C	NDA	58 years	5.5 years (m) 6 years (f)	Threatened 2010
	Beaked redfish		S S	25 cm	58 cm	1.3 kg	350–500 m	69–1,050 m	3°–8°C	0°–13°C	84 years	6–10 years	Endangered 2010 (varies by stock)
Squalidae	Spiny dogfish		S S	64 cm (m) 82 cm (f)	160 cm	9.1 kg	0–200 m	0–1,460 m	6°–11°C	0°–14°C	31 years	11 years (m) 19 years (f)	Special Concern 2010
Xiphiidae	Swordfish		S S	179 cm (f)	455 cm	650 kg	0–550 m	0–800 m	16°–22°C	5°–27°C	9–12 years	3 years (m) 5 years (f)	Not assessed

NDA = No data available   NA = Not applicable   [1] COSEWIC status, unless otherwise stated

FISH COMPARISON TABLE: REPRODUCTION CHARACTERISTICS

FAMILY	SPECIES	EGG BOUYANCY	SPAWNING TIMING	FERTILIZATION TYPE	SPAWNING HABITAT	SPAWNING DEPTH	SPAWNING TEMP.	DISPERSAL TYPE	EGG SIZE	TOTAL ANNUAL EGG QUANTITY	INCUBATION PERIOD	LARVAE SIZE	LARVAE FEEDING
Acipenseridae	Atlantic sturgeon		May–June	External	Natal river bottom	>10 m	13°–20°C	Batch	2.9 mm	400,000 to 8 million every 3–5 years	7 days / 17.8°C	8–14 mm	NDA
	Shortnose sturgeon		April–June	External	Natal river	NDA	8°–9°C	Batch	3–5 mm	12,000 per kg of fish, every 3 years	NDA	8–12 mm	NDA
Ammodytidae	American sand lance		Nov.–March	External	Sand and gravel	9–20 m	4°–7°C	Batch	1 mm	NDA	62–69 days	3.5 mm	Pelagic
	Northern sand lance		Nov.–March	External	Sandy ocean bottom	NDA	4°–7°C	Batch	1 mm	NDA	62–69 days	3.5 mm	Pelagic.
Anarhichadidae	Atlantic wolffish		Sept.	Internal	Rocky crevices	50–500 m	-0.4°–7°C	Nests (several)	5–7 mm	6,000–37,000	3–9 months	17–25 mm	Pelagic
	Northern wolffish		Late fall	Internal	Rocky bottom	400–1,100 m	2°–5°C	Batch	8 mm	42,000	NDA	26 mm	NDA
	Spotted wolffish		Sept.–Jan.	Internal	Sand or gravel	NDA	4°–6°C	NDA	6 mm	<55,000	NDA	21–24 mm	Pelagic
Anguillidae	American eel		Feb.– April	External	Sargasso Sea	To 4,000 m	20°–25°C	Batch	1.1 mm	2–120 million	48 hours	2.7 mm	Pelagic
Cetorhinidae	Basking shark	NA	Mates in early summer	Internal	Mating: near surface	Mating: near surface	Mating: 9°–14°C	Live birth	NA	Litter: 6	Gestation: 30–42 months	Size at birth: 1.5–2.5 m	NA
Clupeidae	Alewife		Spring	External	Lakes, slow-moving streams	Shallow water	11.7°–20.6°C	Batch	0.9–1.2 mm	50,000–200,000	4 days / 21°C 6 days / 15.6°C	5 mm	Pelagic
	American shad		April–June	External	Natal river	Mid-water	12+°–20°C	Batch (of 30,000)	3 mm	60,000–600,000	15 days / 11°C 8 days / 17°C	10 mm	Pelagic
	Atlantic herring		Jan.–Oct.	External	Range of sea bottoms	5–50 m	2°–16°C	Batch	1.2 mm	30,000–250,000	40 days / 3°C 11 days / 10°C	13 mm	Pelagic
Cyclopteridae	Lumpfish		Mid-April–mid-June	External	Coastal waters	27–75 m	4°–8°C	Batch (of 15,000–140,000)	2.0–2.4 mm	100,000–400,000	42–56 days / 4°C	5 mm	Pelagic

NDA = No data available   NA = Not applicable

FAMILY	SPECIES	EGG BOUYANCY	SPAWNING TIMING	FERTILIZATION TYPE	SPAWNING HABITAT	SPAWNING DEPTH	SPAWNING TEMP.	DISPERSAL TYPE	EGG SIZE	TOTAL ANNUAL EGG QUANTITY	INCUBATION PERIOD	LARVAE SIZE	LARVAE FEEDING
Gadidae	Arctic cod		Dec.–March	External	Open nearshore waters	NDA	-1°–2°C	Batch	1.7 mm	9,000–21,000	NDA	5 mm	Pelagic
	Atlantic cod		Mid-Nov.–May	External	Offshore	300–400 m	0°–12°C	Batch	1.5 mm	1–20 million	17 days / 5.1°C 14 days / 6°C	4.2 mm	Pelagic
	Atlantic tomcod		Nov.–March	External	Estuaries	5 m	4°–6°C	Batch	1.5 mm	44,000	24 days / 6.1°C 30 days / 4.5°C	5 mm	Demersal
	Greenland cod		Feb.–May	External	Shallow inland waters	<200 m	2°C	Batch	1.3 mm	1–2 million	30 days / 1°–2°C	4.0 mm	Demersal
	Cusk		May–Aug.	External	NDA	200 m	6°–9°C	Batch	1.4 mm	2 million	NDA	4 mm	Pelagic
	Haddock		Jan.–late June	External	Rock, gravel, sand, mud	50–150 m	5°–7°C	Batch	1.25–1.76 mm	55,000–3 million	15 days / 5°C	2.5 mm	Pelagic
	Pollock		Sept.–April	External	Rocky bottom	90–300 m	5.4°–8°C	Batch	1.15 mm	220,000–4 million	9 days / 6.1°C 6 days / 9.4°C	3.4–3.8 mm	Pelagic
	Silver hake		June–Sept.	External	All bottom substrates	30–324 m	5°–13°C	Batch	0.9 mm	NDA	2 days / 20°C	3 mm	Pelagic
	White hake		Late winter–late summer	External	10–30 m from bottom	290–390 m	5°–11°C	Batch	0.99–1.15 mm	6,000–150,000	6°–8.5°C	2.5 mm	Pelagic
Labridae	Cunner		May–Nov.	External	Inshore	<10 m	>12.5°C	Batch	0.75 m	10,000–60,000	2 days / 22°C 3 days / 12.5°C	2.2 mm	Pelagic
Lamnidae	Porbeagle shark	NA	Mates: Sept.–Nov.	Internal	Offshore	500 m	5°–10°C	Live birth	Capsules <7.5 cm	Litter: 1–5 pups	Gestation: 8–9 months	68–78 cm (pups)	NA
Lophiidae	Monkfish		June–Sept.	External	Offshore	Surface layer	15°C	Batch (veil)	1.61–1.84 mm	<1 million	7 days / 15°C	2.5–4.5 mm	Pelagic
Macrouridae	Marlin-spike grenadier		July–early Sept.	External	Deep ocean	700–900 m	NDA	Batch	NDA	NDA	NDA	NDA	NDA
	Roughhead grenadier	NDA	Late winter–early spring	External	NDA	NDA	NDA	Batch	NDA	25,000	NDA	NDA	NDA
	Roundnose grenadier		Summer–fall	External	Icelandic waters	600–900 m	3°–8°C	Batch	NDA	12,000–35,000	NDA	NDA	NDA

NDA = No data available   NA = Not applicable

FAMILY	SPECIES	EGG BOUYANCY	SPAWNING TIMING	FERTILIZATION TYPE	SPAWNING HABITAT	SPAWNING DEPTH	SPAWNING TEMP.	DISPERSAL TYPE	EGG SIZE	TOTAL ANNUAL EGG QUANTITY	INCUBATION PERIOD	LARVAE SIZE	LARVAE FEEDING
Myxinidae	Atlantic hagfish		Year-round	External	Continental shelf	300–500 m	<12°C	Batch	18–25 mm	1–47	>6 months	NDA	Demersal
Osmeridae	Capelin		Mid-April–early July	External	Coarse sand and gravel beaches	0–280 m	6°–10°C	Nest	0.8–1.1 mm	10,000–12,000	15 days / 10°C	3 mm	Pelagic
Osmeridae	Rainbow smelt		Spring	External	Gravel bottoms of swift-running natal streams	Shallow stream bottom	4°–5°C	Batch	0.9–1.3 mm	8,500–70,000	50 days / 4°C 30 days / 6°C 20 days /10°C	5 mm	Pelagic
Pleuronectidae	American plaice		April–June	External	Near the ocean floor	50–250 m	0.5°–2.5°C	Batch	2.5 mm	250,000–1.5 million	11–14 days / 4°C	2.7 mm	Pelagic
Pleuronectidae	Atlantic halibut		Feb.–June	External	Sandy ocean bottom	180 m	4.5°–7°C	Batch	3–4 mm	Several million	16 days / 4.5°C	7 mm	Pelagic
Pleuronectidae	Greenland halibut		Dec.– April	External	Open ocean	600–900 m	0°–4°C	Batch	3.4–4.5 mm	15,000–300,000	60 days / 2°C	6 mm	Pelagic
Pleuronectidae	Smooth flounder		Dec.– late March	External	Sandy and muddy bottoms, inshore waters	Shallow / inshore waters	NDA	Batch	1.1–1.4 mm	4,600–50,000	NDA	3.4 mm	Demersal
Pleuronectidae	Winter flounder		March–June	External	Sandy-bottomed coves and estuaries	2–72 m	-1°–2°C	Batch	0.8 mm	500,000–1.5+ million	18 days / 2°C	3.2 mm	Pelagic
Pleuronectidae	Witch flounder		May–Aug.	External	Ocean bottom	24–360 m	6°C	Batch	1.01–1.35 mm	48,000–500,000	8 days / 7°C	3.9–5.9 mm	Pelagic
Pleuronectidae	Yellowtail flounder		March–Aug.	External	Sandy ocean floor	30–90 m	4°–12°C	Batch	0.88 mm	NDA	14 days / 4°C 4.5 days / 14°C	2.7 mm	Pelagic
Rajidae	Barndoor skate		Dec.–March	Internal	Sandy or muddy bottom	NDA	NDA	Nest	Capsules: 124–132 x 68–72 mm	42–115	16 months	190 mm	Demersal
Rajidae	Little skate		Year-round	Internal	Marine flats	Shallow	NDA	Single capsules	Capsules: 55 x 35 mm	10–35	6–9 months	100 mm	Demersal
Rajidae	Round skate		NDA	NDA	NDA	NDA	NDA	NDA	Capsules: 33–44 x 24–26 mm	NDA	NDA	NDA	NDA
Rajidae	Thorny skate		Year-round	Internal	Sandy or muddy bottom	NDA	NDA	Serial spawner	Capsules: 34–89 x 23–68 mm	56	<30 months	110 mm	Demersal
Rajidae	Winter skate		Year-round, peaks in summer	Internal	Offshore, rock bottom	<100 m	NDA	Batch	Capsule: 6 x 4 cm	6–50	18–22 months	112–127 mm	Demersal

NDA = No data available   NA = Not applicable

FAMILY	SPECIES	EGG BOUYANCY	SPAWNING TIMING	FERTILIZATION TYPE	SPAWNING HABITAT	SPAWNING DEPTH	SPAWNING TEMP.	DISPERSAL TYPE	EGG SIZE	TOTAL ANNUAL EGG QUANTITY	INCUBATION PERIOD	LARVAE SIZE	LARVAE FEEDING
Salmonidae	Arctic char		Sept.–Nov.	External	Gravel riverbeds	3–6 m	4°–10°C	Nest (excavated redds)	5.2 mm	2,900 / 100 kg	6 months	22 mm	Pelagic
	Atlantic salmon		Oct.–Nov.	External	Gravel riverbeds	>0.25 m	2.5°–12.5°C	Nest (excavated redds)	5–7 mm	1,400–1,600 / kg	28 days / 12.5°C 124 days / 2.5°C	16–19.2 mm	Pelagic
	Brook char		Oct.–Nov.	External	Gravel riverbeds	0.1–1 m	4°–20°C	Nest (excavated redds)	4.2–4.8 mm	295 / kg	144 days / 1.7°C[1] 44 days / 10°C	9–11 mm	Pelagic
Scombridae	Atlantic mackerel		March–July	External	Open ocean	10–200 m	9°–13.5°C	Batch	1.3 mm	250,000–300,000	7 days / 11°C 5 days / 14°C	3 mm	Pelagic
	Bluefin tuna		May–June	External	Open ocean	1–50 m	18°–25°C	Batch	1 mm	>10 million	2 days / 24°C	3 mm	Pelagic
Scorpaenidae	Acadian redfish	NA	March–July	Internal	Water column	<10 m of surface	4°–7°C	Live birth	NA	<20,000	45–60 days	7 mm	NA
	Beaked redfish	NA	March–June	Internal	Water column	<10 m of surface	4°–7°C	Live birth	NA	25,000–40,000	4–6 months	7 mm	NA
Squalidae	Spiny dogfish	NA	Birth: late winter	Internal	Deep offshore areas	NDA	Birth temp. 6°–11°C	Live birth	NA	1–14 embryos	Gestation 18–24 months	22–25 cm (pups)	Pelagic
Xiphiidae	Swordfish		Year-round	External	Open ocean	<75 m	22°–26°C	Batch	1.6–1.8 mm	1–29 million	2.5 days / 24°C <3 days	4 mm	Pelagic

NDA = No data available   NA = Not applicable

Fish Harvesting Methods

GILL NETS

Essentially, gill nets and trammel nets are vertical walls of netting. They may be set at the surface, in mid-water, or on the bottom. Fish swim into a single, double, or triple wall of netting, entangling their gills or otherwise becoming enmeshed. (Single or double mesh nets are gill nets and triple mesh nets are trammel nets.)

Gill nets and entangling nets usually have floats on the upper (head) rope and weights on the lower (foot) rope. The gear can be anchored to the bottom, left drifting untethered, or connected to a vessel. Double gill nets and trammel nets are mounted together on the same frame ropes and may be used either singly or as a fleet of nets.

Traditionally, gill nets were hauled by hand in shallow or moderate-depth water. Mechanical net haulers are now common even in small-scale fisheries.

This type of net is considered to be relatively selective when it comes to the fish species it captures but the incidental catch of non-targeted and often endangered species, such as seabirds, sea turtles, sharks, and whales, is a cause of concern. So, too, is "ghost fishing"—the continued destruction of sea life by lost or otherwise abandoned gill and trammel nets.

In 1991, in an attempt to mitigate the devastating effects of ghost netting, the United Nations banned the use of large-scale high-seas drift nets longer than 2.5 kilometres. In addition, using nets made from new materials that break down or using biodegradable material to attach floats to nets can help reduce the damage done by lost nets that otherwise would continue to fish.

Gill Net (Bottom Set)

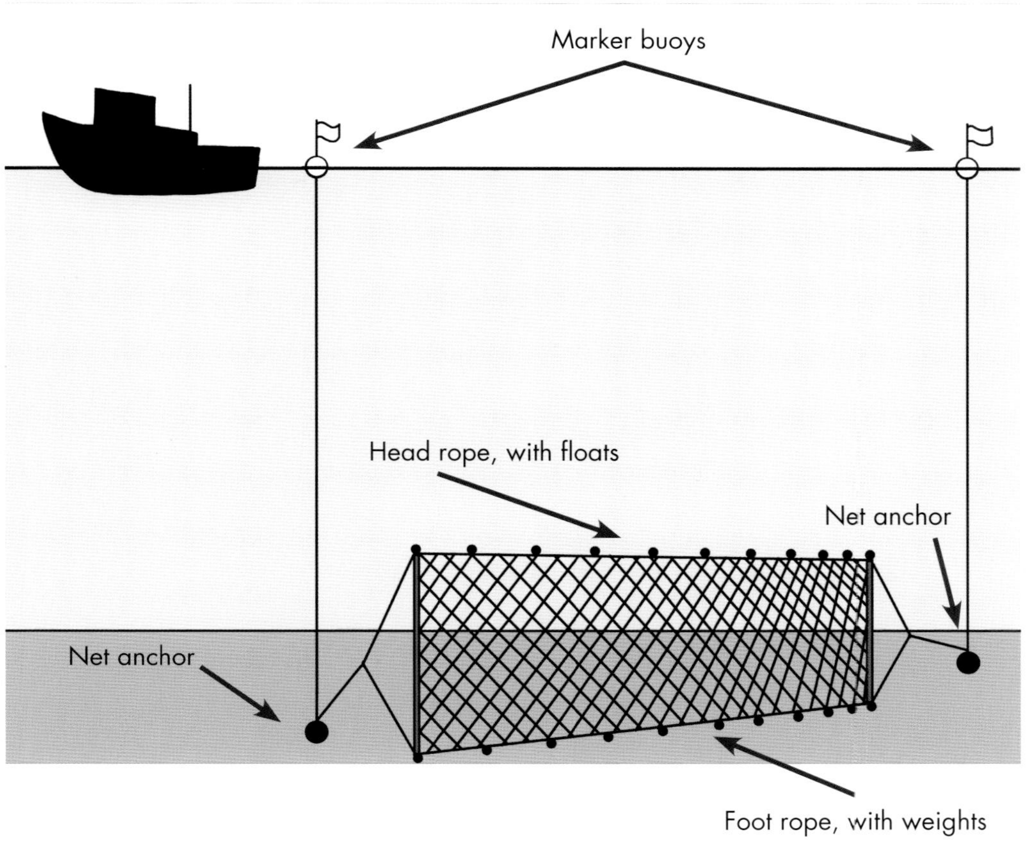

Marker buoys

Head rope, with floats

Net anchor

Net anchor

Foot rope, with weights

Longline

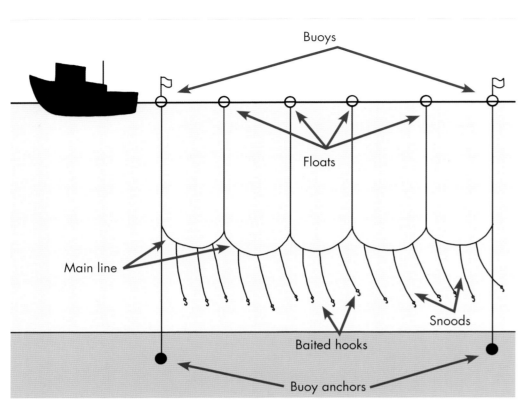

Buoys

Floats

Main line

Snoods

Baited hooks

Buoy anchors

LONGLINES

This effective commercial fishing technique works by luring fish to take natural or artificial bait on hooks that are fixed to the end of a short line (snood). Hundreds or thousands of snoods may be attached at regular intervals by swivels to a long main line, which, depending on the number of hooks, can extend up to 20 kilometres.

Like nets, longlines can be set at the surface, in mid-water, or at the bottom and either anchored or buoyed and left to drift. Longliners use mid-water longlines to target pelagic species such as swordfish and tuna. They use bottom longlines to target demersal species including cod and halibut.

Longlines are particularly effective in waters where the bottom is too rough to use nets. Another advantage of this gear type is that fish are usually alive when the line is hauled aboard. Longline-caught fish have a reputation for freshness.

The longline was the most commonly used groundfish gear for decked boats until the 1960s, when gill nets became increasingly popular (especially during spawning seasons, when many fish stop eating). However, longlines have now surpassed gill nets in popularity among fishers once again.

As with most fishing methods, the longline fishery has become increasingly mechanized. Hooks are most often baited with herring, mackerel, capelin, or squid pieces, although artificial bait is becoming much more common.

Pelagic longline fishing for swordfish and tuna is infamous for incidentally catching and killing seabirds, sea turtles, and sharks and for catching juveniles of the target species. Some estimates say 66 per cent of Atlantic swordfish taken by the American fleet are immature, and the figure goes as high as 83 per cent for females, which means longliner crews must routinely discard up to half the swordfish they catch. Most of the discarded fish is either dead or dies soon after being discarded. The number of sharks accidentally caught each year by longline that later die ranges in the tens of thousands, and the number of Endangered sea turtles caught this way is also too high to be sustainable.

DREDGES

While the target species for these nets is usually shellfish such as clams, mussels, oysters, and scallops, the bycatch of fish species caught by dredge nets is significant.

A dredge is dragged over the bottom. Its "mouth" (which has a heavy rigid frame) and the metal mesh holding bag are designed either to scrape the bottom using short rakes or teeth or to penetrate it to 30 centimetres or more using long teeth or water jets. Some dredges are mechanized to convey harvested organisms from the holding bag to the deck for sorting while the net continues fishing.

Dredger vessels are medium to large vessels up to 50 metres in length and powered by massive engines. Some of the larger dredgers have heavy booms that allow the vessel to operate two or more dredges at a time. Industrial dredgers tow a beam that can be fitted with 10 or more dredges.

Dredge nets, which are used in coastal areas and on the continental shelf, cause high non-target species mortality and damage reefs and other structures, thereby altering the ecosystem in ways that reduce its suitability for native species. If an area is dredged infrequently, and depending on the level of natural disturbance, the sediment type, and exposure to weather and tidal conditions, the impact may be reduced over time. Where dredging is more frequent, however, the seabed and by extension the local ecosystem are unlikely to return to their original conditions.

TRAWLS

A **bottom trawl** is a cone-shaped net that is towed along the bottom by one or two vessels. The gear must make contact with the bottom to operate successfully.

Bottom trawls usually have two lateral wings that extend forward from the net opening. They are often fitted with an extended top panel to divert fish into the mouth of the net. The mouth is framed by a head rope with floats, which hold the trawl open vertically, and two otter boards (or other mechanism), which hold it open horizontally. Depending on the bottom conditions in the fishing ground, the mouth is fitted with ground gear to prevent damage to the net while maximizing the take. A vessel can be rigged to tow one or two parallel trawls from the stern (making it a stern trawler) or from two outriggers (side trawler).

The bottom trawl design catches species living on or near the bottom, whether that is 2 metres or 2,000 metres below the surface. There are three types of bottom trawls, which are named for how the horizontal opening is maintained: beam trawls (commonly designed without wings), otter trawls, and pair trawls.

Because they physically make contact with the bottom sediment, bottom trawls can damage non-target organisms in the marine environment, such as coral and seaweed. Where the bottom is uneven, rocks and other larger objects may be displaced and sediment disturbed. Harvesting and then discarding small organisms and non-target species also take a toll on the marine environment.

Techniques to reduce the impact of these nets include using a larger mesh size in the "cod ends" and deploying other devices in the trawl that reduce the capture of small or non-targeted marine life. Continuing research is required

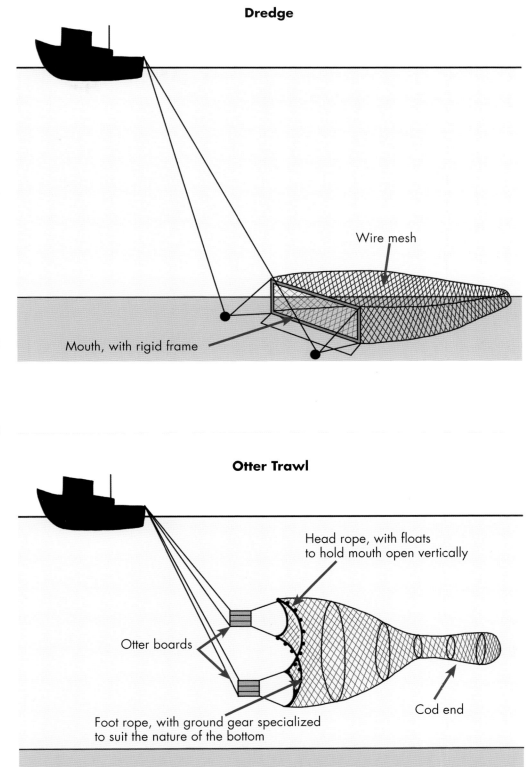

Dredge

Wire mesh

Mouth, with rigid frame

Otter Trawl

Head rope, with floats to hold mouth open vertically

Otter boards

Cod end

Foot rope, with ground gear specialized to suit the nature of the bottom

Beam Trawl

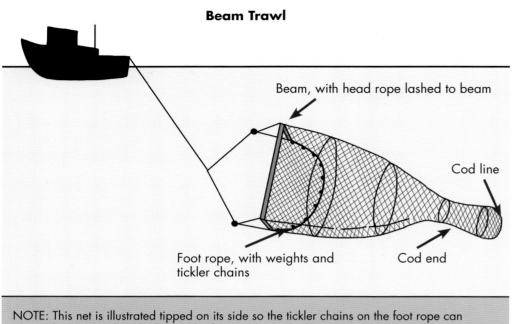

Beam, with head rope lashed to beam

Cod line

Foot rope, with weights and tickler chains

Cod end

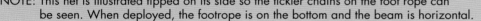

NOTE: This net is illustrated tipped on its side so the tickler chains on the foot rope can be seen. When deployed, the footrope is on the bottom and the beam is horizontal.

into the impact of bottom trawling to clarify its negative effects and seek more environmentally informed methods of demersal fishing.

The **beam trawl**, similar in shape to other trawls, can also be towed over the seabed. The mouth of its net bag is held open horizontally by a long beam. The upper leading edge of the bag net is attached to a strong head rope and lashed to the beam. The under part of the bag, which drags over the bottom, is attached to a foot rope. As the trawl is towed, the head rope is dragged ahead of the foot rope so that when the fish are driven from the bottom they are already under the beam at the top of the net. They accumulate in the cod end, which is held closed by the cod line. When the trawl is hauled onto the vessel, the catch is unloaded by releasing the cod line.

Beam trawls were one of the main forms of gear used for demersal fishing in the days of sail. They are still used in some areas by small inshore fishing boats for commercial fishing and for research. Large nets are up to 15 metres wide but beam trawls can also be considerably smaller.

After a period of disuse in favour of the much larger otter trawls, the beam trawl is experiencing a resurgence in popularity because of modern technology. Today, tickler chains are placed in front of the foot rope to plow the bottom immediately ahead of the net, stirring up fish that would otherwise let the net ride over their hiding places. Electrified ticklers, even more effective, cause fish buried in the sediment to "jump" out of the sand and into the path of the trawl. These electrified chains are lighter than tickler chains and cause less damage to the bottom.

A specialized form of the trawl is the **mid-water trawl**. Similar in construction to a bottom trawl, it is much larger and rigged to operate from mid-water to the surface. The mouth of the net may be held open by otter boards or by two vessels each towing one side of the trawl and operating in sync (pair trawling). In the past, mid-water trawls were held open vertically by attaching floats to the head rope and weights to the ground line. However, larger modern trawls now rely on downward forces from weights to maintain the vertical opening as the net is being towed. Very much a product of the technological age, mid-water trawls are most effective when used with sonar, which enables the captain to detect concentrations of fish ahead of the vessel in time to adjust the vessel's course and the path and depth of the trawl and thus capture more fish.

SEINES

An ancient technique for netting fish is to use a net to surround an area of water (and the fish it contains) like a fence, then tighten the net so fish may be easily harvested. The seine is a type of surrounding net.

Purse seines are used for harvesting pelagic species such as herring and mackerel, which school at or near the surface. The name comes from the drawstring or purse line that runs through a series of rings along the bottom of the net. Once the net is set and both ends joined at the surface (thereby enclosing the fish in a corral of netting), the purse line is pulled tight, closing off the bottom of the net and preventing the fish from escaping. Boats equipped with purse seines are called purse seiners.

Among the negative impacts of this technology is bycatch and the discarding of undersized fish and non-commercial species, which are inevitably caught whenever large nets with small mesh are used.

Danish seines, used for harvesting demersal fish species, have been described as "the poor man's trawl": they have wings, a belly, and a cod end but are deployed differently and have no trawl doors to keep them open.

A Danish seine is operated with a set of tow lines ("warps"). Deploying the seine begins with setting the end of a tow line attached to a buoy. The boat then sails in a half circle, as the first warp plays out. The first wing of the seine is set, the vessel continues to circle, then the cod end is set followed by the other wing. Finally, the second warp is set as the boat returns to the original buoy. The track of the boat during this process forms either a circle, a pear shape, or a triangle. The buoy is taken aboard, the towing lines made fast, then the vessel slowly tows the net while pulling the warps together, before hauling the seine back to the boat.

The Danish seine is not as effective as a trawl when used over rough ground and is not suited to rough seas or strong currents. It can be difficult to operate in low visibility and it requires more work of the fishers. An advantage is low fuel consumption per catch. In addition, the gear is less expensive to purchase and takes up less room than a trawl, which means fishers can operate it from smaller boats.

The Danish seine has been most effective for targeting flatfish, cod, and haddock. It is mainly used in shallow water at depths of 40 to 60 metres. Vessels using Danish seines are similar in size to longliners and gillnetters. The owners of such vessels may switch gear types seasonally, depending on the species they are targeting.

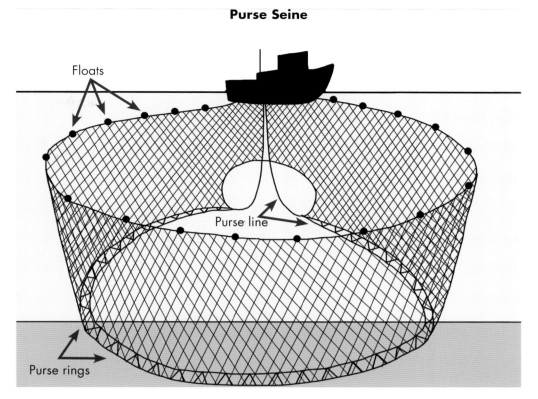

Purse Seine

Floats

Purse line

Purse rings

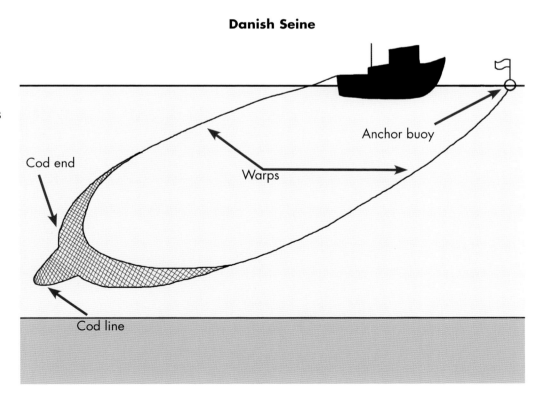

Danish Seine

Cod end

Warps

Anchor buoy

Cod line

Glossary

amphidromous: fish that migrate between fresh and salt water, but not to breed (see also **oceanodromous**)

anadromous: fish that spend most of their lives in the sea and migrate to fresh water to breed (such as Atlantic salmon; see also **catadromous**)

batch spawner: a fish that releases a series its eggs in a series of batches rather than all at once

bathypelagic: belonging to a deepwater zone from 1,000 to 4,000 metres below the surface of the open ocean, but well off the bottom

benthopelagic: belonging to the zone just above the seabed, at depths below 200 metres

bottom feeder: a species of fish that feeds on or near the bottom of a body of water

bycatch: marine life, and seabirds, caught incidentally when another species is the commercial fishing target

catadromous: fish that spend most of their lives in fresh water and migrate to the sea to breed (for example, the American eel; see also **anadromous**)

crus (or **crura**, plural): an anatomical part, usually specialized fins, that resemble a leg (or pair of legs)

crustacean: a member of a marine species characterized by a hard shell, jointed legs, and the absence of a backbone; examples include crab, lobster, shrimp, krill

demersal: on or near the bottom of a body of water; demersal fish live on the bottom (see **pelagic**)

dorsal: in anatomy: of, on, or near the back (compare **ventral**)

dragger: a boat that tows fishing gear along the bottom of the ocean

epibenthic: in reference to invertebrates: those that live on the surface of the ocean floor

euphausiid: a small shrimp-like crustacean (of many species), also known as **krill**, that in huge numbers makes up one of the lowest links in the ocean food chain

fall line: the line dividing a coastal plain from higher ground inland, often characterized by rapids or waterfalls that block inland encroachment of seawater and access for oceanic species

fecundity: the number of eggs an organism produces in a single reproductive cycle; the potential reproductive capacity of an organism or a population

filter-feed: to feed by straining suspended matter and food particles from water, usually by passing the water through a specialized filtering structure

fry: young or newly hatched fish

heterocercal: a tail shape with a long upper lobe and a shorter lower lobe

inferior: in anatomy: the lower side (usually of the head)

krill: from the Norwegian word meaning "young fish," used as the collective common name for **euphausiids**, small shrimp-like **crustaceans** found in all the oceans

landlocked: refers to individuals or subpopulations of a fish species that normally would spend a portion of the life cycle in the ocean but instead live their entire life in fresh water

larvae: the newly hatched, earliest developmental stage of an organism that will undergo metamorphosis; fish larvae differ markedly from the adult stage

leptocephalus: the slender transparent larva of eels

migration: the systematic—as opposed to random— movement of a **stock** from one place to another that is related to reproduction, season, food supply, or water temperature

mollusc: a member of an invertebrate species (such as shellfish) that usually is characterized by one or two hard shells and the absence of a skeleton

natal river: the river in which individuals of a fish species hatch and to which they return as mature fish

oceanodromous: fish that live and migrate in the ocean to breed and to feed (such as Atlantic cod; see also **amphidromous**)

oophagous: feeding on eggs, sometimes (in the case of sharks) on the eggs of potential siblings, during gestation

oviduct: the passage that connects the ovaries to the outside of the body, through which eggs are spawned

ovoviparous: refers to a species that retains eggs inside the body, where the young hatch

pelagic: refers to the **water column**: all the water in the ocean that is not close to the bottom; pelagic fish live in the water column and not on the bottom (see **demersal**)

pharynx: the back part of the throat, the cavity into which gill slits open

recruitment: the number of young fish that grow to become catchable in a species population each year, often specifically the number that reach commercially exploitable size

salt front: the interface between fresh and salt water in a river or estuary

sexual dimorphism: differences in form between male and female members of the same species

sink population: a breeding population that does not produce enough offspring to sustain itself

spawning (biomass): the total weight of all sexually mature fish in a population of a given species

spinule: a small spine or thorn

spiracle: a respiratory opening behind the eyes of certain bottom-dwelling skates that allows them to draw in oxygenated water and pass it over the gills

stock: a discrete population of a species that occupies a defined area separated by environmental conditions or geography (such as temperature or currents) from other populations of the same species

total allowable catch: the total catch of a given species permitted in an area during a specified period, as defined in the management plan for the resource; commonly known as TAC

tubercle: a small, usually hard excrescence or projection, like a wart or lump

tube worms: small segmented marine worms that, as larvae, are free-floating but which, in the adult stage, anchor on a substrate and form calcium carbonate tubes

ventral: in anatomy: of or on the stomach (compare **dorsal**)

water column: the water in the ocean from the surface to just above the bottom, as measured in a conceptual vertical line

yolk sac: a membranous sac attached to an embryo that provides nourishment in the form of yolk to the embryo and to newly hatched larvae

Index of Fish by Common Name

About the Contributors

WADE KEARLEY

During his three decades as a commercial writer and journalist, Wade Kearley has written extensively about the sea and published articles in national and international magazines. Since graduating from the University of Victoria with a degree in Fine Arts, he has written four books: two volumes of poetry, a profile of the legendary lighthouses of Belle Isle (illustrated by Les Noseworthy), and a travelogue of his walking trek across the island of Newfoundland. Mr. Kearley lives in St. John's with his wife, Katherine, daughters, Julie and Sasha, and grandchildren, Luke and Annika.

DEREK PEDDLE

Born in Whitbourne, Newfoundland and Labrador, Derek Peddle has been interested in painting and drawing since childhood. He began his career as a graphic designer in 1986 and worked for several advertising agencies before starting his own, Vivid Communications, in St. John's in 2000. Mr. Peddle's oil, acrylic, watercolour, and graphite illustrations have been commissioned by many clients including the federal Department of Fisheries and Oceans, PetroCanada, and the Fisheries and Marine Institute of Memorial University of Newfoundland.

GEORGE ROSE

George Rose is Director of the Centre for Fisheries Ecosystems Research (CFER) at Memorial University of Newfoundland's Marine Institute. He holds a PhD (McGill) and MSc (Laurentian) in biology and a BSc (Agriculture) in fisheries and wildlife management (Guelph). Prior to the creation of CFER, Dr. Rose held the Natural Sciences and Engineering Research Council of Canada (NSERC) industrial research chair in fisheries conservation at Memorial for 10 years. He has worked for the federal Department of Fisheries and Oceans, the governments of the United States and New Zealand, the Ontario Ministry of Natural Resources, and CIDA-CUSO in Africa. Dr. Rose has published more than 100 scientific papers and books, most on the North Atlantic fisheries.